George,
be
careful

George, be careful

A Greek florist's kid in the roughhouse world of advertising

George Lois
with Bill Pitts

Saturday Review Press
New York

Published simultaneously in Canada by
Doubleday Canada Ltd., Toronto.

Library of Congress Catalog Card Number: 72-80671

ISBN 0-8415-0190-4

Saturday Review Press
230 Park Avenue
New York, New York 10017

PRINTED IN THE UNITED STATES OF AMERICA

To Papa

Contents

George,
be
careful

1 Up from the gladiolas

When I was a kid and an Irishman croaked, I worked my balls off.

My father was a florist in the Kingsbridge section of the Bronx, a lace-curtain Irish parish, directly above the northern tip of Manhattan. We were the only Greeks in Kingsbridge, surrounded by Irish cops, Irish firemen, Irish subway workers, Irish municipal employees and blue-collar Irish families. Their Irish Catholic Church of St. John sat like a big mother among the apartment houses, encircled by beads of saloons with neon names, crowned by blazing shamrocks. On paydays the fathers of my Irish friends jammed the bars and put away boilermakers. By nighttime their Irish laughter was followed by explosive brawls, trailed into the pre-dawn hours by the curses of raucous drunks as they staggered on the pavement and struggled up the apartment-house stairs.

When death came to our Gaelic neighbors, gladiolas moved like hotcakes as the Lois store boomed with orders and bustled with life. We unloaded every last flower in season and all the slow movers that usually wilted in their vases. I hustled to funeral parlors with wreaths and sprays of our bread-and-butter gladiolas, spiffed up with a few asters and chrysanthemums. When the dearly departed was a fawncy stiff, I delivered a high-priced blanket of orchids to drape the mahogany casket of the wealthy mick.

I kept my young Greek nose clean and straight while I worked the funeral trade, but when life returned to normal it was broken nine times, usually in fist fights with my Irish friends because being the only Greek kid, and I mean *Greek*, in an Irish parish, and I mean *Irish*, marked me as the neighborhood nigger.

I was the youngest of three children and the only son of Haralampos and Vasilike Lois. My two sisters were named Paraskeve and Hariclea, and my mother refused to learn English. We talked, shouted and swore in peasant Greek in our third-floor apartment, while the Mediterranean smells of my mother's cooking stunk up the hallway. Fumes of incense that hung from icons in our corridor, burning all day and through the night, seeped out from the Lois apartment, never letting the Irish forget that a hocus-pocus family was a tenant in their building.

Homemade Greek sausages aged on cords from the wooden rack for drying clothes that hung from our kitchen ceiling, while vinegar-drenched lentil soup, my favorite dish, simmered endlessly in the oven on a low flame. When my friends came to visit they were rocked by the strange sights and smells, and by the throaty machine-gun jabber in our native tongue. I was all Greek, inside and out, with the incense clinging to my clothes in P.S. 7, where the corned-beef-and-cabbage Irish christened me "greaseball."

The first time I heard that word I lost my cookies and slugged it out, a beautiful sight to the smiling eyes of the fighting Irish. After that, every kid who loved a fight threw the word at me, and I waded in against gangs of toughs or just one Irishman, no matter how brawny. Until I turned thirteen my nose was unmarked because I was good with my hands, but on my way home one day from P.S. 7, "greaseball" was tossed at me by a kid I didn't know, and I squared off in a sudden rage, watching his right. With his first swing he busted my gorgeous schnozz, but in meeting the first left-handed Irishman of my street career I learned the hard way that not all micks are alike. With the dull pain across my face we bare-knuckled until lefty went down in the center of an onlooking Irish mob, and my stock went up in Kingsbridge. A busy fight schedule followed as every tough in the neighborhood lined up for a crack at the Greek contender. Wingdings with the Irish became a way of life. I took my lumps, but I also became known as a kid who left his mark.

Mrs. Murdock barged into our apartment one night and screamed in her fruity brogue at my bewildered mother—the Murdock kid had arrived home that day with lacerated freckles from a fist fight with the Lois boy, the florist's son. After Mrs. Murdock left, my mother gave me holy hell in peasant Greek and windmilled a broom as she chased me around the kitchen table, grazing a sausage. But my father's quiet stare said more than my mother's broom; he never raised a hand to me. While Vasilike screamed and Haralampos glared, I always sensed a burning pride from the peasant parents of the Kingsbridge kid. Their only son, whether in a Greek mountain hamlet or an Irish parish, was never expected to shuffle.

But it was better by far to be Greek than Jew in the neighborhood school of Father Coughlin's Bronx Irish. The one Jewish kid in our class was brilliant but a nebbish, and our schoolmates never missed a reason to kick the crap out of the class sheeny in the toilets and on the stairwells. He became my ward, and a fight with the kike ended up in a brawl with "greaseball," bodyguard of the jewboy.

In the late thirties the war in Europe made life rough for the class patsy. "*Dirrrty kike*," blared the voice of Mike Quill, the transit workers' union boss, at the corner of 231st Street and Broadway. The sound truck was parked opposite my father's stoore. "*Rooosevelt* wants us to fight for the dirrrty *jooos*, and I'll tell ye why— because *Rooos*evelt is a *dirrrty kike!*" The civil service Irish clustered around fat Mike. The next day their kids belted the Jewish shnook and I came home roughed up after shielding my ward.

The nebbish traveled to P.S. 7 from well-to-do Riverdale, a few miles to the north of Kingsbridge. He had a hundred percent kosher last name which I can't recall, but I remember distinctly that his first name was Preston, very swank for a Jewish kid. His parents wanted to expose him to non-kosher children, but they sent poor Preston out of Riverdale's chicken fat into the fires of Coughlin.

Another parish alien was an Italian kid who spiked the ethnic stew by joining my tormentors. He called me "greaseball" and boasted in front of the Irish that Mussolini's armies would conquer Greece.

The year was 1940, when I was coming into my own as the class artist, showing my Greek-conscious drawings of Evzones blowing bugles and lunging with fixed bayonets. I was finding a way to jab at the guts other than with fists, and I flaunted juicy caricatures of Mussolini, who invaded Greece in October and was pushed into Albania in December by Evzones and peasants. After class I roughed up the Italian kid. After dinner his mother barged into our apartment and screamed at Vasilike in olive oil English about her violent son who had bruised Angelo's mouth for making a few remarks about Greece. Again my mother was completely bewildered —another screaming visitor in her kitchen, another impossible accent in a language she barely understood. But my father listened quietly in the corridor beside the hanging icon of St. George. After our visitor left, my father lifted me up and kissed me. Then he uncorked a bottle of white *retsina* wine and the Lois family toasted the gallant Evzones.

The neighborhood nigger of St. John's parish was gradually accepted by the Irish as I scored on the concrete in schoolyard basketball. Timothy O'Connor and Leon Quinn, foster children of our sternly Catholic neighbors, the elderly Mr. and Mrs. Nielsen, became my closest friends. When they came to dinner in my voodoo Orthodox home they passed up my mother's pungent lentil soup and twitched to the incense. Holding their Mickey Rooney noses, O'Connor and Quinn ran from our apartment as soon as dinner was done, and we played ball until nighttime, when the neon shamrocks bloomed. Lace curtains fluttered from the windows as a garbage can was heaved from a Kingsbridge roof and landed on a transit worker. The son of a cop pushed the can, but it wasn't malicious, only mischief. They called the kid a minor, the transit worker's wife was called a widow—and my father called me to the store for the funeral crush.

My parents fully expected that the family store would pass to me, a belief that was rooted in their peasant heritage, a Grecian tradition that was centuries old. Every Easter Sunday that belief was driven home to me as a religious rite of our Orthodoxy. Over the crust of my mother's home-baked ritual bread, eighteen inches in diameter, my father traced a cross, and as he sliced its quadrants he set the priorities in a Greek family's life with awesome clarity as he chanted to a Gregorian lilt in our native tongue, each word timed to the knife's movements: *"Store . . . home . . . father . . . son."* The store, where a man did his work, always came first.

My father had been a goat shepherd in a primitive mountain hamlet that scraped against the Greek sky, high above the northern rim of the Isthmus of Corinth, a hundred miles west of Athens. In 1911, when he was fifteen, he came down from the mountain on a bony mule and headed for the new world. He went to Coney Island, where he lived with fellow greenhorns, selling hot dogs by day, studying English at night and moving upward into a job with a florist, eventually opening his own retail shop, his *store.* In 1923 he returned to Greece to serve a stint in the Greek army as a full-skirted Evzone, complete with pompons on his military shoes. He also felt the time had come to find a wife, but Haralampos struck out and came back to America in despair. He had his store, but nothing more—until a Greek friend in New York told him about the unmarried sister of an old-country crony, Costas Thanasoulis, who was then a vegetable farmer on Staten Island. Haralampos, his friend and Costas Thanasoulis were all part of a young crowd of immigrant Greek men who worshiped the great scientific wrestler, Jim Londos, their countryman. They rode overnight coach trains in the 1920s from Grand Central to Chicago to watch their Greek idol perform.

In the summer of 1924, young Haralampos and his friend rode the ferry from Manhattan to Staten Island for a visit to Costas Thanasoulis' vegetable farm to look over his sister, the prospective bride for ex-Evzone Lois, the bachelor. Costas called in his sister from the vegetable field to be sized up by the visiting suitor. Vasilike Thanasoulis had recently arrived in America from the same mountain province as my father. The setting was now Staten Island, but the scene was unchanged from peasant Greece.

Unfortunately no dowry, Costas confessed, but what a girl! She was a great cook, he bragged—fed the farm hands, ran the house, excellent health, very Orthodox—and as they bartered over the bride, the humiliated Vasilike ran to hide in the kitchen, where she turned on the faucet at full tilt, sending a rush of water crashing into the sink to drown the sounds. But Haralampos was taken by the fiery Vasilike and a deal was made with her brother Costas.

They were married a few months later in a Greek Orthodox church, and their wedding reception was held in a Manhattan restaurant on Twenty-third Street: Cavanaugh's.

Americanized in name only, Haralampos became Harry to the heathens (as Costas became Gus), and with Mrs. Harry Lois he went to live near his first flower shop on West 137th Street in Harlem, where Vasilike Lois fiercely preserved her Orthodoxy with all of its incense-laced mysticism. Her passionate loyalty to an ancestry of Greekness, aged by centuries of peasant survival against brutal Turks, harsh poverty and mountain primitivism, grew more intense as the years passed in America.

My sisters and I were born in Manhattan and reared as Greeks in a parvenu culture. When a boy was born to the Lois family (I stuck my head out in 1931 and saw Herbert Hoover) all the pent-up yearnings for Greek continuity were funneled through him, the Hellenic *son*, the natural heir to a male-centered tradition, the living embodiment of a Greek woman's mission on earth. A boy child was a happy omen that brought new zest during hard times. The Depression brought millions to their knees, but my father's love for flowers and my mother's absolute reverence for the value of his work and for his supreme authority in our family spurred the florist to weather a gasping economy. While so many Americans tasted bitter failure, the immigrant Haralampos came through the toughest of years. In 1933, alert for even greener pastures, my father sold his Harlem store and we moved north to Kingsbridge, beyond the Greek enclave of Inwood, smack into the Irish heart of St. John's parish, where he opened the store of my childhood among the transit workers and their kids.

We went to mingle with our own people at the Greek Orthodox Church of St. Spyridon in Washington Heights. The clerics of St. Spyridon, those bearded, towering mystics of my Greek childhood, were straight out of an early Christian epic by Cecil B. De Mille. Before receiving communion I fasted for two days, and when at last I came before the giant priest, our *Papathos*, in his formidable black vestments, crowned with a seventeen-inch hat, he nailed me with his Rasputin eyes, I kissed his hands, then I dropped to the floor and kissed his Thom McAn shoes—counting every second until he finished his gorgeous Gregorian chanting so I could grab my chunk of holy bread and wash it down with a sip of ritual wine. Then I ran out of the church and rounded the corner like a Keystone Cop into the Automat, past the crowded tables of coffee-sitters, and shot nickels into the brass slot for a chopped-egg sandwich. Those marvelous charlatans of the Greek Orthodox priesthood celebrated a bravura Eucharist, but with a genuine power to draw emotions to their peak, an inner purging that goes back directly to Aeschylus and Euripides, names my parents never knew. But Haralampos and Vasilike Lois never wavered from a tradition that was molded by the Greeks of antiquity. I was trapped by its hocus-pocus, yet I loved the life of a florist's kid in the 1930s.

Three days a week my father was up at dawn for a buying trip to the flower market, returning with dewy bunches from the wily wholesalers on lower Sixth Avenue. Over the years his fingers sprouted tattoos of scratches from thorns and prickly leaves. I watched him work from the time I was five, when I began my apprenticeship as a florist. He moved swiftly and spoke softly, transmitting to me through the impact of his disciplined silence the rich pride in his work and his consuming love for the smallest details. His scratched fingers twirled tiny wires around clusters of stems with precision movements. I watched as he worked on funeral wreaths, shaving the stems of pink roses until they were smoothed to plastic straws, swiftly inserting wooden struts into their hollows, then binding the clipped ends with perfect balls of wet cotton to feed the flowers beyond the burial. I learned from my Greek father that devotional labor is one of life's values that can never be compromised. Never.

As I grew older I carried the fragrant wreaths on their metal easels that stood six feet high, cradling my father's work from rush-hour riders with my gaunt teenage body in jammed subway cars to funeral homes as far as Ozone Park. Between funerals there were always corsages to be delivered for happier occasions, often double orchids for Mother's Day and weddings, for anniversaries and graduations.

North of the store, in stylish Riverdale, the parish florist's reputation spread among the cultured and the famous. When my father said to me casually, "Go up and see the Maestro," his eyes flashed with pride—long-stemmed roses were ordered for a recital in the home of Arturo Toscanini. I rode the bus from Kingsbridge with Toscanini's precious American Beauty roses resting against my

chest like a breathing infant, passing through the drab Irish parish
into another world. The Maestro's home faced the Jersey Palisades,
overlooking the Hudson River as though it were the Mediterranean, with a vineyard of purple grapes alongside his exquisite resi-
dence. There were florists in Riverdale, but customers who cherished quality called the quiet Greek in Kingsbridge for their expensive dozens of mums or asters or roses. The widow of Fiorello
LaGuardia was a Riverdale customer of Haralampos—also Jane
Pickens, Vincent Price and Madame Chiang. The voice of the
New York Yankees, Mel Allen, was another customer on my route;
my father's adoringly groomed tea roses found an appreciative home
in his swank high-rise apartment.

From the family store, the center of my life, I traveled to mar-
riages and wakes, to the mighty and the meek, catching glimpses of
other worlds. Between deliveries I painted hundreds of vases and
metal flower pots in a beautiful park-bench green, darker than the
neon shamrocks. Each summer I angled a tall ladder toward the
store's high ceiling and stippled its corrugations as the rich odor of
paint blended with the scents of a thousand flowers.

Surrounded by lovely smells and rainbow colors, I was caught in
the magnetic orbit of my quietly authoritative father, with his
piercing flashes of peasant humor that sent me ducking behind the
counter to stifle a sputtering guffaw when a rude customer riled
him. He gloried in his orders from the Maestro because a man of
taste gave meaning to his meticulous artistry, and he detested anyone who tried to direct his knowing fingers as he composed a floral
arrangement. He never raised his voice while saying softly to the
picky customer, *"Ccchyessa,"* a throaty "Yessuh," Greek for "Go
piss on yourself." He would *"Ccchyessa"* very calmly, meanwhile going about his work *his* way. When the customer left the
store I scampered out from behind the counter and rolled on the
floor, laughing uncontrollably as Haralampos smiled, without ever
saying a word.

His father had been the local "doctor" in their native village, a
folk healer in the stark isolation of their mountain hamlet, and that
peasant art had been passed on to Haralampos. When I was nine
and broke my arm, he set the bone, made a pack of eggs and herbs
and bound the break with rope and twine. When my arm healed
and our Irish neighbors heard about the Greek florist's medical

hocus-pocus, they quit going to Dr. Barrow on Bailey Avenue and brought their injured kids to Haralampos. There were vivid days when the Lois store in St. John's parish could be mistaken for a Belfast emergency ward, were it not for my sisters jabbering in Greek as they filled orders while Dr. Haralampos healed the wounded Irish.

Our Greekness flourished in the new world, and it was understood that the only son of Haralampos and Vasilike would finish school and become a florist. But my drawings in P.S. 7 caught the eye of my seventh grade art teacher, Mrs. Engel, who gave me a portfolio as a gift to save my work. In the eighth grade she sent me to the High School of Music and Art for an all-day entrance exam. When I was accepted I knew that I would never be a florist. My parents sensed that I was veering from the store, and their dismay reached my teachers. One day a visitor came to the store—a distinguished caller, the Irish principal of P.S. 7. "No need to fear about your son studying art," said Dr. Callahan to Haralampos. "Your son is talented—and you know, Mr. Lois, art isn't all nudes." My father was immensely proud that the principal had come to his store, but while I went off to study art, my parents prayed to keep me loyal to their Greekness. Basketball helped—and hurt.

At fifteen I joined the Sons of Pericles, an athletic fraternal order for Greek kids, meeting the Irish again when we played against parish basketball teams of the Catholic Youth Organization. To the Irish the city was a patchwork of parishes rather than streets or neighborhoods. "You from Good Shepherd or St. Michael's?" asked the C.Y.O. kids. My father was a shepherd and a good one, I was sure, but when the Son of Pericles said, "St. John's parish," the Irish went "*wow*" because St. John's was a Father Coughlin, Mike Quill, boilermaker Irish parish. And the priest who coached St. John's C.Y.O. team had his eye on the kid from the mother church (we were in business before the Catholics). "Are you the son of Mr. Lois, the florist?" he asked me after a game with St. John's in which the Greek Sons trounced the Catholic Youths.

"Right, Father," I said, not really uncomfortable calling him that because Haralampos was always my *papa;* in fact I felt strangely at home with the whiskey-veined celibate, whose church and its Irish were so much a part of my life.

"Well now, George Lois, your father is a respected merchant in the parish—and very devout, I understand."

"Absolutely. St. Spyridon in Washington Heights. Greek Orthodox."

"Admirable. But tell me, lad—are you not the only son in your family?"

"Right, Father. I got two sisters—Hariclea and Paraskeve."

"Yes, oh yes—very colorful names—and they are both very helpful young ladies, especially when St. John's rents palms for weddings and funerals, as we often do, as you well know, I'm sure." For sure, I knew—the Sunday before I had lugged ten tall potted palms to the church for an Irish wedding, three blocks from the store. I made five trips, carrying a palm in each hand, each weighing a holy ton. Then I made a sixth trip with a gladiola spray. "But tell me—do Greeks not name their sons *Junior?*" he asked, angling for *something.*

"No, Father," I said, playing it straight, "we reverse the names from father to son. My father's name is Harry George Lois, he named me George Harry, and when I get married, if I have a boy he gets named Harry George."

"Fascinating, George Harry Lois. Now tell me this—does your faith permit an alias?" He saw that I was getting the creeps. "Let me put it this way," he went on. "How would you like to play for St. John's—against competing parishes in the Catholic Youth league?"

"Uh . . . I'd *love* to. But I'm playing for Sons of Pericles."

"Ah, but there are times when you're *not* playing for the Greek Orthodox team, am I not right?"

"Well yeah . . . but ain't it blasphemous?"

"Not with an alias."

"Impossible, Father. My name George is so Greek I can't begin to tell you. It's like John to Irish people—like St. John, Father. I'm named after St. George."

"Relax, lad. You will always be *George.* But when you play for St. John's parish we'll call you George *Reardon.*" I winced at the name, but when he added, "We play Good Shepherd tomorrow," I couldn't resist and I showed up the next day as Reardon the Ringer. But just before the warmup the priest said, "I'll have to ask you to remove your medals." My sacred *medals*—I had worn them all my life—two identical St. George medals, one from Haralampos, the other from Vasilike, each with a Greek cross on one side and a majestic St. George slaying a dragon on the other.

"Then I'm afraid I can't play, Father."

"I understand, my boy—you are devout, like your fine parents, but I also know something about your faith. Greek Orthodox parishioners celebrate the Resurrection more fervently than they mourn the Crucifixion. Therefore, lad, not wearing the Orthodox cross will not compromise your devoutness."

"It's not the cross, Father—it's St. George. He's my patron saint. April twenty-third is my Saint's Day. It's more sacred than my birthday."

"I'll protect your medals for you," he said, slipping them off and replacing them with a St. Christopher medal. *"Now let's score for St. John's parish, Reardon!"* We won the game and when the priest returned my medals he told me to keep the St. Christopher: "You've earned it, Reardon."

"Lois, Father," I said, replacing my precious St. Georges. I never told Haralampos—and certainly not the passionately mystical Vasi- like, who found omens in dreams, who worshiped wooden icons and kept the incense cooking, who lived in dread of Tuesdays, a traditional Greek day of doom since 1453 when Constantinople fell to the Turks—on a Tuesday.

No, I never told Mama.

At Music and Art High I played for their varsity basketball team while continuing my ballplaying for the Sons of Pericles and slip- ping into my Reardon alias when the priest cornered me in the church as I delivered their back-breaking rented palms. I played for the Greeks, the Irish and the Artists, working in the store be- tween games and school. But being a Reardon in Kingsbridge was no insurance against being tagged an artist queer when I walked from the I.R.T. subway through St. John's parish with my string- tied portfolio on the way home from Music and Art. "Greaseball" was replaced by "Hi, sweets" plus a chorus of screechy, wind- sucking kisses from a lineup of Gaelic toughs. Like a reflex action, every day during my first month at Music and Art, I placed my portfolio on the pavement, peeled off my jacket and walked into a fast donnybrook. Between the knuckles of my neighbors and basketball elbows, my septum swung across my face with each new break like a pendulum, keeping time to my progress as a Greek in passage from the old world through the minefields of Irish Kingsbridge.

The sons of Jewish immigrants went to college and the sons of the immigrant Irish went to Delehanty's Police Academy or the transit workers union, but the only son of Haralampos Lois was meant for the store. There was a subtle but strong distinction between other immigrant families and the mystique of peasant Greeks. The Jew gave up his guts in a sweatshop so that his kid could become a gynecologist; the Italian peddled off a pushcart on Arthur Avenue so that his kid could build two-family houses or study law; but the work of a Greek father was never a bridge for his son to walk over into a better world than the life of his parents. My father's life was rich with dignity and craft. He was respected by the Maestro and the Mayor's widow and the Generalissimo's wife. He commanded courtesy from the Irish, and when he traded with his fellow Greeks in the flower market he was received as a presence, as a man of strength and honor. He was secure in his Orthodoxy and revered by a tenacious wife who wove a cocoon of Greekness, with his work and their Hellenic heritage at its heart. My sisters were extensions of our mother's Greekness, maintaining links with cousins they never knew in the old country through continuous letters in Greek to nieces and distant relatives on the mountain west of Athens, sharing the joys of each birth and marriage, mourning the sorrows of each death and praying at each illness, all by mail, preserving the peasant lineage of our parents. We were unscarred by the Great Depression because the work of my father sustained us while the culture of his fathers, with its proud Greekness and its firm Orthodoxy, fed his inner certainty about our way of life.

And like my determined father, I dreamed of the day when I could assert *my* talent and *my* power, but unlike my father I collided early in life with the roughhouse Irish, using bare knuckles to prove myself. I beat them at their own game and then I joined them as Lois-Reardon. I identified with Jews. I discovered a villa of striking elegance when I went up to see the Maestro. And I loved the speed and sweat of ballplaying even more than the old world warmth of my father's store. The pace and breadth of my life was carrying me beyond the role of a florist's son.

As a child I thrilled at the force of a graphic image on an unsuspecting eye. When the neighborhood nigger in P.S. 7 drew a picture on the blackboard of a hawk-nosed Columbus for the Irish kids who still hadn't discovered America, the eyes of my classmates forgot about "greaseball" and shifted to my work, preserved in chalk for months by our teacher—an honor of honors. I was evolving my own pictorial language that came to its point with simple images, but always with a squirt of vinegar to burn the senses. Mussolini was a clown, Columbus was a bird. The Irish laughed, the teacher nodded, nobody touched the blackboard—and the nigger connected.

Later, at Music and Art I pored over art books, storing away details of the Renaissance masters and marveling at the courage of Braque, Picasso and Walter Gropius. I was deep into man's oldest language and I knew that I could distill it to immediate images so that ordinary kids like Murdock and Quinn and O'Connor and Angelo could get my message. The High School of Music and Art was one of the great monuments of Fiorello LaGuardia, a dazzling leap for me out of the provincial parish of Kingsbridge, where I met strong Jews and sensitive Italians, where the Maestro himself came down from Riverdale and mounted the podium to lead the student orchestra, where young Lennie Bernstein was also a guest conductor—where we could tingle in his theatrical presence while saying as adolescent students in a free high school that this guy still ain't as good as Toscanini.

In the autumn of 1949 my father woke me at four in the morning to go with him to the flower market, but I had passed my entrance exam to Pratt Institute in Brooklyn and I was ready to move in earnest toward a career in art. "I can't go anymore, Papa," I told Haralampos in the overnight fullness of our incense-drenched apartment. "I'm starting college today." My career as a florist had ended after thirteen years. Haralampos shook his head slowly, realizing finally that his store, the business—my Greek patrimony—was rejected by his only son. He left for the flower market without me, concealing his awful sadness with a stoic silence. But there was a further break that cut even deeper.

It was fully expected that I would marry a bona-fide Greek girl in St. Spyridon, where my sisters later married Greek men amid the pomp and soaring ritual of an Orthodox ceremony. Hariclea, the younger of my sisters, married a Greek with the virile name of Anastasis Tracosas, and while we called them Ricky and Ernie, their marriage was true to our heritage. My older sister, Paraskeve, whom we had called Paraskevoula since our early childhood and then Voula for short, married a Brooklyn Greek named Vasile Chirgotis, whom we called Bill. And certainly any real Son of Pericles was destined to marry a Greek Orthodox girl—surely as Greek as his sisters.

But on my first day at Pratt Institute I met a girl from Syracuse. In a curiously intuitive way I knew she was the girl I would marry from the first second I saw her. Blond, tall and intelligently animated, she was talking to a fellow freshman. I walked up to the two Pratt students and said to the girl, "Get rid of da creep." Instead she tried to get rid of me, but I followed her from school that day, which was against the rules. We parked on the stoop of the girl's dormitory and I introduced myself: "Hi. I'm Lois. George Lois. Me Tarzan, you Jane."

"Me Rosemary," she said. "You arrogant."

"No—Greek Orthodox. I love you."

Rosemary Lewandowski was a second-generation Polish-American whose devoutly Roman Catholic parents danced polkas. She came to New York to build a career and meet cultured people. Instead she met me—but intruding the way I did was the smartest move of my life. When I saw Rosie I *recognized* her. I knew I had found the woman of my life.

We sat together in classes and took an introductory course in advertising, given by Herschel Levit, a maverick teacher who played Mozart in class and described the pleasures of a lobster feast. Two months later I had saved enough money to take my girl to a five-course dinner. The lobster that night was the finest course I ever took in advertising.

I was still living in Kingsbridge, commuting by subway to Brooklyn and moving conspicuously out of my Greek orbit. My parents got wind of my blossoming romance, but they hadn't met Rosie. One day my mother saw her photo as I was going through my wallet. "George, be careful," she said. "Go with other girls . . . take your time . . . no rush to get married." She was groping for the right way to tell me to stay single if I couldn't find a Greek Orthodox girl. Then she looked at the photo again and shouted in

Greek, *"You're throwing your life away with that Irish bum!"* I never told Rosie.

I paid my way through Pratt with the tips I had saved over the years as the florist's delivery boy, plus a basketball scholarship. But in the middle of my second year Herschel Levit told me I should be working in advertising, that I was wasting my time at Pratt, and he sent me to a tiny lady named Reba Sochis, whose nose was broken as badly as mine and cursed up a storm, certainly like no woman I had ever known. She proved to be the third most important woman in my life. Miss Sochis studied my portfolio and offered me a job as an artist in her promotion studio at $35 a week. I quit school and went to work. A few months later, during the summer of 1951, I eloped with Rosemary Lewandowski. We were married in Baltimore in the home of a Lutheran minister, my St. George medals the only visible remains of my Greek upbringing. Before we left New York I called the minister to see if he could handle the ceremony—Greek Orthodox groom, Roman Catholic bride, Lutheran joiner. "Give me good material, I'll do a good job," he said. Our wedding was scheduled for three o'clock in the afternoon. We arrived two hours too early and went to a Jerry Lewis movie. Its title still stays with me: "That's My Boy."

We returned to Brooklyn as man and wife and moved into a pocket-sized apartment a few blocks from Pratt in the Brooklyn Navy Yard district. We shared the hallway john with a sailor's family. The corridor of my new home was bare of icons and free of incense.

We were married while my parents were in Greece for their first visit in twenty-seven years. I rode the subway from Brooklyn to announce our marriage to my older sister, Paraskeve, who was running the store while Haralampos and Vasilike were on their pilgrimage to the mountain. I told her the news and my sister fell into a ritual swoon among the easeled sprays of gladiolas—a few hours earlier she had learned by cablegram that our mother lay in a hospital in Greece, felled by a stroke.

My stricken mother partially recovered in her native land and then came home to Kingsbridge, where her daughters ministered to her selflessly, although her stroke was one of a series to follow that would gradually turn the powerful, perpetual-motion matriarch into a permanent invalid. On her return from Greece, the marriage of her rebellious son—the ordained heir to the store, to our faith, to her Greek mystique—was kept a secret until she was strong enough to absorb this new shock in her odyssey from Greece to Kingsbridge. She knew, however, without being told; the mystical Vasilike, who collected omens and found clairvoyant signals in dreams, announced to me, "You got married." Then she said, "Bring your wife."

"Better than Greek wife," she said after she met my Roman Catholic, Polish-American bride.

"Better than Polish mother-in-law," said the new Mrs. George Lois.

"Better than most eligibles," said the draft board as the Korean War raged.

Shortly before my Greetings arrived, Rosie also quit Pratt and got a job as a designer with a small ad agency. I was only twenty, but I was already married and leaping ahead in my work with a fat jump in salary and a new world of knowledge in my chosen craft. I had broken away from my family—symbolized as fact when the lentil soup recipe of Mrs. Harry George Lois was handed down to Mrs. George Harry Lois. My wife held her nose but mastered the vinegared soup and fed her ambitious Greek. Life became an idyll, with my parents becoming reconciled to my break from tradition, while my wife and I were pursuing parallel careers. But I blew my deferment when I dropped out of Pratt in leap-frogging to an early apprenticeship for the advertising life. I knew what I wanted and I was willing to pay the price. I was drafted into the army to fight in Korea.

When they shanghaied me to Asia to kill gooks, the army had no idea that I'd already gone through the most basic training in life by fighting micks in the Bronx. I was therefore ready for a two-front war: against the official enemy in Korea and against the brass whenever they would try to crap on my dignity. I may have rejected the flower shop and turned my back against the Ortho-doxy of my parents, but I was still a Greek in my bones, still the son of a male-centered heritage.

But I had to come through the war in one piece, because if this young Greek punk got his ass shot off, too many Irishmen in St. John's parish would laugh their balls off over boilermakers after ordering gladiolas from the store I might have owned.

In basic training I talked back crudely when spoken to rudely.
During my sixteen-week cycle, ten weeks were therefore occupied
by company punishment. After a day of training under the scorch-
ing Georgia sun I was sent to the kitchen to scour ovens and polish
vats. "I'll clean the grease traps while I'm here, okay?" I asked the
mess sergeant. He looked at me cross-eyed: "What the fuck you
up to?" "I like to clean grease traps," I said. He squinted suspiciously, but I did all my chores until the penalty was paid.

The army thought I was a malingerer at first; then they thought
I was missing a few marbles when I gave them a gleaming kitchen.
But the mess sergeant loved my work after just one night. "Hey
Lois," he said on the chow line the next morning, "ah needs mah
floors waxed. Pull some more punishment, willya boy?" We
neighborhood niggers don't like to be called boy, so I gave it back
in spades: "Up yours, man. After I give you the cleanest fuckin

ovens at Gordon, how dare you serve this dogshit to a human being?" That night I waxed the floors to a super sheen.

When they ran out of kitchen chores I was put on rock cleanup duty with three other incorrigibles. We collected every rock in our punishment area, loaded seven barrels and dumped them in another part of Camp Gordon. The next day a noncom ordered us to put the rocks back in the seven barrels, then dump them again in a *new* area. I suggested he go fuck himself, and he hauled me in to the major. "Explain yourself, soldier," snapped the major. "Sir, I'll do anything that makes sense," I said. "I'll scour your ovens, I'll polish your vats, I'll clean your grease traps, I'll wax your floors, I'll paint your barracks—I'll do anything. But I ain't gonna pick up rocks that go from here to there, then move them to another place. I just won't do it, sir, because it's not *productive*." The major came around from behind his desk, glanced for a moment at my lopsided nose, then he swatted me on the back and said firmly, "Good man!"

I walked away with my dignity, but a few weeks later I jerked back my elbow into a captain's ribs after he chewed me out for a chickenshit infraction. I thought he was no longer standing behind me, but I hoped I was wrong. When he doubled over I drew three days in the Gordon stockade, where most of the prisoners were black. They policed the pen better than any acre at Gordon, and their drill exhibitions drew crowds as the fuckoffs outsharped the boys outside. "*Sheet*," said the stockade leader, "we'll show them mothers we got rhythm." When I joined them in the "stockade strut," I hardly felt like the neighborhood nigger while serving time.

When I came back rehabilitated, I led the platoon in drill session and marched into more trouble. Our sergeant had one bad eyeball, permanently looking up. I had the platoon going fine to stockade rhythm and after a few "Hut, two, three, fours," I began to chant, "Sergeant Finch came astruttin' *by* . . . cased his squad with one good *eye* . . . he kept a check on the big blue *sky* . . . with his fucked-up shif'less *eye*." The sergeant charged at me, the boys tumbled into each other, and I was sent back to the grease traps.

After another round in the kitchen I was back in time for a spit-and-polish inspection by a visiting major from the inspector general's office. I was in my sixth week, but with all my company punishment I never drew a weekend pass. The major was a spiffy demon—pointed wax mustache, classy boots, riding crop. I was sixth man in the second row. As the major went along the first row, followed by the sergeant, he gigged everyone for nit-picking stuff, a deliberately cute performance to bring the trainees to heel. When he came to Private Lois the major stuck his eyes so close to my chin that his eyelashes brushed my skin. "Did you shave this morning?" he snarled. I stared straight ahead and said, *"Ccchyessa."* There was a long pause. He stepped away slightly and studied me closely. "What did you say?" he asked. I looked down this time, catching his eyes. *"Ccchyessa,"* I repeated. He leaned up close to me again and asked in a whisper, "Son, are you Greek?" With the trace of a grin I said it again. He backed up a foot, twirled his riding crop over his head and barked, "Now *here's* what I call a good-looking soldier—and this happens to be one damn good-looking outfit. Entire company gets a weekend pass, including all you men I gigged." He walked away briskly, leaving the sergeant with his one good eye popping out. "What'd you *say?"* the boys asked me. I told them the truth: "I just said to the major, 'Piss on you.'" All I heard on our weekend was, "Ahhh, Lois, you're full of shit." If I had told them it was a Greek-meets-Greek coincidence they wouldn't have believed me. When some of the Crackers heard I was from the Bronx they thought I was Jewish, and I never denied it; it was a sure way to get a brawl going, and I missed the clean fun of St. John's parish. When they called me jewboy it was like old times again behind the barracks.

"Lois! On the double," barked a noncom from company head-quarters. What now? What for? What punishment? Instead I was handed a telegram: "HARICLEA GAVE BIRTH TO NINE POUND SON JON. WE ALL SEND LOVE AND PRAY FOR YOU. GEORGE BE CAREFUL. VOULA." That night I wrote a letter in Greek to Vasilike, congratulating her on the birth of her first grandchild—a son, a fine omen, a sign of fresh luck for the Lois clan. Maybe some of it would rub off on me. Our training cycle was ending and my record was a beaut. What now? Where to? What for?

My civilian classification as "commercial artist" suddenly worked to my advantage as the army tried to decide what to do with me. I was sent to a rinky-dink post in the heart of Atlanta, where the commander ordered me to paint a mural on the Signal Corps. I was given an empty wall as big as *Guernica* and a blank artistic check.

I chose a Renaissance theme with nuances of Gordon, where we lived and trained with blacks. Racial integration was official policy, but I noticed that the black GI's were always the pole climbers while the whites worked the phones, on the ground. In combat, any GI who climbs a pole makes a ripe silhouette. If the pole climber is dumb enough to stop a bullet, the white communications man on the ground phones in fast to say there's a bleeding spade dangling from the straps.

I painted a desolate field with a white GI set in a Christlike pose on a ghostly pole while a black GI knelt in the foliage like Mary Magdalene, on the phone. After a few days the underpainting was done. The post commander checked on his artist-in-residence and picked up my Renaissance theme as fast as any curator in a Florentine gallery: "What in the Christ goes on, soldier?"

"My mural, sir—in tribute to the United States Army Signal Corps. This is the underpainting and now I'm ready to finish it. Ain't it a knockout, sir?"

"Hold it, Lois. I see a white soldier on the pole and a nigger on the phone."

"You're right, sir, but this painting tries to communicate the haunting mood of the Crucifixion. The GI on the pole has a Christlike feeling, right, sir? And Christ was white. *Ccchyessa*, he was a *white* man."

"I see a white man on the pole and a nigger on the phone. Paint it the other way around, boy."

"But that violates my artistic freedom, sir."

"Put that nigger back on the pole or you'll be court-martialed for disobeying an order."

"I can't, sir. That would compromise my conscience as an artist."

"Conscience, balls. You're confined to quarters."

Rollers were dipped in Dutch Boy and the mural was whitewashed. Instead of a court-martial I was sent to Fort Sam Houston in San Antonio, a manicured golf course where records went astray and mural painters strolled unassigned in civvies on its country club lawns. When I ran into Abe Becker, N.Y.U.'s great basketball star of the '50–'51 season, I knew the army goofed in shipping me to Fort Sam. I was deep in the heart of jockland; and since I majored in basketball at Pratt Institute, I was a natural for an army athletic scholarship. Basketball was high-priority action at Sam, where a career officer's future was built by his ballplayers. Six feet six was the army's enlistment limit, but Fort Sam's basketball team rented taller ringers, regardless of their height, creed or color. I made the team, wore my St. George medals and played at army camps and college campuses across the Southwest. One black ringer was given a seat in the black section at Louisiana State University, where only whites were allowed on the court. I sat that one out and pulled Becker with me to nigger's heaven where we watched the game with the silent ringer. "Never met a nigger-lover I could understand," said one Caucasian teammate. "Never met a bigot I didn't like," said the Son of Pericles. We ended the season undefeated, the ringers went home to pump gas and I was ordered to Asia from Texas via New York by boat.

After forty-five showerless days and 9,300 miles at sea via the Panama Canal we arrived in Japan. Combat veterans who fought in Korea indoctrinated us on the wiles of commie gooks and the tricky ways of Charlie's oriental mind. I tucked away every word on how to survive against those evil slant-eyed Asian butchers. A Catholic chaplain beefed up morale at our benediction: "Look around you, soldiers. Every other one of you is a dead man." I looked at the dead man on my right, but he was pitying the dead slob on *his* right. Then we were shipped to Korea and boarded an antique railroad train, made in Japan. Fifty-caliber bullets smashed through the ceiling planks and opened the stuck windows on the first morning of our picture-postcard ride north through the paddies to the line on the map where the human waves from above the Parallel met the might from the south. From the parish of John and the playing fields of Sam, the Son of Pericles had finally arrived.

"This is your bunker, keep your weapon clean and stay alert," said the sergeant. We were evicted fast from our home in the defoliated hills by a great gook rampage over the Parallel. We pushed back and rescued our bunker until the enemy regrouped and pushed us out a second time. But we drove out the commies again and got our sandbagged bunker back. Soon we were sitting out a lull between artillery barrages and counterattacks. When butterflies fluttered near the bunker it was safe to reach for one. Whoever fired first would bring on the mortars and shrapnel, an unwritten rule. Through the slits of our bunker one morning I spotted a Chinese soldier six hundred yards away, hanging his laundry in the bright Korean sun. "Fire on that man," barked a new shavetail in our unit. He was one day old on the Parallel and couldn't read the unwritten rules. I was writing a letter in Greek to Vasilike and ignored the looie. "I won't say it again, soldier," he shouted at me, "*fire*." I drew my diagonal slash through the squat circle of *phi* (ϕ) and finally said, "Listen, why make trouble?" He began crowing about a court-martial so I explained the facts of life: "If I fire just once, Lieutenant, they'll start a barrage and we'll get our asses blown to hell. Yours too, sir." The dumb ϕuck quit hounding me, I finished my letter and the enemy finished his laundry. Here's how I remember Korea: I earned thirty-six points for combat and wrote thirty-five letters in Greek. I was a gladiator and a classicist. It was a Renaissance experience—and while I was wounded in the guts by their side, I didn't let my balls get busted by our side.

After five months of give-and-take on the Parallel I earned five days in Japan for rest and recreation. I was late coming back because the line at Tokyo's airport for return flights was three days long. "You're AWOL, Lois, a serious crime," said the sergeant. "Don't worry, Sarge, I'll get me two commies and make up the time." The enemy let loose again to take back our sandbags and a shrapnel daisy tore my stomach. There went my benediction— "Every other one of you" was odd man Lois. I was moved to Seoul, where surgeons sliced and stitched. I lost some intestines but my ass was intact. "Should have no effect on your intestinal fortitude," said the medics. I went back to war to earn my thirty-six combat points for freedom, four per month. Back at the bunker the non-coms were falling like flies and over their dead bodies privates rose in the ranks. "Dear Rosie," I wrote from the Parallel, "I'm now a sergeant first class. Spend more."

I was loading supplies for a new push north as the Korean sun sizzled. After two sleepless days and beat by the heat I peeled off my shirt. A major waved his swagger stick and ordered me to get in uniform, but I ignored him and continued loading. When he drew his sidearm I waded in. The major's pistol fell to the dirt and he flopped on his stick. "You'll be court-martialed for sure," I was told. "For what?" I asked. "Who's the goddam enemy?" The major was a black market profiteer. A garrulous old warrant officer who had taken a shine to me and knew the score asked him if he was clean enough to dirty my record. I lost my stripes but kept my gun. The barrel of my weapon could be held to the sun and not a grain of dust would block the light. I nursed my steel and I got me my commies, but there was always something more to defend. "Dear Rosie," I wrote, "I didn't keep my shirt on. Spend less." When letters from Korea arrived in Brooklyn, my war bride glanced first at the top left of the envelope to check my latest rank, a very up and down situation.

The war was a special torture to the worrisome matriarch Vasilike, made more unbearable by her paralysis, which bottled her fiery emotions. Her only son was back in combat. In addition, Hariclea's husband, Ernie Tracosas, was serving as an artillery officer in Korea, after having been wounded twice in the Marines during World War II. "If I bump into Ernie," I wrote Hariclea, "I'll be sure to congratulate him personally about Jon. Besides, Greek officers are the only ones who talk to me."

I never saw my brother-in-law in Korea, but I later crossed paths near the Parallel with a Boston Irishman from an artillery outfit. "Who's your company commander?" I asked him. "Captain Tracosas," he said. "Holy *shit*," I shouted. "I hear he's the worst prick in Korea."

"*Worse*. Roughest motherfucker of them all. Drives the guys out of their skulls—toughest company commander in the artillery. That sonofabitch is buckin to become the first Greek general in the army."

"Listen pal, I'm Greek too, so I'll give you a friendly tip. If you wanna make points with Tracosas, instead of saying *yessir* to the prick, say it Greek style and he'll love you." I coached him on how to pronounce *Ccchyessa* until he said it better than any Irishman in the world.

After nine months I had earned my thirty-six points and left Korea. The boat from Inchon made it to Seattle in fourteen days on murderous seas, then our human cargo plane to New Jersey feathered two engines on the way to Chicago and we stopped for repairs at O'Hare. No coats, class-A uniforms, ten degrees below zero during the frigid flight, and now a twenty-four hour layover in the Chicago airport with a planeload of war-weary GI's, twiddling their frozen thumbs, waiting for freedom. I felt so near and yet so far. The wait at O'Hare—the faceless, timeless agony in the airport—was the last straw. I exploded in a nonstop fury at all the horseshit, bullshit and chickenshit. In New Jersey I was restricted to base for insulting the army (I went AWOL), while my name kept slipping to the bottom of the discharge list. Eventually it climbed to the top and freedom was in sight for Lois, George Harry; son of Haralampos and Vasilike; husband of Lewandowski; alias George Reardon; killer of commies.

"Blood test, men. I punch your vein and the blood fills up each man's vial. Round the room I go and I'm back to you before the vial is full. Then *I* pull the needle. No man pulls the needle before I'm back. Clear?" It was a big room with about forty GI's bleeding for a slow-moving creep. My vial filled up and he was only halfway through. I pulled the needle and he charged at me, livid with rage, out for blood. He grabbed my vial and poured it on the floor. My last round with the army ended this way: I swung at the honcho and missed, but he slipped and fell on his butt in a pool of Greek blood.

The captain called me in. "Why soldier, *why*," he asked, "when you're so close to discharge?"

"My blood, sir. My dignity."

The captain looked me in the eyes and *saw* me. My papers stayed at the top of the list and I left the same way as I came: rank E-2, very private.

When the men returned from war the *ouzo* flowed in Kingsbridge. Rosie and I subwayed to the family reunion from our new Brooklyn apartment, a larger joint with a *meros* all our own, Greek for "the place"—the can. "In my village," said Haralampos, "we still have no *meros*, even today. Everyone goes to the cypress grove." Papa wasn't his quiet self on this happy day.

Voula, Ricky and Rosie charged around the apartment like peasant wives, dishing out food and helping the invalid Vasilike enjoy her first moments of peace since her stroke in Greece. As she fondled her first grandson, Jon Tracosas, her eyes sparkled with a new zest. The kid was built like the Trojan horse, a *very* good omen.

Haralampos, Bill Chirgotis and Captain Ernie were sipping Metaxa in the dining room. "Hey Papa, I found out why Eisenhower *really* went to Korea," I said. "He wanted to stop Captain Tracosas from invading China. Your son-in-law was becoming the Greek MacArthur, and I've got a witness to prove it."

"Listen, Papa, you won't believe this," said Ernie, ignoring me. "One day in combat I'm telling this Irish kid in my outfit to give me a fast inventory of our ammo while they're laying mortar all over us. Well, may God be *my* witness, he says to me, '*Ccchyessa!*' So I promoted him to corporal on the spot, but I warned him that if he ever said that to me again, I'd bust his ass. He told me a Greek GI near the Parallel taught it to him. He said this joker had a crooked nose, a New York accent, talked real fast and was just broken from sergeant. Your son Georgios, Papa."

"*Ccchyessa*, Anastasis," I said.

Finally Haralampos got around to my career, my *work*. "You're back again with the very nice lady?" he asked. My job was waiting and Reba Sochis offered me a partnership when I returned, but I wanted to spread my wings as an art director. Reba was like a third sister and took me in hand wisely. She told me to keep away from Madison Avenue until I had perfected my craft. She referred me to CBS, a West Point for young designers. Bill Golden, the network's coiled-spring boss of TV advertising and promotion, a co-worker of Dr. Frank Stanton, was giving the network its incomparable graphic class. I showed my portfolio to his senior designer, Kurt Weihs, who thought Golden should see it. "Test him," said Golden after scanning my work. Weihs gave me a set of photos for a current TV series and asked me to do a few ads. When I submitted my work, Golden looked it over and told Weihs he made it too easy for me. He crabbed and fidgeted, but he hired me. Golden turned out to be an unusual boss—a perfectionist who was absolutely fearless.

When one of his projects was turned down by the president of CBS Television in a room loaded with vice presidents, Golden tore up his designs, tossed the confetti on the floor and charged for the door. He was so enraged he pulled the handle clean off the door, bolting himself in the room with the brass.

When Jack Benny saw his face in a CBS ad sketched by the great illustrator René Bouché, he blew a fuse and demanded that only authorized photographs run in future ads. Golden said screw him, commissioned a second sketch by Bouché and ran it without Benny's okay. That sketch became his famous trademark.

When one of Golden's designers brought a sketch by Bouché to Jackie Gleason for "The Honeymooners," Gleason tossed the designer out of his office. Bill went to see Gleason and they almost came to blows. Finally, a Gleason aide came down to talk it over in Golden's office and the sketch was approved, but only after the roughest shouting I had heard since parish days. Golden then walked Gleason's man to the reception area, and as they waited for the elevator, Golden said sweetly, "I suppose this is where I should apologize for blowing off, but how could I possibly apologize to someone like you, with taste for shit?"

He was a model of integrity for a young designer, but breaking the ice with him was no simple process. Two days after I joined CBS, my first project was ready for Golden. His secretary, Teri Kerner, looked up at me from a massive dictionary and smiled nervously when I asked to see him. "Go ahead in," she said, looking more edgy. Off in the distance at the far end of a long room, Bill Golden was at work. He was a tall man, with wide scarecrow shoulders, wearing a jacket that was a size too large, sleeves flapping as he moved his pencil in sudden strokes over the layout on his crowded desk. I walked to within four feet of his desk and waited for him to look up, but he kept on working, his eyes riveted to his layout. His hair was long and his fingernails were black, yet he radiated a certain elegance.

I began to feel like a fool, standing there without even being acknowledged, so I began to time his cute act. Thirty seconds elapsed, but it felt like an eternity. I cleared my throat but Golden kept working, his eyes always on his desk. I stepped closer, I cleared my throat, I coughed. Then I leaned forward and held my layout almost in front of my knees to catch his eye. But Golden just kept working, his left shoulder jerking with a slight tic. He knew I was there, and I knew he would never look up. I walked back quietly to Miss Kerner. "May I borrow your dictionary?" I asked.

"Tell me the word and I'll find it for you," she said. "It's very heavy to shift around."

"It's a four-letter word," I whispered, and I lifted the hulk from her desk. I went back into Bill Golden's office and stopped three feet from his desk as he kept to his work. Fingers raced over a tracing pad, his tic flashing. I held the dictionary chest-high and opened my hands. It fell to the floor with an ear-splitting smash. The pencil flew from Golden's hand and his face jerked up.

"Oh, George—can I help you?" he asked. His tic had stopped.

"Uh, yes. I'd like to show you this ad." I handed him the layout and he looked at it briefly. "Good. Very good," was all he said. I took back the layout, picked up the dictionary and left his office. "I found the word for Mr. Golden," I mentioned to his secretary as I returned the dictionary. I cupped my hands to her ear and whispered, "*Lois.*"

Later we locked horns over a priest. When "$64,000 Question," the biggest quiz show of them all, was slated to bring back the famous priest Alvin Kerschaw for the jackpot shot where he pockets the $32,000 or goes for the $64,000, a last-minute decision was made to run a large ad for that show. It was getting late and only Bill's production manager, Ed Side, was around. I did a simple ad of the priest's face, which everyone knew, with the question that everyone was asking: "Will he go for the $64,000?" That was the whole ad—I had left out the CBS Eye, the channel and the time; but the priest was so famous I wanted the ad to look like a news story. "George, be careful," said Side. "Golden will murder you."

After the ad appeared, a blizzard of angry calls and memos descended on Golden from the network brass for allowing it to run that way. The Eye in particular was sacred to CBS, and certainly to Golden, who designed that world-famous trademark with Kurt Weihs. He was furious at me for omitting it and his tic ran wild. "But Bill," I said, "it's the most famous show in the world. You don't have to tell anyone who, what, when or where because they *know.*" But he was still plenty pissed. To pacify the brass he actually circulated proofs throughout CBS with the missing line. When the storm blew over he stopped by my office and with a devilish smile he waggled a finger at me: *naughty, naughty!* He liked the ad and respected its eyeless moxie, but he couldn't allow his feelings to come out in words.

A few months later Golden ripped six tries at a layout by designer Tom Courtos. Finally I asked Tom to let me handle Golden. "Bill, I'd like you to look at this job," I said. He thought Courtos had thrown in the towel—that I was showing him *my* design. "Nice job," he said. I scooped up Tom's layout and headed for the door. Then I suddenly turned to the wonderful tyrant and said, "I brought this in for Tommy. He wasn't feeling well today." Golden again waggled his finger at me: *naughty!* I waggled back: *enough!*

Bill Golden had created a designer's paradise at CBS, where a young artist could cut his teeth and learn the disciplines of his craft. Ed Side, for example, was so devoted to precision that he checked out the size of every ad with a chrome-plated ruler. "You're off by a thirty-second of an inch," Side told me one day when I gave him an ad to be engraved. I knew that even $20 German rulers weren't sized identically, but Ed Side swore by his chrome-plated master. "Check the ruler," he said. I loved Ed Side and hated to upset him. He worshiped details like Haralampos at a wreath, and his face had the appealing fullness of Franklin Delano Roosevelt. But I couldn't resist: "By *your* ruler, Eddie, it's off by a thirty-second, but by *my* ruler it's on the button." The next day Ed Side circulated a memo asking everyone in the network who used a ruler to send it to him so that CBS could work with standardized rulers once and for all. They came flying into Side's office from every shnook in every nook of the world's largest network and his room turned into a lumberyard. But Ed Side himself checked out every last ruler against his chrome-plated master—because Golden our boss had chrome-plated standards.

I worked closely with Kurt Weihs, designing booklets, mailers, letterheads, theater marquees, program notices and ads for hundreds of CBS shows. The work flowed into Golden's office in torrents, and he respected this passion for work while he raised the standards of American graphics and gave CBS its visual class by using the talents of superb illustrators like Felix Topolski, John Groth, David Stone Martin—and Ben Shahn.

Golden commissioned work from Ben Shahn during the McCarthy years when he was blacklisted in the communications industry—until things *really* got hot. At that point (the peak of the McCarthy hysteria) Bill was ordered not to use Shahn. After the historic Edward R. Murrow television show that helped break the back of McCarthy, Shahn resumed work for CBS. It was a great day for art, CBS, and America.

Young designers were falling over themselves for a chance to work in Golden's universe, enriched by giants like Kurt Weihs and Mort Rubenstein. Lou Dorfsman, an alumnus from Bill's department in charge of the network's radio advertising, added further strength to that elite circle. But after a few years I got ants in my pants for an ad agency job—while Madison Avenue art directors were beginning to notice my work in the art journals. So I began to scout around. The creative director of an agency that handled a famous cigarette account looked at my work, picked out a few of my best ads and said, "Bill Golden did these ads." I shot back angrily, "Everything here *I* did—*me!*" He asked to keep my portfolio for a few days, but I warned him he could hurt my relationhip with Bill Golden if my boss knew I planned to leave. "Why of course," he assured me. A few days later Bill Golden mentioned that the creative director called him about me. "I was just looking around, Bill," I said. "I'm not unhappy." Golden dropped the subject; he could never accept the idea that anyone wanted to leave his universe, and I'm sure he erased it from his mind. But I was incensed.

"I looked you in the eye. I was very, very clear about keeping the confidence," I told the creative director. "Well I'm sorry," he said, "because I can't recall the conversation. But my speaking to Bill Golden did you no harm. I won't tell you what he said, but I'll tell you this—*my* boss would like to meet you." His boss was a runty bird with fishy eyes. He closed the door tightly and cased the room for hidden mikes. He moved like a thief onto his oversized leather chair and leaned across his enormous desk, looking me over through his great black-framed eyeglasses. "I'd like you to come in as our Number Two creative man under our creative director, who is Number One in that area," he said. "But while you'll be working for *him* and not for *me*, you'll really be working for *me* and not for *him*, because I've got plans, *big* plans." I grabbed my portfolio and ran to Jerry Fields, the central job-jump station of the advertising business. "Very promotion, very designy," was entered in my dossier. "Fashion or allied" was listed as my area of expertise. I was twenty-six and typecast. I was sent to Lennen & Newell, an advertising agency that wasn't considered a "design" agency and had no fashion accounts. But I took the job. L&N was one of the country's top twenty agencies, with $45 million in billings. I was offered a salary of $18,500 to start. For a young kid that was hot stuff. I told Bill I was leaving.

For a brief period CBS had used a big agency to create and place small ads for local programs. Bill Golden detested their advertising and reassigned the creative work to his staff. Most ad agencies were whores to Golden. He felt they corrupted talent, and he was convinced they knew nothing about *communicating*. "Nobody's beat them yet," he told me. "You'll have a terrible time out there. Think about this decision. George, be careful. It's your career, your life." He spoke at length and with feeling. I was deeply moved, but I was twenty-six and he was forty-six. The next day we had a shorter conversation. He wanted to know what accounts I would be working on.

"American Airlines," I said proudly. "I think it's a great opportunity to do creative advertising."

His tic suddenly acted up.

Suren Ermoyen's droopy-lidded eyes seemed to have been painted on his face by El Greco. Ermoyen, a bald Armenian, was senior vice president and art director at Lennen & Newell, Inc., 380 Madison Avenue, U.S.A. My new boss, an aristocrat of style, looked the part of a high-powered advertising man. He wore a ritzy blue shirt with striking white cuffs, and he sported a lush Dean Acheson mustache under his long Byzantine nose. His office was furnished like an Arabian tent, with arching potted palms and gorgeous oriental rugs.

A sharp rummager of the art annuals, Suren was familiar with my work and knew my name. "Exciting stuff happening here," he said when we met. "Need great talent . . . terrific atmosphere for creative ads . . . perfect place for someone with your ability . . . you'll be doing original work . . . great environment . . . terrific, terrific. . . ." He sang all the siren songs I wanted to hear: "American Airlines is a major account . . . national advertiser

. . . receptive to fresh thinking . . . you'll be doing original work
. . . terrific, terrific. . . ."

I was now ready to become a real art director in a real ad agency.
First I would score with my American Airlines ads, then I'd branch
out to L&N's other big clients like Colgate-Palmolive and Benrus.
My future looked *terrific*, and on my first day at work I buttonholed an account man for information about the airline industry,
but he turned right around and asked me, "Aren't you an art director?" I found out fast enough that a young artist was expected to
learn his place at L&N. Mine was a large room off the bullpen;
writers popped in and handed me slips of paper with fortune cookie
headlines from which to "execute" ad layouts. I didn't go through
my apprenticeship with Reba Sochis and Bill Golden for *this*—
but maybe I didn't understand the agency's style. I checked in at
the tent to consult with Suren Ermoyen. My boss was going over
some material with a few creative types—and to watch the way
Suren's team agonized, it was obvious that they cared about their
work. I decided to speak with Suren another time, but as I turned
to leave, one of the creative fellows shouted at Suren, "No, goddamit, if you want to bet that kind of dough, raise the fuckin
odds." Another star shot back, "Well for chrissakes, Snider's out
of his slump—what do you want, *eight* to five?" Suren brushed the
edges of his noble mustache and I went back to my office. I shut
the door and made ads, working late at the agency then resuming
at home. My office was soon papered with campaigns, a one-man
show of drive and rage. If only because of its quantity my work
would have to be noticed.

"*Fantastic*," said Suren, admiring my wall, "remarkable work
. . . just what we need . . . wonderful ideas . . . very creative
. . . terrific, George, terrific." He shot his cuffs and returned to
the tent. "Very *interesting*," said the account boys, "stay with it
. . . we'll give it a shot . . . interesting, *interesting*."

"They like my work," I told Rosie. "It takes time and I know
I'm in a hurry, but I'll click soon. My office is exploding with great
campaigns, but big agencies like L&N move slowly. I'll speak to
Suren tomorrow." I popped into Suren's tent and asked him when
my work would move off the wall and start showing up in newspapers. "Be patient," said Suren. "Keep at it, George . . . your
stuff is fabulous . . . the account group will come around . . .

we'll sell 'em . . . don't stop . . . the ads are terrific, terrific."

As the weeks went by my layouts butted up against the ceiling. Entire campaigns and concept ideas stuck to my wall, but one or two timetable ads slipped through the account group and were okayed by the client. An ad that made it was dumped on my drawing table one morning as a voice snarled, "Did you do this goddam thing?" I looked up at a gnarled face with fiery eyes. "Yeah," I said, my hackles rising, "why?"

"Because as of now you're in trouble, Lois. This ad is too *good* for this place." He grabbed my hand and shook it hard. "I'm John Cholakis, traffic man." He herded ads from the art director's layout to the art bullpen to the engraver to publication. I leaned over and whispered, *"Hellene?"*—the Greek way of asking, "Are you one too?" When I heard his tooth-smashing name I knew Cholakis was no Swede, but he didn't suspect that Lois could be the name of a Greek. Again, I was taken for an Italian or a Jew, with a name that may have been shortened from Losicelli or Lowenstein. Also, having been raised in the city, I use words like *kvetch* and *va fa'n culo* more naturally than smooth Madison Avenue phrases like *neat, nifty* and *you're right, sir.* The name Lois comes from a Greek clan called Loe, a mountain family that goes back three hundred years. They named their hamlet Loes—thus it was *lengthened* to a four-letter name. At Ellis Island a few Irish immigration clerks kept it as Loes, but the others spelled it Lowis, Loys, Lewis and Louis. Haralampos was the only one to become Lois.

L&N's traffic man was not only Greek but a fierce Hellenophile, and my name was instantly recorded in the Book of Cholakis, his mental directory of every Greek in the industry. He knew a marketing man at J. Walter Thompson, a copywriter at Benton & Bowles, an account executive at Young & Rubicam and a goniff at an engraving house called Achilles the Heel. At lunch we exchanged notes on Madison Avenue's Greek underground. "Don't worry," I reassured him, "we Greeks will take over the world—*again.* First we'll get the Jews by poisoning the food in Chinese restaurants. *Then* we'll go after the Irish."

I once spotted Cholakis in the art bullpen with a man in a repulsive flowered tie. They seemed to be gabbing about one of my few ads that was okayed to run. Cholakis called me over and goosed me. He said to the flowered-tie wearer, "I'd like this young fella to hear your comments." Then Cholakis rolled his eyes and announced loudly, "This gentleman, George, sells a lot of printing to our agency. He agrees with me, as I mentioned to you the other day, that an ad such as this one is wrong." The vomitlike flowers on the salesman's tie screamed to be plucked. "I was explaining to Mr. Cherokees," he said, "that this American Airlines ad is in poor taste. Now let me tell you why—" I clutched the tie and yanked it up fiercely. His face turned blue when the flowers met his eyes. "Look, schmuck—with taste like *this*," I growled, "you're criticizing *my* work?" Cholakis told him I was a florist's son and that I became very emotional when I saw artificial flowers.

My impatience also began to show with my aristocratic boss. While I was in the bullpen with an assistant, adjusting a strip of headline type on one of my ads, Suren strolled by with a few clients and stopped at our drawing board. Without actually seeing what I was doing, he curled his mustache and told me to move up the headline. "I like it down *here*," I said, flattening out the strip of type. Suren reached over, peeled off the headline and moved it up an inch. "No, I think it's better up *here*," he said, playing to his clients. "It's shit up there," I said, moving it down but not looking up. Suren kept at it: "No, I think it should be up there, and I *want* it up there."

"Well if you want it up there," I said, "take the goddam layout and shove it up your fuckin Armenian rug-making ass." Then I picked up the ad, which was pasted down on a slab of rigid cardboard, and broke it over my knee with a sharp crackle as a gust of howling laughter went up from the bullpen. The clients giggled, Suren smoothed his mustache, and I went back to my office.

After several months of being mickey-moused, I barged into Ermoyen's tent and spoke my piece: "Suren, *I* want to show my ads to the account supervisor of American Airlines." Suren was in a spot because his art directors were expected to go through channels. But I said if he refused I would call the account supervisor myself, and if *he* refused to see me I would walk in without an appointment. Realizing that I was dead serious, Suren promised to arrange a meeting. I stripped my wall and delivered all my layouts to the Arabian tent. A few days later my phone rang. "Mr. Smith would like to see you in his office," said a crisp voice. Suren had delivered.

C. L. (Bill) Smith was a senior vice president and management account supervisor. He was a very, very big wheel at L&N, with an office as big as a ballfield. His brother, C. R. Smith, was the head man at American Airlines. I almost flipped when I saw the richly carpeted floor of C. L. Smith's enormous office covered by my layouts. They were neatly aligned in parallel columns with two-inch separations, the right width for a tiptoe stroll among the rich fruits of my labor. It was a proud moment in my career. I was in the office of mighty Smith at *my* request, along with an important copywriter, an important marketing man and an important account man. Also Suren. I smiled at my boss with a grateful gleam in my eyes, but his El Greco lids were droopier than ever—and his eyes looked somber.

"Lois, ah want to talk to you about your work on American Airlines," said C. L. Smith.

"Terrific, Mr. Smith. I've been looking forward to this opportunity."

"Well fine, Lois. Now ah've reviewed your work carefully and it's come to mah attention . . ." He was walking as he spoke. He was walking *on my work*, not even trying to edge along the canals of carpeting between the layouts.

"And so ah've given a great deal of thought to your ideas, Lois, and ah've decided . . ." He was planting his feet in the *center* of my ads, grinding his shoes into my work, squishing what I had made, killing a cockroach. Instinctively, I cased the joint. The important faces were all tense. Suren covered his eyes and turned away.

My movements were catlike. I walked quickly in long soundless strides around the entire perimeter of the room so that I could reach the first ad of the first column without trampling on my work. Smith stopped abruptly to watch me, suddenly confused. I kneeled down and swiftly rolled up my ads, column by column, until I had them all in a tidy cylinder under my arm. The diagonally positioned desk of C. L. Smith sat like a fortress in the far corner, behind me. I had salvaged my ads, but I was still in a blind rage, incensed at the way my work was defiled. I gripped the overhang of Smith's desk and with all the strength of my furious mood I flipped it toward Smith's corner. The fortress landed with a deadly thunk on its forward side as drawers slid open and were jammed back into the falling hulk. My cylinder of ads was safely tucked under my arm as all the debris from the top of Smith's desk crashed to the floor. My action was so sudden that a streak of ink actually surged from the desk's executive well and hit the wall like a Rorschach splotch. But I had my ads, my *work*—and without looking back I quietly walked out of the room.

I had no doubt that my career at L&N was finished, but as I began to pack, C. L. Smith came by to see me. "Hey Lois, you a goddam pistol," he said. "Stick around boy, don't get pissed. You and ah gonna git along fine. Ah'm a king-maker . . . ah'll make you a king—a *king*, you hear, boy? You a goddam pistol, Lois."

I kept my job, but they kept the hot-headed kid at arm's length. Later, one out-of-wedlock ad, my only work of value, was found in my office and survived. Talk was in the air of moving the Dodger baseball franchise from Brooklyn to Los Angeles. As the story became big news, an emergency call came through for a rush ad to promote flights to Los Angeles. I posed in a Brooklyn baseball cap, my head pointing west. The photographer developed the shot while I waited, and a few hours after getting the assignment I gave the ad to Cholakis to be engraved. The caption said, "Thinking of going to Los Angeles?" The following day Cholakis brought me proofs. "Beautiful," he said. "Beautiful," I agreed. "But it got killed after the engraving," said Cholakis. "Then why was it engraved?" I asked. "Because it doesn't deserve to die, so *I* engraved it," said my subversive Greek ally. "You'll get in trouble, John," I warned him. "You'll get a prize, George," he predicted. "But it has to *run* to win a prize," I explained. "It's dead, so hang it on your wall and forget it," said Cholakis.

"Gotta have something to show for my sweat." I tacked the proof on my wall. An account man from American Airlines soon noticed it hanging there. He ran the ad and it later showed up again in one of the art annuals. That was my body of work at Lennen & Newell: one proof.

Even after the desk episode I might have made a go of it at L&N if I had shaped up and acted like a proper Madison Avenue gent. But to see my work go to waste was the cruelest fate I could imagine. After about six months I dropped into Suren's tent to tell him I was leaving. "What the hell, George," he said, "it is a rough business. Maybe an ad agency isn't where you belong. I think you came in here with stars in your eyes."

I left the agency with memories of vivid personalities: Suren the Armenian aristocrat; Cholakis the Greek partisan; a smart blond copywriter named Bunny Wells who often stopped by my papered office to look at my ads; Bob Wall, the art director on Old Gold butts, whose office was next to mine—Wall would drop in to look at my ad-covered room, pat me on the back and shake his head with sympathy; also Mike Wollman, a fellow art director who watched me bleed and nursed my wounds. But while the place had its colorful cast of characters, my first job on Madison Avenue was a bust.

As I walked out of Lennen & Newell, having thrown in the towel at the first of my big-time ad agency jobs, I thought of Bill Golden's Cassandra words: "Nobody's beat them yet. You'll have a terrible time out there." Now Suren had told me the same thing—but I wasn't ready to pull in my tail. I belonged in an agency where the art director was a respected advertising craftsman. The pickings were lean in 1957. There were only two agencies where ads were made with a sophisticated sense of graphics and with a genuine respect for the man at the drawing table: Sudler & Hennessey, a pharmaceutical products agency, and Doyle Dane Bernbach, the first "creative" ad agency, in the best sense of that abused word.

I would sink to my knees on the steps of the Acropolis, but never on Madison Avenue. I wasn't about to compromise my standards, and when I called Haralampos to tell him I had quit my job—at a salary of $18,500, an incredible income for my father to contemplate—he asked me to come to Kingsbridge so that he could find out what was wrong.

"It's the *work*, Papa. My work is born every day and it never gets off my wall. It dies. It's like bringing American Beauty roses to the Maestro, and he says 'Beautiful, Mr. Lois, but I don't want them.' "

"Never—the Maestro would never do *that!* But what will you do? A man must work. A man must bring home dollars. A man must support his home."

"I'll find a Maestro."

"They are very rare."

"There's one, but I'm not ready. His name is Bernbach."

"And until you meet Maestro Burnbucks?"

"There's another place that respects good work. I'll try them."

We drank *retsina* and he wished me luck. "Eighteen thousand five hundred dollars—tsk, tsk, tsk—a fortune," said Haralampos. "I won't tell Mama."

"Please, George, control your temper at the new job."

"Please, Rosie, mind your own business."

"Please, George, go easy at Sudler & Hennessey."

"Please, Rosie, I am what I am."

"Please, George, don't remind me."

No sooner was I at the new job when I saw Matt Hennessey moving through the cubicles of the art department bullpen. I knew he was up to something that was none of his business even if he *was* the executive vice president of Sudler & Hennessey. I knew he was diddling with my ad, and Hennessey was no art director. I took off for the bullpen and found him leaning over the shoulder of one of my assistants, telling him to change my layout. My voice bellowed through the floor: "Don't *touch* it, Matt. You want to change my work, tell *me* what you have in mind, but get your goddam hands off my work!" A sea of eyes stared in shock. Hennessey flushed, glared furiously at me and stormed out of the bullpen.

Then he called me into his office to dress me down. Matt Hennessey was a founding partner of the agency, a man in his forties—and here was this young punk art director blasting him out of his art department. But I felt personally defiled.

In his office I was more clear-headed. I admitted that I should have spoken to him privately. (But apologize? Not a chance.) "If you think something's wrong with an ad," I said, "tell me and I'll see if I agree with you. *But don't you ever touch a job of mine.*" Hennessey was enraged, but his hands seemed tied. I had been hired by art director Herb Lubalin, the agency's deeply respected creative boss. I never became a favorite of Hennessey, but his tasteful shop was a charming place to work and I kept my new job.

Arthur Sudler and Matt Hennessey, both formerly with Squibb, started their agency in the forties. They picked up a string of ethical drug accounts like Ciba and Upjohn. When Herb Lubalin later joined Sudler and Hennessey he gave it the pedigree of a fine *atelier*. Pharmaceutical companies, with their elegant brochures for the medical market, were among the first advertisers to seek out the starkly expressive graphic style that Lubalin helped pioneer. He brought stature to Sudler & Hennessey as innovators in design. But by 1957, when I was hired by Herb Lubalin, this distinctive shop was branded as an ad agency that knew how to handle only ethical drug products.

I was one of several key men on a new consumer products team that would transform S&H into an agency that talked to consumers as well as to doctors. We were the new breed. Our emphasis on breakthrough campaigns and our youthful fire were expected to bring in juicy consumer accounts like beer and soap. Under the tasteful creative leadership of Herb Lubalin, S&H attracted a bright, antic crew. Our magic password was *new business*. Jim Collette, a smooth cookie with rich pals and top-level connections, was our new business chief. The agency's chairman, Arthur Sudler, was one of those benevolent older generation types who believed that new accounts would drop through the transom if enough Ivy League asses were kissed by his new business boys. On Mondays his client-hunters gave us the lowdown on their *terrific* progress over the weekend: "We were guests on his yacht on Long Island Sound. Slept eight. He gave us a shot at the account. He personally controls a $400,000 budget. Let's get a presentation going—marketing plan, selling theme, ads, new product ideas. It's a real shot, a real shot!"

Someone may have shacked up in a boat on Saturday night, but somehow those $400,000 nuggets weren't rolling in. New business-men can convince themselves that when a flunky says he's thirsty you can get his account if you're first to shove a drink under his nose, which may explain why all those "shots" never struck gold. But there were dollars to spend on presentations because S&H was very profitable. The agency turned out brochures that looked like a million bucks and yielded much fatter margins than the usual 15 percent gross profit on time and space, the measured media of "pure" advertising. We were able to do eye-boggling pitches on speculation, but when our dazzling work was brought to the hot prospect who was going to give us a real shot, we were lucky to finesse the presentation past the crap pile on the assistant marketing manager's desk. We had shots, ins, pals and chances, yet the formula of guys-who-know-guys never seemed to come off. But patient Arthur Sudler never lost faith. He stuck keys into the backs of his new business boys, wound them up every Friday, and sent them strutting to bag new clients. Ambitious projects were set in motion, but the agency stayed put with Upjohn and Ciba.

After I had a bellyful of fruitless presentations, I submitted a proposal: once and for all let's cut out the costly pitches based on hoohah connections and wild shots. Instead, let's zero in on a New York advertiser who spends about $100,000—and let's offer to do his ads *free*. We'll turn out *visible* work and national advertisers will see our ads in the New York media. They'll want to know who's turning out that great stuff. Then we'll start getting calls from advertisers who want to talk turkey.

The agency decided it wasn't prudent to spend money so loosely. The old ways of hunting business went back into gear as Jim Col-lette's boys went off to their lunches at the Ivy League clubs to make connections. On weekends they sailed on Long Island Sound with new top-level wheels. They chased rainbows, and fantasies bloomed like wild daisies. Nothing happened. But Sudler & Hennessey was still a charming place to work.

Herb Lubalin attracted bright people, including a creative consultant who dropped by my office shortly after I joined the agency. He had Park Avenyoo class—sweetly fawncy, with a graceful set to his clothes and a perfectly dog-eared jacket. The consultant had bright eyes and a puckish smile. "Are you Lois?" he asked. "I'm Fred Papert." He handed me a sheet of paper with copy for a Ciba ad. "I work with the agency," he explained. "Herbie told me you're the new art director. Can we work together on this ad?" He was an extremely likeable smoothie, but I found myself beginning to boil. Lubalin never told me there was a creative joker in the deck, and suddenly here's this sweet consultant, with his fortune cookie copy, expecting a layout. I told him to take his goddam paper off my table. But he smiled nicely and listened like a patient gentleman when I explained how I preferred to work. I said we should get the full story on the product, then talk over the job together and pinpoint its chief strengths. Then *together* we would come up with an exciting idea.

Before he became a consultant, Fred Papert had racked up an impressive record as a copywriter with some of the most prestigious agencies in town. But even to a pro like Papert it came as a new idea that an art director should be considered as more than a "designer"—that he owned a brain as well as two eyes. Experienced as he was, Papert listened as though I might not be entirely cuckoo. Papert and Lois began to work like partners on Herb's happy team. We became Freddie and George, feeding the spunky spirit at Sudler & Hennessey.

The charm of Dave Herzbrun, copy chief of our consumer products team, was hard to pin down. He came on like a Fuehrer and could throw you off. Herzbrun moved into a power position swiftly, installing himself as a confidant of Chancellor Sudler. He seemed to be moving with blitzkrieg speed to annex all of Sudlerland. After he got the lay of the land he came into my office and closed the door behind him slowly. He leaned over my drawing table and laid it on the line, his eyes flashing: "I had dinner with him last night. He plans to retire next year. He told me himself. When he retires he'll name *me* new president of the agency. It can happen within a year. Now here's what I want to know, Lois—are you with me or are you against me?" Matt Hennessey was already against *me*, so I couldn't afford to make an enemy of our copy chief. "Hell yes, I'm wit ya," I said. "When's da *putsch?*" Herzbrun became another teammate, adding further spice to the joint with his *achtung* act.

Cholakis was also a key man in Sudlerland.

When Herb Lubalin was interviewing me for the job he asked if I knew of a good traffic man. I referred Cholakis to Lubalin and he was hired, too. But after my blowup with Hennessey I warned Cholakis, "The minute Matt finds out I was the guy who sent you here, you're dead—so don't get close to me, John." We both played it cool and Cholakis went about his work, ignoring me. He turned into more than just a traffic man; Hennessey loved his work and made him the unofficial "efficiency expert" of S&H as Cholakis streamlined the agency with skill and speed. He stuck a pencil behind his ear and cased the joint with a loaded clipboard. His gnarled face scowled up from the water cooler, scaring the pants off some of the stiffs who padded the payroll. Matt Hennessey began to swear by Cholakis while I swore to Cholakis that I would never tell Hennessey we were friends.

But Cholakis came between me and one of our account men after Lubalin's doggedness finally paid off. We landed our first consumer products account, a discount retailer in New Jersey called Carr's— not quite Procter & Gamble, but a refreshing change from Upjohn and Ciba. One morning an engraver's proof was placed on my drawing table, one of my first finished ads for Carr's. Warning signals began to flash as I leaned closer and noticed that the proof was different from the way I had designed the ad. My work had been tampered with. *Personally defiled*—it was the only way to describe my feelings at such moments. I turned pale with rage. Gerry Schaflander, the account man on Carr's, was with me. "What happened to this ad?" I asked him. "This wasn't the way I sent it through."

Schaflander was tall, with a restless manner. He jabbered back nervously, "I didn't like that piece of type so I changed it, moved it up . . . the ad looks better . . . client likes it, and it's too late to change . . . already plated . . . running tomorrow." Cholakis overheard what was brewing. He dropped his clipboard and scooted into the room. I had just grabbed Schaflander's lapels in a blind fury and lifted him off the floor. I was actually holding him in the air, cursing at him with the roughest words I knew from my gutter-Kingsbridge arsenal.

Cholakis, about five feet nine, slipped in between us and poked his head up through my outstretched arms. "George," he pleaded, "calm down, for chrissakes. Control yourself." But I was too incensed, and I raised my pitch, the blood rising in my face as I boomed out a volley of filth that would have shaken the toughest of toughs in the schoolyard of P.S. 7—at the very moment when Arthur Sudler happened to stroll by with a few new business prospects. I spotted Sudler as I held on to Schaflander, by now sinking into his collar, with Cholakis' head between my arms as he tried to shove me away. Without skipping a beat Arthur Sudler said to his guests, "As you can see, gentlemen, our people get very excited about their work at our agency."

They strolled away and I kept my job. I worked hard and seemed to be settling down. But after ten months my life changed. Rosie and I had our first child in September 1958. The kid had dark eyes and a deep Mediterranean look. When I had told the priest of St. John's parish team that my boy would be named Harry George, reversing my George Harry, little did I realize that I would have a Polish father-in-law named Joe with a vested interest in the baby equal to Papa's. We named him Harry Joseph, one name per grandfather. *"Store . . . home . . . father . . . son"* was being realized. We had moved from Brooklyn to a handsome apartment in Greenwich Village, and I was now the father of a half-Polish son who looked more Greek than me. But I began to grow restless at my job. If and when the store ever materialized, I would need experience in the big leagues.

After a year's diet of charm and style at Sudler & Hennessey I felt imprisoned in a gorgeous cage. I sent a letter to the Maestro. Bill Bernbach was founder, president and creative boss of Doyle Dane Bernbach, the first and the only "creative" advertising agency in the business. DDB was less than ten years old, a relatively new shop. But Bernbach was changing the look and language of advertising as no man had ever done before. He was placing all his chips behind breakthrough campaigns—advertising that was *seen*, that appealed to people's intelligence. He had elevated the art director to first-class citizen of the advertising world. His emphasis on stunning visuals and simple, truthful copy was making unknown brands famous and famous ad agencies ashamed of their shoddy work.

My letter to Bill Bernbach caught his attention. I was referred to Bob Gage, his chief art director and one of the charter members of DDB. Portfolios were stacked in a wobbling heap in the corner of Gage's busy office. My letter came at the end of a long search for a new art director. I got the job.

Leaving Lubalin was sad, but I couldn't stay. He knew I was going to the one ad agency where I should be working. I left with the rich experience of a year with a pioneer, a giant, an *art director*. I gave Herb my graceful Thonet hatrack before leaving, but someone had copped my beloved brass spittoon; my two vintage pieces stayed behind.

"Hey Cholakis," I said on my last day, "you want a raise? Before I take off for Doyle Dane I'll tell Hennessey I think you're the biggest fink in the agency."

"I'll miss you, *Hellene*. Your next job will be your last. After Doyle Dane Bernbach you'll have no place to go. You'll have to start your own agency." Some Greeks, according to some Greeks, are supposed to be clairvoyant. That night I called Haralampos. "Hello Papa," I said, "I'm leaving the agency."

"*Again*, George? Why are you so restless? Why can't you sit still?"

"I'm leaving the agency for the one job I was telling you about . . . with the Maestro. Doyle Dane Bernbach. You remember?"

"Aha, *aha*. Now listen to me, George. I want you to listen to me. Stay long at your new job. If your Maestro is a man of taste he will respect your work. I wish you good luck with Mr. Burnbucks."

6 The matzoh and the Nazi car

With my first assignment at Doyle Dane Bernbach in early 1959 a posse was out for my neck because of the Ear.

Bill Bernbach asked me to come up with a newspaper campaign for a new product called Kerid ear drops. I was eager to prove that I could measure up to the three big-gun art directors at DDB. My chubby boss, Bob Gage, had been knocking out so much of that great work for Polaroid, for Ohrbach's, for the Dreyfus Fund with its trademark lion, for Chemstrand—and for just about every account at the agency. Bill Taubin did the famous campaign "You don't have to be Jewish to love Levy's." Taubin's personal warmth in that great advertising showed the breadmakers that a message can be powerful when it's human. The art department's third big gun was a complex kraut named Helmut Krone with a dour, Buster Keaton face. He was a fidgety perfectionist who worked with deadly Teutonic patience. A ferocious talent, Helmut Krone had done the first great Polaroid ads, including the memorable ad por-

trait of the classic clown's face. The giants of my profession were
Gage, Taubin and Krone. Even the other art directors at DDB—
their so-called second-string team—were worlds ahead of most so-
called top talents in the larger ad agencies. And now I was part of
this great agency's awesome first-string lineup, itching for action.
It began with the Ear.

Kerid's research showed that people poked around with pencils
and bobbie pins to clean their ears. I pushed the moral to its graphic
brink by showing a colossal closeup of an ear, sprouting all those
pencils and pins. The visual warning was inescapable: don't tinker
with your ears, use Kerid ear drops.

When I brought the Ear to Bernbach his eyes lit up. But some of
his creative people thought it was downright disgusting. The corridors buzzed with angry talk. I shut my door and holed up to
complete the campaign. I knocked out enough layouts for Kerid
to cover a wall. My room was converted into a gallery of ear
posters. But some of the elitists at DDB had become zealots
about the "tasteful" tone of their new-wave advertising. A posse
gathered and went to Bill Bernbach. They were ashamed, they said,
to see the Ears of twirp Lois come out of holy DDB. Bernbach listened. Then the campaign was presented to Kerid and they ran off
with the Ear. The campaign ran and sold drops. But I learned from
that first assignment that I would have to fight for my work—*again*,
even in my Maestro's paradise. With the matzoh poster I almost
lost my life.

Bill Bernbach revolutionized the creative process in advertising
by encouraging his artists and writers to work together without
account men jamming fortune cookie copy into the blend. But this
meant that a great ad could be harpooned by a client if the account
man couldn't sell it. My matzoh poster was a classic example.

"He didn't like it," said the account executive when he returned
from Long Island City. "He killed it, George." My poster was
rolled up in a thick cardboard tube. "It's dead, George." He
chucked the tube into the corner of my office. "I tried, George."
In the tube was a stunning eye-stopper, a visual symbol that was
so clear even the Irish of St. John's parish would buy a box to nib-
ble with their beer.

I showed a huge, gorgeous, realer-than-real color blowup of

a matzoh. Above the matzoh my headline said, "Kosher for Passover," which may sound like nothing much—but the headline was lettered in Hebrew. And the poster was scheduled to run in New York's subways just before Passover. In Hebrew lettering my headline was as clear as a shamrock. There wasn't a person in New York who didn't know that these hieroglyphics meant kosher. But because the matzoh poster was so obvious, I should have known it would need imaginative selling for the average client to buy it.

"You gotta give me a reason," I asked the account man. "No reason," he said. "He just didn't like it." I went to Bernbach.

"I don't understand, Bill," I said. "The client killed this poster and they didn't give a reason."

"Well obviously they didn't like it," he said.

"But I want to know *why* they didn't like it. I don't think it's right for any account man at Doyle Dane to come back with a fat *no* and no *reason*."

Suddenly he bristled. "George Lois," he said softly, "why do you insist on calling me by my first two names?"

"Sorry—Doyle Dane *Bernbach*. But I still don't know the reason."

"I don't know either. What did the account man say?"

"They just killed it, period."

"Well I'm sure he made every effort to sell it."

"I'm *not* sure, Bill. If he really understood the concept he would have sold it."

When I first showed the poster to Bernbach his eyes feasted on it as though I had sprung the Maltese Falcon for Sydney Greenstreet. But now he was reluctant to undercut his account man by contacting the client himself. And the agency had an unwritten rule: when the account man strikes out, the art director takes his lumps and tries a new approach.

"Well if you think you're that smart, *you* go sell it," he said.

"Thanks, Bill. I will." The Maestro knew what he was doing.

"I'm going to sell it," I told the account man.

"Oh no you're not."

"Oh yes I am. Bill told me I could go."

"*Bill* told you?"

"Yeah."

"Well then you call up right in front of me, right now, and make the appointment."

He gave me the number. I made an appointment to review my poster personally that afternoon with A. Goodman & Sons in Long Island City. The account man was miffed. But he was also tickled to have me poke my crooked nose into the matzohland buzzsaw. The old man at Goodman had the reputation of a master *kvetch*, a very obstinate customer.

The word got around fast that I was headed for disaster. In the john I overheard a media man tell an account man, "Did you hear? Lois is going to Goodman *a cappella* to sell his matzoh poster!" The account man said, "Bernbach is smart. He's throwing him to the wolves. When the old bastard in Long Island City says no, that's it. Lois will get his ass racked and he'll crawl back to his office." When the media man said, "Maybe he won't come back, God willing," the account man shot back, "*Nobody* ever quits Doyle Dane." The pious creeps were getting under my skin. "Doyle Dane *Bernbach*," I said, slamming the door as I left. That was the best imitation of Bill Bernbach where account men shoot the shit.

The matzoh monarch's office looked out onto a network of glass cubicles so that every clerk could be seen by their boss. He was an Old Testament patriarch with a harsh manner, but a warmth lurked in his sullen eyes. His staff surrounded his imperial desk like a family gathering. They all greeted me with a friendly warmth.

The patriarch hunched over his desk, heavy eyebrows draping his Talmudic eyes. His dialect was boardroom Menasha Skulnik. His favorite sentence was "I dun like it." And his favorite word was "No." But he was an attentive listener. He leaned forward as I said, "You're on the subway and you see this gorgeous Goodman matzoh poster . . ." and just as I unfurled it he said, "I dun like it."

"I *love* it," I said, "because you want to *stop* people when they're in a hurry. You want to make them *see* the Goodman. And you don't need lots of words, because you don't have to explain matzoh. When people rush around in a subway they don't have time to *read* a poster." A head nods with approval. "It's just before Passover," I went on. "Everyone who buys matzohs is probably

Jewish, and it's a joyous holiday, right? There's food and wine on the table, and everything's kosher, right? So you say something that fits the holiday. This poster says it!" Another head nods, encouraging me to continue: "You don't say, 'Listen, buy my matzoh because I make a terrific product' and all that stale hoohah that nobody reads. You just use a few Hebrew letters to remind people of the spirit of Passover, so when they think of matzohs they think of Goodman." A secretary nods. Even better, the patriarch waves his hand and harrumphs a frog. He speaks: "*I dun like it.*"

"I don't care. This poster will sell Goodman matzohs because it's a simple message that will reach masses of people, and they'll buy. *That's* what I care about. It's fresh, it's provocative, it's fast, it's clear, it's attractive and its says *matzoh*. It also says kosher, it also says Passover. And that's the best way to say and sell Goodman."

More heads begin to nod. I'm winning the staff but the king still *kvetches* no no no. The matzoh monarch won't budge. But I won't quit and I keep at him: "Take my word for it—this poster is so strong you'll sell more matzoh to *goyim* than during a bread strike. The Hebrew headline dots the i. It says that Goodman is the most Jewish matzoh you can buy. So even if you're not Jewish—if your name is Angelo Cappella or Preston Reardon—you stop in your tracks when you see this poster and you say, 'Maybe that's for me because when I buy matzoh I want real *haymishe* matzoh.' If you do it this way you'll be the *only* matzoh in town."

I had them all nodding now, but the old man was still shaking his head. I picked out the face of the boldest nodder and winged my words at him, but he interrupted me to say, "Please, Mr. Lois, don't talk to *me*. I happen to love the poster." That was my breakthrough. The patriarch suddenly perked up, took a ballpoint pen and tapped the desk for silence. He sipped from a glass of water that was shoved into his hands. He leaned forward and spoke: "*No. I dun* like it."

He folded his arms across his chest, slumped back in his chair and shook his head at me sadly. Nothing would move him. But nothing could hold me back from breathing life into my gorgeous work. Time was running out. I had to make a final move. I saw the window. "There must be *some* way I can sell you on this"— and I rolled up the poster and headed for the window. "I dun vonna tuck abott it no more," he said, as I raised the window. "Neither do I," I shot back. "We shouldn't be arguing about this master-piece in the first place. It speaks for itself." As I began to climb through the open window he shouted after me, "You're going someplace?" I stepped through the open window and shouted at him, "I'm leaving."

They gaped at me as though I were some kind of *meshugenah*. I was poised on the outer ledge high above the pavement like a win-dow washer. I gripped the raised sash with every tendon of my left hand while I waved the poster with my free hand. One of the Good-man men was slapping the big desk, trying to hold in the laughter, grabbing at his crotch. He crossed his thighs and doubled over, cup-ping his mouth. His bladder would go if he held in the guffaw, but if he let it go *I* would go. The others stopped him before he could slap the desk again, and nobody made a sound. Any noise might loosen my grip and the matzoh corporation would have to cart away a crumpled art director from the concrete. I screamed from the ledge at the top of my lungs, loud enough to be heard in all of Long Island City:

"YOU MAKE THE MATZOH, I'LL MAKE THE ADS!"

"Stop, *stop*," said the old man. "Ve'll run it, ve'll run it. You made your point already. Come in, come in, *please!*" I climbed back into the room and thanked the patriarch for the nice way he reviewed my work. The doubled-over guy ran to the toilet. As I was leaving, the patriarch shouted after me, "If you ever kvit edvertising, young men, you got yourself ah job as ah matzoh salesman."

"*This* is my work," I shouted back as I raced through the cubi-cles of glass, holding the cardboard cylinder. I saw a flame burning from the top of the tube.

My heart was still thumping as I stepped off the elevator back at the agency. Casually, I walked to my office. "What happened?" came voices. Account executives surrounded me. "We had a quiet chat and he bought it," I said coolly, chucking the tube into the corner of my room. "He's a very sweet, reasonable gentleman."

Passover of 1959 was a very kosher season for Goodman as sales crackled in. And I had given life to the work that I loved.

After the Ear and the Matzoh came the Tie. By then I had be-come a great actor. All I risked with the Tie was being found out!

From the first day at DDB my Bronx accent and parish ways marked me as a slob, mostly with Bill Bernbach's broads, my Maestro's lady copywriters. They reported to Phyllis Robinson, the agency's brilliant copy chief. To many of her girls she was the Mother Superior and I was the parish incorrigible. With my Kingsbridge accent and my crooked nose, some of the women with whom I was paired on ads thought I could read no further than a headline. When I went over their copy and said, "This part here sounds like horseshit," they ran to Phyllis in tears. I was the impossible art director with a filthy mouth. I decided to be more careful with the girls and I worked at it.

I was at my finest with the Tie:

I was assigned an ad on a fabric that made men's ties *washable*. Before I met with my copywriter-wife I roughed out an ad showing two fat men wearing bibs. They were ready to start an eating orgy of suckling pig at a table heaped with rich food. What made the ad unusual was the way their ties were worn: *outside* their bibs. My headline said, *"now! ties made for eaters."* I completed the ad and shoved it in my drawer. Then I met with the copywriter to do the ad—again. I fed my creative partner clues: "Can you figure out *some* way we can show a person wearing a bib without covering his tie?" More clues followed. After lots of careful goosing I jockeyed her to the point where she hit on the headline, *"now! ties made for eaters."* I jumped out of my chair and terrificked her for coming up with that marvelous ad. I asked her to give me twenty minutes to do the layout. "We just did this *marvelous* ad," she sang to an account man in the corridor. I buzzed for my assistant to order photostats of the completed layout in my drawer.

I ran into another obstacle on the Tie when I gave the account man my bare-bones sketch of the ad to show the client. Layouts were usually submitted as fancy pastel renderings. I could have had a board man in the bullpen with green eyeshades render a fancy color "portrait" of the bib-wearers, but the client might gag at the rendering and reject the concept. I volunteered to go along with the account man to explain the ad, but after Matzohland I wasn't that welcome. He took my layout instead of me and sold the concept. The Tie finally made it.

I ran into the reverse problem with Julius Hochman of the International Ladies Garment Workers Union, another DDB client.

When I showed him my rough drawing of an old lady cradling a baby for an ad on the early struggles of labor unions, Hochman wanted to frame it. He was David Dubinsky's right-hand man, an old warrior of the sweatshop era. "Dott's *arrt*," he said. "Dott's ah *messterpiece*." When I told him we'd shoot a photo he was shocked. A charcoal sketch to Hochman was sacred, like the earthy proletarian art of Käthe Kollwitz. In an earlier ad on the promise of America I showed him a sketch of two symbolic hands: one held an ice cream cone, the other was the Statue of Liberty's hand, holding the torch. He almost wept when he saw it—and I shot the photo. When he saw the ad in finished form he was upset: "Dot's not vot I saw. I vant de drrawings, de *drrawings*." I had to shift gears on Seventh Avenue with this old labor lion who worshiped *arrt:* "It's ah pleasure to talk to an arrtist and not to ah commoicial man, Lois." *Oy gevalt.*

Joe Daly, for some reason, hardly found it a pleasure to talk to me. Daly was a power in the agency—vice president and account supervisor on Polaroid and Chemstrand, two accounts that added up to a hefty chunk of DDB's billings. I had done an ad for Acrilan, a Chemstrand fiber. Bill Bernbach okayed it, the account man Len Press liked it, and the client bought it. I shot the photo and prepared the final artwork. Then the ad was killed by Daly. I bitched to Bob Gage. He told me to leave the ad with him, that he would try to work it out. Bob called me to his office the next day and I walked into a roomful of faces around his table, studying my layout. In a corner behind Gage I noticed a tough-looking bird with a military crewcut. His muscly arms bulged in his short-sleeved shirt as he sat and watched. We weren't introduced, but I knew I was looking at Joe Daly.

Len Press went through the motions, explaining why "we" vetoed my ad. I knew he was in a spot; Daly was obviously calling the shots. I cut him off and played the wounded innocent to bait Daly: "Len, I don't understand *any* of this. The account group liked it, Bill Bernbach liked it, the client liked it, I shot the photo and that was approved. Now I'm told 'we' don't like it without any *reason.* It's not 'we,' it's Joe Daly. Now who in the fuck is Joe Daly?"

"Who the fuck are you?" roared Daly, rearing up like a cougar and coming across the room at me. Gage and Press grabbed Daly as I squared off, waiting to see if he led with his left. "Joe, Joe, what are you *doing?*" came a voice. Daly huffed, I puffed, then I walked out and snarled at him, "Any ad I do for you is *my* work, not yours." The ad finally ran, but the grapevine quickly spread the word about the Greek tough who would one day get his from tough Joe, who was no slouch. Never a dull day at Doyle Dane Bernbach.

The joint was always jumping with absorbing work. I kept an alarm clock in my office to go off at midnight or I would never stop. I loved the pace at DDB. Working late may have marked me as Bernbach's pet beaver, but it was Bill's partner, Ned Doyle, the agency's executive vice president, who took notice. The agency was on Forty-second Street, a few blocks from the Algonquin Hotel, where Doyle often held late dinner meetings. After his full Irish quota of booze he often made a special trip back to the office. When he got off the elevator he tiptoed down the corridor, he edged open the door to my office, poked in his hawklike face and blared out, "Goddamit, Lois, if you knew how to organize your fuckin time, you wouldn't have to stay late every night to finish your work!"

I was making my mark in the world's best ad agency, but many at DDB were members of a new religion and the agency was their church. "You painted my balls back on," said one of the creative guys. The world's best agency had some of its stars worried. The do's and don't's of Bernbach's self-appointed disciples could turn men into eunuchs. One way to shake up a Madison Avenue church is to bring in an art director from Kingsbridge. Another sure way is to hire a writer from Aqueduct.

When the nags were running, Julian Koenig, the judge's son, was often at the track during working hours. But any man who comes up with ads like "Think small" for Volkswagen doesn't follow rules. They called him the Dartmouth Beatnik. He wore horn-rims and rumpled suits. At one time he managed a semi-pro baseball team. When Volkswagen chose DDB as its agency, Julian was assigned to write the copy. He refused. It was hard to forget that Hitler himself was directly involved in designing the Volkswagen. Even though the Fuehrer was helped along by the Austrian car engineer Dr. Ferdinand Porsche, the cute Volkswagen in 1959 reminded lots of people about the ovens. Julian was Jewish and wouldn't forget it. Bill Bernbach's agency was all set to explode with its first car account. VW's budget was tiny by Detroit standards, about a million bucks, but Bernbach was determined to show Detroit that breakthrough advertising could sell cars as well as rye bread. Julian hardly gave a damn—and, in fact, I doubt if anyone in the agency knew at the time how talented he was.

The art direction was to be divided between Helmut Krone and me. I was asked to work on the station-wagon ads, but Volkswagen was as much a Nazi car to me as to Julian. I told Bernbach I couldn't work on the account either. Bill respected our feelings, although he couldn't quite understand why a Greek would feel as strongly as a Jew. I never told Bill that my guerrilla cousins on the mountain luckily decimated Hitler's advance column just a few miles before they could reach the native villages of my parents. Bernbach argued that circumstances had changed, but our feelings ran stronger than his logic and we stayed off the account. Meanwhile, orientation junkets were underway to VW's plant in Wolfsburg, Germany.

A short while later West Germany sold a fleet of jets to Israel. Julian dropped by my office and we agreed that circumstances *had* changed. We spoke to Bernbach and he sent us to Wolfsburg with the VW account executive, Ed McNeilly. His Irish eyes were assigned to watch the Jew and the Greek among the krauts.

We weren't the most polite guests of our German client. We asked our guide, "Would you please point out the ovens?" We told VW's head man, Dr. Nordhoff, that a picturesque church spire looked like a V-2 caisson, and he never spoke to us again. One VW guide had fought against the Yugoslav partisans. I asked him if he had ever tangled with Greeks. "Kreeks are mountain animals," he said, and I invited him to join me on a hike. It was hard to forget that our newest account was the famous Nazi car.

Meanwhile we kept hearing about a mysterious room at Wolfsburg where some of the first VW prototypes were stored—from the earliest Porsche version to the millionth VW, a gold-plated museum piece. We bugged the VW people to show us these historic models, and after incessant pestering by Julian and me they led us down to a cavernous basement room where a large fleet of cars was draped with tarpaulin. They peeled off the tarpaulin from the Porsche version, then from the very first Volkswagen, and then from the gleaming millionth, plated in gold. I wanted to see the other cars, but they kept ignoring me. I told Julian to keep our guides busy while I slipped away and studied the exposed tires under the tarpaulins. I spotted one VW's tires that stood out starkly from the others—wide-gauge, heavy-duty rubber with blitzkrieg ferocity. I peeled off the cover and found a Nazi jeep with mounted machine guns. I slipped into the jeep, trained a gun on our group and in a chilling imitation I broke the quiet conversation with an "*ach, ach, ach, ach,*" swinging the empty gun on its swivel mount. Julian stepped forward, raised his hand, stuck out his chest like Goebbels and said, "Und ve almost *did.*"

"Get de fuck out off de vay," I shouted at Julian, swinging the gun and going "*ach ach ach*" until I thought that Ed McNeilly was about to be mowed down by mortification. When he finally brought us home to Bernbach without having lost Volkswagen, McNeilly looked immensely relieved.

But we learned that Hitler's "people's car" had a lot going for it. Julian saw it as a dumb, honest little car—but a marketing enigma. Bernbach could have turned out lousy ads for Polaroid and the product would have made it; Volkswagen called for unusual moves. New York was the biggest market for our new account—that's what made it so tough. None of us had the answer when we got back from Wolfsburg, but the marketing problem was absolutely clear to Julian and me. We summed it up this way:

We have to sell a Nazi car in a Jewish town.

In the church of Bernbach, where long copy was generally taboo, Julian Koenig wrote the longest copy in the history of car advertising. He often wrote at night. Aqueduct, newly opened in the fall, often occupied Julian in the afternoon. In the morning he casually dropped phrases like "Think small" and "The beetle." Helmut Krone, the Teutonic precisionist, was shook up at first by Koenig's work habits. Helmut liked to closet himself with writers until the last bead of creative *schvitz* was drained. Koenig was an easygoing Robert Benchley, flipping out words and ideas without sweat and at odd hours. Our unlikely chemistry worked. Soon the ad campaign of the century came into being. Its creative trio was as unforgettable to me as the campaign: a Jewish horseplayer, a kraut perfectionist and a Greek ballplayer.

We sold the Nazi car in a Jewish town by junking all the rules of car advertising. It could only have happened at Bill Bernbach's agency. And we drew attention from major advertisers to DDB with our Volkswagen campaign.

Solved and sold: the Ear, the Matzoh, the Tie, the Nazi Car. My life at Doyle Dane would be complete if only Joe Daly could learn to love me!

Koenig and I had worked out a TV spot for Chemstrand tires. Bill Bernbach loved our approach. He asked that we show it to Daly. We brought the storyboard to Daly's office. He killed it. I asked him why. He turned to Julian and said, "I'll talk to *you*, but not to this punk." I exploded. He got to his feet, clenching his stubby fists. I squared off again. Simultaneously we both winged rights, both missing—but it was a lively scene, for sure, as shadow swings sliced the air. Julian was sitting at the far edge of Daly's desk. He pressed his nose against the oak, his eyes swinging back and forth through his shell-framed glasses, fists whizzing overhead. A crowd swelled at the entrance to Daly's corral. Finally, Koenig lifted his head and ordered, "Stop," shoving us apart. I rolled up our storyboard and went to Bernbach. "Definitely can't work with Daly," I said. "Whatever you hear about us is true."

It was also true that Joe Daly was going places in Bill Bernbach's agency. His chief competitor was another vice president, Eddie Russell. They jockeyed for succession, but tough Joe held the aces: Daly was close to Ned Doyle while Bill Bernbach was close to Daly.

Russell was a beautiful dude, as different from Daly as an eel from a bulldog. A boutonniere should have sprouted from Eddie Russell's lapel. His wardrobe was pre-Meledandri, post-Menjou, and his slick hair lay flat against a crafty noodle. Russell was a tasteful power in the agency. While others kept sloppy offices (Bernbach was no Burnbucks when it came to decor) Russell furnished his digs with lovely antiques and a classy bar. Creative people felt an easy kinship with the elegant Russell. When creative problems arose, Russell was the right rabbi to see. The joint was teeming with colorful talent, exciting people.

Bunny Wells, who studied my airline ads at Lennen & Newell, was now in the copy department at DDB. She was now Mary, not Bunny. She moved like a swan among brass and clients. When she leveled an opinion, her words came out like 50-caliber bullets

—and Mary knew her way around. You could tell that Mary Wells would never end up with wrinkles in a writer's tower.

Under the sunlight of Bernbach, the talented flowered, the powerful mellowed. At a private Christmas party in 1959 for the agency's key staff in Eddie Russell's apartment, Joe Daly waggled a cocktail under my nose. He smiled at me. I watched his free hand—was he getting ready to wing one at me in Russell's lush joint? "Kid, I gotta admit," said tough Joe, "it was an exciting year with you in the agency. I've changed my opinion about you, Lois." I returned the compliment. "I'd run my accounts the way you do, Joe," I said warmly, clinking glasses, "if I were an account guy— with no talent." He drank to that, but I got away fast before Daly downed his gulp—if we came to blows at the party, one of us might land on Russell's elegant Thonet chairs. It might have been me because Daly was no slouch. And that was hardly the way to end an exciting year at the agency I loved so much.

A few hours earlier, at the official Christmas party in a hotel, we all heard a memorable toast. I sat with Julian Koenig as Bill Bernbach spoke about the year that was ending, glorious 1959. It was a year of great advances. I thought of my kid, Harry, taking his first solo steps a few weeks before. When Bernbach raised his ginger ale I expected the usual stuff about teamwork and creativity. Instead his words telegraphed a different message. His eyes darted toward Julian and me, and we buried our faces in our VO's as Bernbach spoke of a change in attitude toward the agency's work during the past year. Then he mentioned the names of two men who deserved much of the credit: Julian Koenig and George Lois. We held on to our seats as the joint applauded. We looked up from our VO's and exchanged cautious glances.

In the world of art directors the equivalent of an Oscar is the Gold Medal of New York's Art Directors Club and 14,220 entries poured in for work done during 1959. When the winners were named a few months after the year ended, twelve Gold Medals were awarded. Of the twelve, Doyle Dane Bernbach won four. Of the four, three were for the following ads: the Matzoh, the Tie, the Nazi Car.

It could only have happened with the Maestro. And it happened more than a dozen years ago. But I remember him clearly.

7 Maestro Bernbach

When I went into Bernbach's office he looked at my hands and I looked at his fawns.

Bill expected a kind of magic from his art directors. A new ad was like pigeons from a sleeve. But it was tough to concentrate with that Kresge glass zoo of does and fawns on Bernbach's window, his mementos of middle-class life in Brooklyn, where the great Maestro still lived when I joined his agency. "Are those *yours*, Bill?" I asked, pointing to his amazing glass animals. "Those are for Brooklyn, Bill, not for Manhattan." But he stuck to his baubles, brushing aside my needling. His eyes were glued to the layout in my hands. I clutched at my throat. "Hey Bill, can we look at my work away from your room?" I let out a gagging *acchhhh*. "I get .sick when I see those Bambis." Bernbach ignored my clowning.

"Stick with me," he would say. "I'll make you rich. You'll be wearing diamonds." He was the president of a $27 million agency. He was the advertising innovator of his age. But those five-and-dime fawns *belonged*. He may have looked like an accountant or a history professor rather than an impresario of advertising, but to many in his agency he was the Pope. To greet him was to kiss his ring, to meet with him was to have an audience, to eat with him was a sacred event. "You had lunch with *Bill?*" the boys asked in awe. "What did he *talk* about? What did he *say?* What did *you* say? What did *he* say when you said *that?*" When I said it was routine stuff, that Ned Doyle was there, that Bill had a tuna fish sandwich and we talked about the usual things—that wasn't good enough. Not when you broke bread with *Bernbach!* "Yeah, I forget. We had these wafers and wine. Then this blind cripple came to our table. Bernbach blessed him and the guy ran out of the fuckin restaurant with 20-20 vision."

If some of his staff didn't actually tremble in his presence, they fumbled. He seemed to look right through you with his piercing, crystalline eyes. And when Bill Bernbach himself came up with an ad idea, who could question his word? Koenig looked sick when he showed me a headline written by Bill: "You'll find the label six inches up." Bernbach's line was for a campaign that would remind people to buy clothes with the ILGWU label. In women's dresses it was sewn inside the garment, about six inches above the hemline.

"Bill *Bernbach* came up with that? That's real funny, Julian— I never realized he had that kind of humor." I thought Bill was kidding us along, but the next day Julian came by for the layout. "Julian, it's dirty," I said. "Doesn't he realize that?" Julian assured me that Bill was serious, that he actually thought it was a great headline. But I still couldn't believe it.

The next day Bernbach dropped by my office. "How's ILGWU coming?" he asked.

"Hey Bill," I said, "are you serious? You really want to say in an ad, 'You'll find the label *six inches up*'?" I squirmed up my face as I quoted his line. He ignored my taunting. "Yes, that's correct," said Bernbach. "The label is always in that area. It's a provocative phrase and it draws immediate attention to the location of the label. *Why*, George?" I scratched my head and gawked at him. "Six inches up," I repeated, "*six inches up*. Don't you understand, Bill? It's *dirty*." A shadow of impatience crossed his eyes. He knew I wasn't all wrong, but I knew he wasn't raised in St. John's parish. " 'Six inches up' is *dirty*, Bill. It says *prick*."

He blushed for an instant. Then he looked at me directly and lashed out, "The only thing wrong with you, George, is that your mind is in the gutter." He turned away and left my office. But he quit hounding Julian and we forgot the ad.

Bernbach may have been deaf to the dirty phrase, but his rising influence kept the industry's ears and eyes on his creative agency, with its remarkable work on little-known accounts. In 1959 even Polaroid was a comparatively new product. Chemstrand was mostly soft goods, a low-prestige category in those days. Ohrbach's was a department store in only three cities. He had no business from General Foods and nothing from Detroit. He was without toothpaste or gasoline or aspirin or soap. He had an airline, but not Pan Am. He had a candy account, but not Whitman's. He had bread, but no Wonder. He had Levy's Rye, Barton's Chocolates, El Al of Israel and the ILGWU. In 1959 Bill Bernbach was still sitting in the back of the Madison Avenue bus. But he was some traveler! With his maverick accounts, many from Seventh Avenue, he crafted glorious campaigns that earned the respect of major advertisers in *Fortune*'s "five hundred." He treated advertising as an art. He encouraged his art directors to be strong by his open admiration for our ability to sell with images. He treated us with total respect. He was generous with his praise. And he put up with hijinks that would have brought out the worst in a smaller man.

A crash campaign was under way to unload a big inventory of leotards made of Chemstrand Nylon. The hour was late and I was the only art director in sight. A double-page ad was needed for *Women's Wear Daily*, the soft goods industry bible, to announce Chemstrand's blitz. Traffic manager Ray Ponterotto found me at my drawing table. "George, George, thank God you're here," he said. "We gotta push leotards." As Ray said those words he *wrote* the ad. I sketched a man's hand pushing against the snug behind of a girl in a leotard. The headline said, "We're pushing leotards." John Fenyo, the account man, showed it to Chemstrand. He rushed back with a quick okay and the ad was completed the next morning. Joe Daly was out of town, so he never had a chance to kill it; Bernbach was busy, so he never had a chance to approve it. As soon as the ad ran, orders for leotards flowed in. Fenyo later told me it was Chemstrand's most successful trade ad *ever*. Bernbach saw the ad shortly after it ran and called me to his office. He was holding

"We're pushing leotards." I was one proud art director to be standing in front of the Maestro as he admired my work. Tea roses would have been ideal for that glowing scene.

"Disgusting," said Bernbach. "Think twice before you ever do an ad again with this flavor. Certainly I'll expect that you'll see me about it first." For a moment I was stunned. Then I let loose: "Hey Bill, you're completely wrong. First, the ad was exactly right for the marketing problem. Second, it was a tremendous success. Third, it's a provocative approach. Fourth, I love it. Fifth, everyone else loves it, including Chemstrand. And sixth—the only thing wrong with *you*, Bill, is you're a *prude*." He turned away. But he never turned his back on me.

Bill Bernbach understood that man's first written words were symbols. He personally revolutionized the alphabet of advertising. One day as he studied my ads he said, "I've worked with the two greatest art directors of our industry, Paul Rand and Bob Gage. George, you're a combination of both." Heady stuff when you're twenty-eight. Paul Rand was one of America's graphic pioneers and Gage was the very best in the business. But Bernbach was unstinting in his praise when his art directors brought him visual magic.

He was a sensitive teacher and a bold leader, a man whose impact on my life is retained with respect and love, fawns and all. I worked for the Maestro and matured professionally during my one year in his brilliant presence. One year. Because one day I had a visitor.

In November 1959 a caller came to my office with a chart. I cleared the Volkswagen layouts off my table to give him room. It was a dazzling graph. A line starting at zero took off slowly, then it rocketed off the page. At the end of Year One, he explained, the new ad agency should be doing business at an annual rate of X and growing at a pace of Z. I asked him why. My question was a big mistake. His gift of gab was overpowering and he sprayed the room with velvet sell. His sweet, puckish face tingled with excitement. Then he asked me what I thought. He was too persuasive for evasive talk. I answered sincerely, "Listen, don't bullshit a bullshitter."

My visitor had started an ad agency with an art director named Bill Free. It didn't work out and Free left. I dropped by his office in the Seagram Building after Free was gone. He was good at keeping up appearances, but the black orchid of bankruptcy was blooming near his desk. He asked me then to team up with him and start a new agency. His visit to my office wrapped up a month of sell. With his charming jabber he was hard to resist, particularly with that hypnotic chart. At age thirty-three, old for advertising, the creative consultant of Sudler & Hennessey, Freddie Papert, was on the comeback trail.

As I looked at his wild graph, rocketing to heaven, I dropped an offhand thought: "If Koenig comes in I might do it." Freddie's composure went to hell: "Koenig? Koenig? *Who's* Koenig?" Papert expected that he and I would be the writer-artist team. He hadn't heard of Julian. "You're now the *second* best writer in the world," I told him sadly. "The best is Julian Koenig." Papert grabbed his beat-up Princeton hat and said, "Koenig? I'll get him for you. Where is he?" I grabbed his sleeve. "Hey schmuck, Julian and I have been working together for a year. You don't have to *get* him for me. And right now he's in Los Angeles shooting a commercial for Volkswagen." He dashed out of my office shouting, "Los Angeles? I'll get him for you." He left his chart behind. It looked less insane every time I stole a glance.

That night my phone rang at home. A voice boomed, *"Who the fuck is Freddie Papert?"* Koenig was calling from Los Angeles. Papert had reached him. Julian thought the idea was crazy, but he wanted to know how I felt. I said, "There's only one creative agency in the country, Julian. With you and me working together and with Papert hustling to bring in accounts, it just might work."

By the time Julian returned, Papert had learned of his reputation and began to lose his mind dreaming of getting Koenig too. On a Sunday morning in December, Papert pressed for action. We met at my apartment. Freddie and Julian recognized each other from the track, and they kicked around race-track jargon until the smell of Aqueduct filled the room. My apartment was already stunk up by the vinegar fumes of Greek lentil soup; Sunday potluck for our last-minute guests had been simmering in the oven since Thursday, infesting the joint with its grand heroic fragrance. Rosie stuck a full bowl in front of Freddie. The twinkle in his eye gave way to a sickly grin. Julian peered at my wife, his nose twitching. "It's a traditional soup," she said. "I cook it for George every Christmas." Papert pecked at a clump of lentils like a sick bird. Julian braved a few swallows and quit. When Rosie saw that Freddie was near keeling over, she said, "George won't go into business with anyone who hasn't tried his favorite Greek lentil soup." Papert licked the bowl, then he ran to the kitchen for a gulp of water or he might have gagged at our war council.

By the end of 1959 anyone who spent a dime on advertising was needling his ad agency to "come up with a Volkswagen campaign." One advertiser who had good reason to watch those VW ads was Victor Elmaleh, a Renault-Peugeot distributor with an ad budget of \$250,000. Freddie contacted Elmaleh and asked him, "Suppose I get you the two guys who did Volkswagen?" When Freddie mentioned Julian Koenig, Elmaleh smiled; he had apparently known Julian for years. Elmaleh didn't commit himself with a blood oath, but any second thoughts Julian might have had about leaving Doyle Dane Bernbach evaporated when Freddie told him he just met an old friend of his with an ad budget of a quarter million bucks. (It may sound like a lot of moolah, but since ad agencies work on 15 percent commissions, we were really talking about \$37,500 of gross income to cover our fancy rent and all our other expenses, usually damn high when you start *any* new business. Salaries come last, if there's anything left to divide among three partners. Even so, Elmaleh's budget was not to be sneezed at.)

By Christmas of 1959, one year after I joined DDB, the plans for our new agency were settled. We all agreed that Papert should be first on the masthead. Julian suggested Papert, Lois, Koenig. But I was keen on last place. The name became Papert, Koenig, Lois, Inc.

After the holidays Julian and I asked to meet with Bill Bernbach. "Let me handle this," said Julian. "You'll screw it up." I felt a twinge of doubt; Julian sometimes choked up with Bernbach. We walked into Bill's office wearing jackets, which no self-respecting creative man ever did. And this time we had no ads for the Maestro. He sensed immediately that this was an occasion. "Yes boys, sit down," he snapped. He studied us carefully. I waited for Julian to speak, but his cords jammed. We sat through a tortured silence until Julian blurted, "Bill—George and I are starting our own agency." Julian was thirty-eight. I looked up to him as my mature partner. But he muffed our big line. Bernbach's eyes swung from Julian to me as though we were two thieves who had been finagling with his accounts. I knew he would get rough. Out it came: "Good —I'll send you business."

"Bill," I said, "we're forming our own agency with a man named Fred Papert. We want to see if we can come anywhere close to this creative agency in ten years." Bernbach alternated between fatherly concern and naked rage. "Now *who* is this Fred Papert?" he asked at one point. "You mean to tell me that he's thirty-three years old, he's always been in advertising *and I've never heard of him?*"

More than anything I wanted Bill Bernbach to know that our hands were clean. For the rest of my life I would have the deepest respect for this man. To leave a germ of distrust behind would be intolerable. "I must try it before I die," I said. "Bill, I must have the experience of starting the second creative agency in America." Suddenly his kingly poise returned. "Talented as both of you are," he said softly, "do you *seriously* believe that the two of you can do what I've done?" I said we were doing it *after* him—that it might even be done in *five* ad agencies on his model. "*Never*," he said, with total certainty. "This was done exactly right. The chemistry will never happen again." Even Bill Bernbach, whose agency was regarded by almost everyone as a "creative freak," was giving credence to that myth.

The cord was cut. For a farewell toast, the agency brass gathered to see us off in Eddie Russell's stylish office. All eyes shifted to Bernbach as he was handed a glass. But something still seemed to trouble him. I wondered if he thought we were playing the Madison Avenue con game of resigning, followed by an account or two pulling out, followed by a news item that the two men who pulled out got the resigned business. "I don't understand," he began. "Knowing you as I do, George . . . and knowing your personality as I do . . . I don't quite understand your allowing Mr. Papert and Mr. Koenig to place your name last on the masthead." The Maestro couldn't have fed me a sweeter cue.

"Because a few years from now, Bill, when we've really made it . . . when people will be calling our successful agency to say, 'Congratulations, George—Papert Koenig has hit $20 million,' I want to be able to say, '*Why do you insist on calling me by my first two names?*'"

A new decade was dawning, a new ad agency was launched.

"*Store . . . home . . . father . . . son*" was now becoming the story of my life—on my terms. I had my first son. I was doing the work that I loved. Now I was opening my own store. I called Haralampos to tell him the news.

"I'm leaving the Maestro, Papa," I told him in Greek.

"George, George—*again* you're changing jobs? You spoke so warmly of Mr. Burnbucks."

"Papa, listen—you remember my telling you about the *Hellene* I worked with . . . Cholakis? When I went to work for Bernbach he told me it would be my last job. He told me I would be starting my own agency, and that's what's happening. I'm starting my own advertising agency with two partners. My own business, Papa."

"Aha, *aha*—your own *business!* Wonderful, *wonderful!* Is Cholakis your partner?"

"No. Julian is one, the writer I worked with on the Nazi car. And the other is Freddie Papert—terrific businessman."

"George," he asked, almost in a whisper, "they're Jewish?"

"Well Julian's Jewish, you know that. Freddie is *kind of*, if you follow me. He's a Park Avenue type. Very classy. We have an expression—'He used to be Jewish, but he's all right now.'"

"George, be careful."

"Hey Papa, c'mon. Bernbach's Jewish and he gave me the best year of my career. I owe the man more than I can begin to tell you."

"Yes, yes, I understand. Your *own* business. Wonderful, George. I wish you great success. I'll tell Mama."

Later we had a family outing at the home of my Uncle Gus on Staten Island—Costas Thanasoulis who bartered with Haralampos thiry-six years back over his unmarried sister, Vasilike.

"I hear your partners are Jewish," he said. "George, be careful."

"Hey Uncle Gus. The Jews are more like Greeks than anyone, you know that."

"That's why I'm telling you to be careful."

"Would you be happier if my partners were Irish?"

"God forbid."

We started the new decade in style. In January 1960 the shingle of our new agency was hanging in the swank Seagram Building. We had some camp chairs, a few potted plants, and our $250,000 account. Papert, Koenig, Lois was in business—PKL, my own store.

We pulled out the stops for Renault, helped by our inside scoop about Volkswagen. We always knew, for example, that VW's heater was cool. When we found out that Renault's heater was hot stuff, we showed a VW saying in an *achtung* accent to a Renault, "Ah heater dot *heats?*" Julian took dead aim at VW in another ad: "First you thought small. Now think a little bigger." My favorite never ran: "Why I traded in my Nazi car for a Renault on V.E. Day." We were rolling along with Renault-Peugeot, but as often happens in the dreamworld of Madison Avenue, our rosy quarter million turned out to be more like $60,000—or $9,000 of gross income—not a lot of bread to support three grown men, including two horseplayers.

The infant agency needed fast feeding or we might have starved in our camp chairs. Along came Dr. Spock to beef up our formula. Freddie was collaring every prospect on his endless list, including Charles and Beatrice Gould, who published *Ladies' Home Journal*. After the Goulds heard about Papert and his Volkswagen guys until our names were running out of their ears, they gave us an advance copy of the upcoming issue of LHJ and told us to try some ads. We plucked out a story on Spock's childhood and we did an ad with a picture of an old-fashioned two-year-old kid. "What kind of a baby was Dr. Spock?" asked the headline. Another story in that issue dealt with meddling mothers-in-law. We showed a powerful mama, built like a Green Bay tackle, crushing her grown son against her forty-eight-inch chest. The ad was captioned, "What can a wife do when her mother-in-law won't let go?"

Freddie showed our work to the Goulds and he called back in a delirium—we got the account. A big budget was headed our way and the whole world opened up. But the next day we were scratching for business again. LHJ's space salesmen raised all kinds of hell when they heard that a small unknown ad agency was now in the act. Magazines usually assign their advertising to big agencies because ad pages are sold easier that way to captive clients. Our ads were strong, our clout was puny, and our hearts sank. But the Goulds were still in love with Baby Spock and the Green Bay mama. Things began to look up again. They gave us a monthly creative fee while paying their big agency the fat commissions they would normally get if we weren't doing LHJ's ads. While Renault was our first account, the first ad that was actually run by PKL was the first of the decade's Jewish mothers, built like a Green Bay tackle—years before Greenburg's expensive manuscript, which I'll get to later.

Ladies' Home Journal was a showcase account for a new ad agency. We set up a stage in Grand Central Station and hired models to pose as housewives sitting on their lovely butts reading the Goulds' magazine while vacuum cleaners ran wild and toast burned. The gals were concentrating on their reading. Advertising men from Connecticut and corporate brass from Westchester

County choked the concourse to catch the action. It might have been the hottest show in town if the bathtub had arrived, but the Goulds scratched our plan to put a naked housewife in the tub with their magazine. They also vetoed our two-inch newspaper announcement:

Admen:

There's a nude

in Grand Central Station.

She works for

Ladies' Home Journal

We were aiming for more than the commuters. We wanted to catch the network news editors and have them send camera crews. A two-minute shot on network news would have been worth more than a dozen ads. The simple premise of our commuters' show was this: *people like to watch people.* Instead of the nude I used a fully dressed model, just swaying in a rocking chair. And people stopped to stare . . . and stare. (Advertising isn't all nudes.)

Meanwhile, back on Madison Avenue a doctor named Sheckman was making house calls on ad agencies, searching for creative ideas to sell two products. He had a million bucks to spend and a list of ten agencies to screen, but PKL wasn't on his list. Agencies outdo Busby Berkeley when a million dollar prospect walks off the elevator. At one joint the doctor was shown a reel of slick, finished commercials, but Dr. Sheckman wasn't conned by razzle-dazzle or by fancy stiffs in nifty clothes. He was looking for *ideas.* When Julian got wind of it—he seemed to know as many names as Freddie—our agency was added to Dr. Sheckman's list.

Dr. Edward Sheckman was the maverick president of Pharmacraft Laboratories. He had a cold-relief product called Coldene. He was also testing a new product for allergies called Allerest. He wasn't exactly in love with the work his agency was doing for Coldene, while a major competitor of Allerest owned about 95 percent of the market.

We went to see him at night in his Fifth Avenue co-op apartment. He was a ringer for Eric von Stroheim, with a bald, bullet head. He was wearing red pajamas and slippers—and he was furious at all the bullshit he had plowed through during the past weeks. "I don't want any more fake stuff," he told us, "just creativity.

I'll give you a month to show me what you can do. But remember,
no horseshit." The doctor didn't seem to care that Julian's pants
needed a pressing or that I sounded like a cab driver. He fed us all
the facts about his products, and we left his apartment. Over the
weekend Julian scrawled and I sketched. By Monday we were
ready. The doctor's office was a few floors below us in the Seagram
Building. We called for an appointment and went down to meet
with him and his lieutenants. "What do you want to know?" he
asked. "What further information will be of help to you?"

"No, no, Dr. Sheckman," we said. "You don't understand. We're
ready to show you our work." He stared at us incredulously.

We showed him about fifty ads and TV storyboards—not beautiful stuff with color illustrations and crisp lettering, but rough
pencil sketches that only Julius Hochman would have wanted to
frame. "I asked for some ideas," he later told a trade magazine, "and
they showed me fifty, all roughed out in pencil on plain paper.
I was stunned by their informality and delighted by their ideas."
When advertising men talk about doing fifty ads and storyboards
overnight, divide it by ten for puffery and subtract two for booze.
The work we showed Dr. Sheckman was done in a passion, and
after his safari among the big agencies he tore up his list and gave
us his business—our first million bucks of billing. One ad gives the
full flavor of our work in eighteen words. You open the page of a
magazine and you see this—

You don't have a cold!
I DODE HAB A CODE?
You have an allergy.
I HAB AN ALLERGEE?

—plus a picture of Allerest. All I need is a dozen more words to
show why Dr. Sheckman went for PKL. This was for Coldene.
White words on a black page and nothing else, not even a photo
of the bottle:

"John, is that
Billy coughing?"

"Get up and give
him some Coldene."

PKL's maverick approach was clicking; we carved out a 72
percent share of market for Allerest, making a shambles of the old

95 percent by its rival. Later we were assigned other products and another million from Pharmacraft. We were moving faster than the line on Freddie's chart. But it was Dilly Beans that became our Volkswagen—a far-out product that was pickled in the holy water of my life: vinegar.

While we were pulling out of Doyle Dane, two smart young girls in a small New Jersey apartment were stinking up the neighborhood with four-hundred-pound barrels of that heavenly juice right in their living room. There weren't any Greeks around to appreciate that fine stink, so the neighbors raised hell with the health department and out went the barrels and the babes. They were building a business in their apartment by pickling strips of raw string beans in vinegar and dill. Their product was a gourmet item called Dilly Beans. Sonya Hagna and Jacqueline Park moved out before the cops moved in, formed a company called Park & Hagna and began to sell their crazy beans in Washington, D.C. The girls came to our new agency a few months after we started. With Dilly Beans we startled Madison Avenue. The girls had a small budget, about thirty grand, but we gave it the muscle of a cool million. And out of the vinegar came overnight fame for PKL. We whacked out a classic campaign to make an unknown product famous. Shortly after our work ran, friendly grocers bitched to New York's radio stations to call off our advertising.

Julian was scribbling and mumbling and I was drawing and shouting—our ad-making method at PKL. I was sketching a TV storyboard, showing a woman holding a Dilly Bean like a cigarette. I lettered in, "Break the smoking habit, eat Dilly Beans," jabbering between layouts, "We oughtta tell people to do something wild, like getting them to knock something off the goddam shelves when they don't find DB's in the store"—and out came this radio commercial: "If your friendly neighborhood grocer doesn't have a jar, *knock something off the shelf on the way out.*" The commercial ran and real nice ladies on the fancy East Side charged into their supermarkets like looters. They shoved cans and jars off the shelves—and the radio stations caught hell from New York's grocers. We were forced to tone down the message. We changed it to *"move to another neighborhood."*

Dilly Beans changed our lives. Julian quit going to the track to case Madison Avenue's favorite saloons. He buttonholed bartenders to place tent cards on their tables for a new cocktail, the Dillatini —a martini plus a Dilly Bean. You stirred the drink with the DB and ended up eating the stirrer. "Ask the waiter to bring you one," went the copy of Koenig, "and warn him to leave that damn Dilly Bean alone." On television a gorgeous gal was about to jam two DB's in her mouth, a vulgar way to eat. We asked tastefully, "Is it vulgar to put more than one Dilly Bean in your mouth?" We found out that the DB had 1.2 calories compared to 7.2 in an olive. Our secretary, Diane Shugrue, was put on a crash weight-gain diet of DB's and we announced the findings of our consumer research in a tiny ad: "Diane Shugrue ate 3925 Dilly Beans last month. She didn't gain an ounce." We could have ended the line at that point, but it would have made a bum ad. We tacked on: "Is *she* tired of Dilly Beans!"

New York suddenly went ape for Dilly Beans and many stores jacked up its retail price by 20 percent. Highbrow radio station WQXR gave PKL a special award for "unusual, imaginative and effective use of radio advertising on behalf of Dilly Beans," the third such award in their low-keyed twenty-five-year history. "The Dilly Bean's success," wrote *Time* magazine, "is a tribute to the power of advertising."

Sonya and Jacqueline finally told us to ease up on the advertising until their supply caught up with demand. They yanked all their ads out of Washington to fill their orders in New York. Six months after we got the account, *Advertising Age* said, "Much of the credit for the Dilly Beans success story belongs to the agency, Papert, Koenig, Lois." While PKL was still too young to be known, talk began to fill the air in and out of the ad world about "the Dilly Beans agency." Doors were suddenly flung open to us. But you don't always know what waits behind those free-swinging entrances. We were asked to pay a visit to the Ronson Corporation, named after and run by Louis Vincent Aronson II. Julian saw from our first meeting that the chemistry between Aronson and me was sure to bring out the parish streetfighter in his young partner. I stayed away from Ronson, but in his mature way Julian did fine without me.

After we had turned out a carload of ads for our big pitch to Ronson in their New Jersey office, Aronson hammered away at one of our full-page ads: "What would it look like as a *half*-page ad?" he kept asking. Julian held up the full-page layout and said, "Here's how it would look"—and he tore it in half. I was never so happy to hear that my work was ripped apart. Our ads must have been plenty zingy to survive Koenig's caper because PKL came home with about $400,000 of Ronson business. I was proud of my mature partner and I got to enjoy our new account after all. I never set headline type with more zest than these lovely words for Ronson electric shavers: "No brush. No lather. No blades. No blood. No push. No pull. No bull." I thought these were even lovelier: "We don't roll. We don't adjust. We don't float. We don't lo-speed. We don't flip. We don't raise. We don't lower."

Ccchyessa!

We were quickly becoming the red-hot creative agency, with fancy accounts like Seagram, Xerox, the New York *Herald Tribune* and National Airlines. We kept our informal ways by adding brilliant mavericks, like the Irish itinerant peddler.

Ron Holland was folding Chinese stewards' freshly laundered Jockey shorts at Groton, Connecticut, in his older brother's laundromat near the submarine base. Ron was twenty-nine, with an IQ of 155. He had a college degree and had served in the army's Counter Intelligence Corps. He also had a New York City license to work as an itinerant peddler, selling ice cream off a truck. His brother Charles told Ron to get off his can and make a career for himself before he hit thirty. "But my life has color and variety," said Ron. "I sell to Jews in the Bronx, to blacks in Harlem, and my Puerto Rican landlord charges me exorbitant rent for a shitpot room, forcing me to moonlight on weekends by folding underwear for Chinese sailors." Charles, a savvy guy and a hot jazz pianist, urged the kid to find a job in advertising. He told Ron there was an agency in New York doing radio spots for Dilly Beans, which he kept hearing up there in Connecticut. "Find out who does that clever stuff," said Charles, "and try to get a job with them. What you're doing now is no way for a bright Irish lad to spend his life."

When Ron Holland got back to New York he ran into an illustrator friend who not only knew PKL but also knew Fred Papert. "We'll be glad to talk to him," said Freddie, "but we don't take trainees." Ron boned up on John Gunther's book, *Taken at the*

Flood, the story of advertising's pioneer Albert Lasker. Then he wrote two short stories, sent them off to "Fred Koenig" and asked for an interview. His letter got to Julian, who liked his writing— and was equally impressed by his Good Humor job. He thought Ron should be a copywriter. But the words "account executive" from Lasker's book had grabbed Holland—he was, after all, an executive in the ice-cream business. Koenig sent him to PKL's new marketing vice president, Norman Grulich. "What do you know about intaglio prints?" asked Grulich, sizing up the itinerant peddler. "I shouldn't wear one to the office," said Ron. "Hired!" said Grulich—and Holland became an assistant account executive.

A former Good Humor man who screws up the name of his new employer had the stuff of a great account man at carefree PKL. Norm Grulich was also thrown by our name when we first contacted him. We weren't known and he thought we were an insurance company. With Pharmacraft in our shop we needed a marketing pro who knew their business and could supervise our accounts. We put out feelers with several top echelon men, including a vice president of Benton & Bowles who was a rising star in that big agency while PKL was a small potato. The rising star came on like a patronizing sonofabitch with a Machiavellian odor. He said he couldn't *possibly* be interested himself; instead he talked up another *excellent* man at Benton & Bowles named Norman Grulich. "I think the prick gave us the name of his chief rival," I said to Julian. "Grulich must be good." He sure was. Norm Grulich ran the $12 million Crest and Prell accounts at B&B for Procter & Gamble. He was one of the best drug marketers in advertising. He joined PKL and recruited our account staff as we grew. But Ron Holland became the square peg in Grulich's round holes; the Irish ice-cream hustler wasn't cut out for account work. Julian and I encouraged Ron, who was no square, to become a copywriter. One day I gave him a patient, fatherly, Ned Doyley word on his performance: "Holland, you're without a doubt the worst fuckin account man in the history of the world." But Holland was no quitter and he tried for six months. Grulich finally blew the whistle.

On a Monday he told Ron, "I'll give you until Friday. If you can't come up with an idea to help sell Coldene by then—even if it's a simple tie-in premium offer, *anything*—I'll have to fire you."

When Friday came, Holland walked into Grulich's office and without trying to fake his way out, he said he had nothing. Grulich kept his promise and said, "Fired!" They shook hands and Ron scooted down to Koenig. "Do you really think I should be a copywriter?" he asked. "Yes I do," said Julian. "Then I will be, because I was just fired," said the smiling Irish peddler. "Hired!" said Julian. "Move your debris to writers' row."

I began to work closely with Ron. At a presentation before a group of advertising women, Ron and I explained how we did all that hot stuff at PKL. "You start out by hiring people who are creative, then just give them room to do what they want," I said. "You just sit down and *work* with guys. Also we try to hire people who will disagree with us, isn't that right, Ron?" The Irish copywriter answered with deadly accuracy, "Yes sir, Mr. Lois, that's *absolutely* right."

Holland was at home in writers' row at PKL, a hothouse of some of the smartest smartasses in town. The bearded monologist, Monte Ghertler, fascinated Ron. "Why is it, Monte, that I'm always interested in what you say," Ron asked him, "even though what you say is not necessarily interesting?" Ghertler explained: "It's that mysterious something that separates interesting people from bores. Now on any given morning you, Ron, could walk in and say 'Gee, it's hot today,' and that wouldn't bore me. But another guy in the agency could say, 'Guess what, Monte? I was leaving my house this morning and saw a growling lion running down the street. Suddenly a bull elephant came charging out of my back yard, caught the lion, mounted it and fucked it. Then he stomped on the lion and knocked over three passing cars.' Well you see, Ron, halfway through that story I would have dozed off."

Ghertler wasn't too happy with his beard. One day he told Ron why he kept wearing it: "I would shave this off right now if I didn't think they'd cut $10,000 a year off my salary."

Another copywriter, Milt Trazenfeld, was a thrift-shop addict. Trazenfeld was always elegantly dressed, but he never shelled out more than $2.50 for a suit. For a tie he would go as high as $20. "Drop what you're doing and come with me," he said to Ron one morning. "I'll explain later." Trazenfeld hailed a cab to LaGuardia and ran with Ron through the terminal onto a shuttle flight to Boston. "This is the day for values," he explained on the plane.

"It's the end of final exam week. All the students at Harvard and M.I.T. are trading in their wardrobes for cash to survive through summer." When the plane landed at Logan Airport, Trazenfeld shoved Holland into a cab and barked at the driver, "The thrift shop in Cambridge, *and step on it!*" He found a suit for $2.00 that was traded in by a Cabot. Back in Manhattan he bought an $18 tie. Trazenfeld and Monte Ghertler then exchanged notes on tailoring:

"The silhouette of your trousers is classic, Milt. Where did you purchase that remarkable wardrobe?"

"Only in those thrift shops, Monte, that most closely approximate the standards of Savile Row."

"Gentleman's Resale?"

"Thrift shop off Harvard Yard. This suit cost two dollars."

"A reasonable value. The tailoring is brilliant."

"You do understand, Monte, the correct way to style trousers? At the waist—snug, yet ample. Lines descend to the knees in perfect parallels. Slight kick outward at the knees. Then a tapering toward the ankle, ever so minutely."

"Ah yes," said Ghertler, "a good deal like the Parthenon."

The first of Madison Avenue's red-hot creative agencies attracted more lovely mavericks. When account man Paul Keye got ants in his pants at David Ogilvy's fine shop, his friends told him that PKL might be a jollier joint to hang his hat. Keye went to see Papert, and when Freddie asked who sent him, Keye said, "God." We hired him fast. Bill Murphy, who was recruited by Grulich to head up PKL's media department, solved calculus problems at lunch for relaxation. "Like nearly everyone on the staff," *Television Age* commented in 1961, "Mr. Murphy is utterly easygoing, shy of publicity and unbefouled by mannerism." Translation: *loosey-goosey*.

Ally the Turk, meanwhile, unbefouled by work, was beating the Madison Avenue bushes. Most Turks, as all Greeks know, suffer from an intrinsic lack of character. But Carl Ally lacked a job and was a model candidate for the PKL scene. He came from Campbell-Ewald in Detroit, where they made him a troubleshooter and new-business specialist. According to the Turk in an interview with *Ad Age*: "They'd say, 'Ally—we're about to lose that account—go over there and see what's wrong.'" He was such a smash they sent him to their New York office, where he brought in $3 million in new business. Then something went sour and Ally was canned. "I walked around the streets for a year," said the Turk. "It got so bad they turned off the lights, disconnected the telephone. . . . I walked around and saw everybody and couldn't come up with a thing." *Ad Age* described Ally as a person with "the humility of a professional lion tamer." When he came to PKL for our first meeting, his references were hairy. But with enemies like Ally's he was made for our agency. And it's not an everyday event when someone comes to a job interview with a Turkish bellybutton peeping out of his shirt.

When I first met Carl during his interview with Julian, we asked a few pointed questions about his past. We had important accounts for Ally to handle; we wanted to be sure that what we heard about him was *true*. Quick-tempered, boiling with energy and a ratatat talker, Ally shot back, "Fuck you, I don't need this horseshit." I told Julian, "I love him, let's hire the guy fast." The fat Turk joined us as a vice president and account supervisor. Also as PKL's pilot.

He had worked his way through the University of Michigan by stunt flying and crop dusting. He was a fighter pilot in World War II and was called back to fly jets in Korea. He convinced us that a company plane would be cheaper than commercial travel so we leased a Beechcraft Bonanza. Its pilot was the Turk.

Ally worked with Ron Holland briefly on the *Herald Tribune* account while Ron was still struggling to become an account man. According to Holland the chemistry between them was lousy: "Carl never liked me. He thought I was always sucking around Julian. I couldn't figure out why, until I realized that I *was* sucking around Julian." When I saw what was brewing I called John Cholakis and told him we had a triple parlay in the works: a crazy Turk who was pissed at a smiling Irishman for asskissing their Jewish boss. "Get 'em all into a Chinese restaurant *fast*," said Cholakis, "and we'll blow up the joint." Good thinking. I hired the Greek as a producer in our TV department.

But thanks to the *Herald Tribune*, our worst account man, Ron Holland, became our best copywriter. In 1961 the *Herald Tribune*'s circulation was 330,000, a weak second behind *The New York Times* with its tremendous 800,000. John Denson, last of the Ben Hecht editors, was brought in by the *Trib*'s publisher, Jock

Whitney, to make it a vital force in New York journalism. When PKL was appointed as the *Trib*'s ad agency we came up with a delicious strategy:

Four nights a week, exactly at eleven, we ran a one-minute commercial immediately before CBS News, then featuring newscaster Doug Edwards. The "star" of our commercial was the next morning's front page of the *Herald Tribune* that was just hitting the newsstands. Our TV spot was made up of teasing references to the news behind the headlines. "Stay tuned for Douglas Edwards and the news," said the CBS announcer a few seconds before eleven, "but first this message." As the videotape cameras scanned over closeups of the *Trib*'s front page, we said, " 'James Meredith starts classes at Mississippi.' That's the headline—but there's more to the news than the headline, because now there's a new way to edit a serious morning newspaper—the *Tribune* way. It gets rid of long gray columns of unevaluated news." We hit the high spots, raising questions about reactions from Governor Barnett, the NAACP, the Justice Department—but never actually telling the news. Instead we said, "There's more to the news than this headline—*and there's more to it than you're going to hear on this program*." Then Doug Edwards came on with the evening news.

At 8:15 each night in the *Trib*'s city room, less than three hours before air time, Ron and I got the first proofs of the morning's front page. We worked out the commercial as Ron belted out words and we planned shots together. We were allowed thirty minutes taping time at the CBS studio to complete our sixty-second spot—almost no time for *any* one-minute commercial. We worked with three cameras and brought to life a flat sheet of newsprint. That was no easy stunt. Every second counted between the first page proof at 8:15 and the stroke of 11:00 when the commercial ran. We barged out of the city room and shuttled crosstown in a cab to the taping studio. Carol Reed, the first of TV's famous weather girls, came on after Doug Edwards. She rehearsed her segment at 10:45, on the heels of our allotted half hour of taping time. "Have a happy" was her trademark. Ron usually caught hell from Carol when we ran over our time until we were completely satisfied with the final tape. After one runover too many she screamed at Holland, "You black-haired sonofabitch!"

"I told you it would happen," Ron said to me, "but at least she got the color of my hair right."

Each night I was home by eleven to catch the finished commercial on my TV set. I watched in amazement as the announcer said, "There's more to the news than this headline—*and there's more to it than you're going to hear on this program*." Then came Doug Edwards, right after our put-down. I couldn't believe that CBS was actually letting us get away with it night after night. Carol Reed came on with the weather after Doug Edwards. A storm was brewing, she said, but have a happy. The storm came from William Paley, board chairman of CBS. He finally saw one of our spots, and when he heard the line he was horrified. He called PKL's board chairman, told Freddie Papert to watch our language on his network, and he ordered us never *ever* to use that line again. We quit using that introduction, but it was fun while it lasted—and the *Trib*'s circulation had begun to rise.

John Denson was the best of the no-bullshit editors—which may explain why he regarded advertising men as charlatans. He must have suffered through years of phony promises and slick talk. Suddenly in walks Ally the ratatat Turk with his shirttails hanging over his fat ass; Lois the Greek with his Bronx yeah yeahs; and Koenig in a crinkled suit. Denson looked us over as though some joker stuffed the Marx Brothers, the Ritz Brothers and the Three Stooges into a barrel, spun it around and sent him the first three who came out standing. But he seemed to like what he saw, especially our work—although traces of anti-adman bias stuck to Denson's ribs, and Ron caught the worst of it. But he was fast on his feet.

At a meeting with Denson and his front-page editors, Jock Whitney introduced Ron Holland as the ad agency writer who would be sucking around there every night to pick their brains. But Whitney said it graciously, like the patrician that he was: "Ron Holland will be working with all of you, and I'm sure he'll try not to get in your way. I would appreciate anything you can do to help him, because his efforts will be part of our push to rebuild our newspaper." When Whitney left the meeting, Denson fiddled with his eyeglasses—a sure sign he was about to let loose a ballbuster. He looked closely at the black-haired sonofabitch ex-itinerant peddler and asked, "Is it true that all you Madison Avenue guys are fags?" Holland shot back, "Well I don't know about the others, but *I* am." Denson doubled over. He and Holland became buddies instantly.

The new *Trib* that Denson put together looked so different and so unusual that it was almost suspect to many readers—until we came up with the line *"Who says a good newspaper has to be dull?"*

But Denson quit suddenly after an internal flap and was succeeded by Jim Bellows, an elegant Damon Runyon. By the time Bellows took over, Freddie and I had come up with a plan to build readership on Sundays—when the *Trib*'s circulation died while business zoomed at the *Times*. The *Times*' Sunday magazine section was popping its buttons with ads and original articles, while the *Trib* carried a skimpy syndicated insert. We met with Jock Whitney and Jim Bellows to show them a new magazine we had created to compete with the *Times*. It was a combination *New Yorker* and *Cue*, with articles that would appeal directly to people who lived and worked in New York City. No such magazine existed. *The New Yorker* was for highbrows and college kids, more a national magazine. And while the *Times*' magazine was Sunday's drawing card, it was dull and deadly.

Our Sunday magazine for the *Trib* was called *New York, New York*, out of my love for this wonderful town. Jimmy Breslin and other *Trib* staffers had pitched in with articles for the prototype. Whitney listened carefully to every word we said. But he clammed up completely and finally walked out. I was absolutely baffled. A few days later Bellows called me to say that Whitney okayed it. "Only one thing, George," said Bellows, "Jock Whitney doesn't want to call it '*New York, New York.*' He thinks it should be called just plain *New York.*"

"Not half bad," I said. *New York* was born.

I made a special point of urging Bellows to set aside a hefty piece of his budget for a top-flight art director, and I recommended a tasteful pro, Peter Palazzo. When I mentioned the salary that a guy like Palazzo would command, Bellows thought it didn't make sense to pay *New York*'s art director more than its editor. "It's about time it happened," I told Bellows. Palazzo was hired, he gave the magazine a special graphic class and *New York* was on its way. But the sixties was a rough decade for newspapers in our town. The 114-day strike of 1962–63 hurt the *Trib* badly. Before the

strike its circulation had climbed steadily. After the strike its price
had to be raised, circulation slipped, and in 1966, after a second
strike, Jock Whitney closed its doors. All of us who had helped
the new *Trib* grow shared Gentleman Jock's obvious sorrow in
shutting it down after his spunky fight. But its new magazine section, *New York*, was later revived by Clay Felker and converted
into an independent weekly. *New York* magazine is now a thriving
publication—the fruit of one of my most cherished concepts.

PKL's spontaneous ways paid off. We had no committees to
slow us down and our business sizzled. We hit $8 million after two
years and $20 million after three. We were sure-fire newsmakers
and our phones were constantly ringing with calls from reporters.
When Freddie Papert got on the line he charmed the pants off
PKL's callers, setting off a blizzard of publicity. I once mentioned
to Julian, "If Freddie talks to you for five minutes he'll convince
you you're a girl." From some of the stories that ran I began to
wonder if Freddie had convinced himself he was our father. One
day I saw a three-column piece in the *New York World-Telegram
& Sun* on Papert and PKL. I was described by the writer as someone who had been "toiling one year for demanding Doyle Dane
Bernbach." Julian was referred to as a "radio writer and semi-pro
baseball promoter before he went into the ad business." Koenig
and Lois were labeled as "assets" of Papert. I shot off a letter to the
newspaper, pointing out that "Fred Papert is a great advertising
man, but giving him all the credit is like giving Tony Lazzari
credit for the 1927 Yankees and barely mentioning Babe Ruth and
Lou Gehrig." I later learned that a PKL secretary had been rushed
over to the editor's desk after my letter was mailed. She inter-
cepted the envelope.

We went about our business like no other ad agency, always
volatile, never stiff. Julian spilled the beans about our top-secret
creative formula in a talk to the Advertising Writers Club when
he explained, "If you look at your ad and you want to puke, the
chances are it's a bad ad." Our work flowered in this breezy atmosphere. Example: We were visiting a furniture factory in Fall River,
Massachusetts, where the chairs of Harvey Probber, Inc., were
precision-made. Each chair was placed on an electronic test platform to be sure it was absolutely level. "Got a book of matches?"
I asked Julian, a heavy smoker. He handed me a matchbook and

I slid it under one leg of the chair on the test platform. "I've got the ad," I said. " 'If your Harvey Probber chair is crooked, straighten your floor.' " Julian scowled and shot back, "Asshole—'If your Harvey Probber chair *wobbles*, straighten your floor.' " That was the way the ad ran and that was the way we built the first red-hot creative agency.

We added another floor and junked the camp chairs. I redecorated the agency with Breuer chairs, marble tables and antique taborets for our art directors. We worked in a spacious, open environment. I hung an oval picture of Haralampos in his Evzone uniform behind my drawing table. His pleated military skirt and the pompons on his shoes seemed more brilliant than any color photo could possibly convey, despite the portrait's faded daguerreotype hue. His Mediterranean eyes watched over me as I worked at my business—at my *store*.

To work at PKL was a never-ending joy. I was involved with gifted people, each ad was a thrilling challenge, the joint was unbefouled by mannerism—and nothing could stop us. I was in love with my loosey-goosey paradise. We worked late because it was painful to leave its carefree atmosphere, where everyone was always so wide awake.

Bronfman snored.

"*Massa Sam*," I said, louder than usual, slapping the conference table. His eyelids opened. The mighty tycoon of the liquor business often snoozed at meetings while the boys carried on with their presentations, but I'd be damned if anyone conked out on us while we showed *our* work. Even Samuel H. Bronfman, the fabled boss of Joseph E. Seagram & Sons, Inc., would have to lose some sleep over our ads for his whiskey. If he expected his staff to keep talking while he slumped in his chair and snored, that was okay with me. But I wasn't about to play the foot-shuffling adman who swallows his pride and does a jig for a dozing client. So I whacked the table and Bronfman quit snoozing.

During PKL's first year we became one of the lucky ad agencies that worked for this powerful man they called Mister Sam. He was not only the boss of Seagram, but our landlord as well; his corporation also owned Pharmacraft. That made three reasons to be *very* respectful. Our work for Dr. Sheckman was admired by Mister Sam's son, Edgar Bronfman, and we were given a chance to show how PKL's approach could help increase sales of Wolf-schmidt vodka, a very sensitive subject to Samuel Bronfman. Smirnoff was running a smart campaign that dominated the market. "Leaves you breathless," claimed Smirnoff—very astute copy. If a respectable businessman put a load on at lunch, his telltale breath might hurt his career or knock over his secretary; so when Smirnoff came out with those clever code words, lots of noontime boozers switched from their usual hooch to vodka martinis or straight vodka on the rocks.

Whether it was Smirnoff's smart advertising or Bronfman's stubborn attitude, he regarded vodka as the black sheep in Seagram's stable. He considered it hokey stuff that wasn't a real liquor. But Edgar Bronfman liked our racy style. He seemed to look forward to having us show our stuff to his old man.

In my roster of client-tyrants, Samuel Bronfman rates a special laurel because he was a surprisingly sweet tyrant. If most advertising guys could shake off their shivers and treat a tycoon like Bronfman in a man-to-man way, they'd discover a fine human being behind his awesome power. But a crafty wizard like Bronfman could detect fear like a bad smell and decide here's one more nervous advertising schmuck, so I'll grab my nap while he goes through his bullshit; and if my staff says yes while I'm sleeping, I'll say no when I wake up and have my fun—because it's such a pleasure to rough up Madison Avenue's con artists. In dealing with Bronfman you had to grab his interest and hold it, even if it meant slapping his desk or addressing him slightly off key, but squarely on target. That's why I rarely called him "Mister Sam."

"*Massa* Sam," I said, showing him a Wolfschmidt ad headlined "Taste my screwdriver." He looked at it cross-eyed, not quite sure what to make of it. "This is for California," I said. "They'll read it both ways out there. It'll grab their interest twice." He leaned forward and smiled.

His staff usually watched him for their cues. If you blurted out the wrong words while Bronfman was deciding, you might look like a jerk when he made up his mind—and his mind was hard to change once it was made up. Even when the old man was wrong he wasn't shy about insisting on his right to be wrong. Julian once defended a PKL ad so convincingly that one of Bronfman's staff spoke up and said, "Koenig's right, Mister Sam." "Fine," said Mister Sam, "let him be right someplace else." But he apparently liked the campaign as well as the relaxed style of his offbeat tenants at our first big presentation. Some of our ads for Wolfschmidt that would have gotten us tossed out of most tycoons' offices grabbed Mister Sam's interest. "You're some tomato," said a vertical Wolfschmidt bottle to a luscious red tomato. "We could make beautiful Bloody Marys together. I'm different from the other fellows." The tomato answered, "I like you Wolfschmidt. You've got taste." Mister Sam smiled again.

He understood that the campaign made marketing sense by telling people that his vodka had a taste. We were saying that you *could* tell one vodka from another—the direct opposite of Smirnoff's breathless booze claim. Then we showed a follow-up ad and stressed the point that it should run one week after the "tomato" ad. The copy reveals why: "You sweet doll, I appreciate you," said the Wolfschmidt bottle, now lying horizontally, pointing to a ripe orange. "I've got taste. I'll bring our your inner orange. I'll make you famous. Roll over here and kiss me." The orange answered, "Who was that tomato I saw you with last week?"

Mister Sam was known to be hooked on ads that showed beautiful people in swank penthouses, but when he saw his stepchild Wolfschmidt vertically erect with a tomato, followed up by a horizontal scene with an orange, he never asked for a penthouse. Instead he told us to wait outside while he thought it over. We didn't have to wait too long before Edgar came out and told us that Mister Sam said yes.

We walked away with a client of towering prestige, an ad agency's jewel. Seagram was the world's biggest distiller, with about $1 billion in sales, but a sweet old man lurked behind the curtain of wealth that made him such a feared presence. He was also far more flexible than many on his own staff suspected. Bill Bernbach might have sliced off my Wolfschmidt phallus before I could sneak the ads out of his office, but Bronfman didn't mind at all. When I said, "They'll get the hots for Wolfschmidt, Massa Sam," he knew what I meant.

Mister Sam never got a *Ccchyessa* from me because he was always a gentleman. But he owned the world's biggest whiskey plantation, so I always made sure to call him Massa. After a while he seemed to catch the ring of it even if he may have thought he was hearing me wrong when I first said it. As I became a familiar face in his conference room he began to squint at me with a devilish, searching look that seemed to say: "Hmmm—*Massa Sam*. It does sound more obedient than *Mister* Sam. You're up to something, but I'll figure it out." (Yes suh, all dem words.)

He was a short, nondescript man, neatly tailored, about seventy, and actually meek in his outward appearance. You couldn't tell Massa Sam's book by his modest cover even though he was richer than many countries and more powerful than real kings. But when something caught his personal interest, no matter how small, he didn't delegate his ballbusting power. I found that out on a left-field project for Leroux cordials, a minor brand assigned to us after Wolfschmidt. Seagram's ad manager, Sandy Greenwald, asked if I could improve Leroux's labels. He thought they were slightly ugly. I thought they were absolute eyesores, so I designed new ones and brought them to Greenwald.

"Let's show these to Massa Sam," he said. I didn't like the idea of Greenwald picking up my "Massa." Dat wuz *mah* word and he wuz *mah* Massa—but when we met with Bronfman, Sandy said, "Mister Sam, here are some new Leroux label designs that Lois did for us."

The old man wasn't his usual sweet tyrannical self when Sandy mentioned new labels. He looked suspicious, a treacherous frame of mind for even the sweetest of tyrants. I decided to lay off the Massa Sam stuff and play this one cautiously. "The labels you have are fine," I began, "but I think if you study these new designs you'll see that the name Leroux comes across with more style." I went through a no-nonsense, no-wisecrack explanation, but each time I used a phrase like "more tasteful" or "better style" he seemed to become more upset. Then it hit me: by a grunt and a glance I realized that Bronfman himself had actually supervised the design of the old labels. I began to back off, trying to use neutral words about the old labels while selling my new designs. But before I could go much further he eased back in his chair, cut me off with a wave of his hand and turned to Greenwald. "Sandy, what's your opinion?" he asked. "Well Mister Sam," said Sandy, "I think I agree with the agency on this," and he picked up where I left off to sell his boss on my new designs. Bronfman leaned forward and calmly asked Greenwald, "Who do you work for—me or this *pig-fuckin agency?*"

It connected like a kidney punch and I fell to the floor, doubled over with laughter. The old man stretched his modest frame over the table and stared at me as I rolled on his carpet, grabbing at my stomach and guffawing uncontrollably. "Why are you laughing?" he asked. "I just insulted you." But I couldn't stop. "Oh Massa Sam," was all I could mumble, rocking in convulsive laughter at his feet, tears streaming from my eyes. He stood there, just staring at me. Finally he leaned toward me again and said, *"You* I like." Not too long after that, the labels that were designed by my Massa Sam were replaced by the new designs from his pig-fuckin advertising man.

Massa Sam owned de whole plantation and he sure knew it, yes suh. One day I was in the conference room with his staff, but there was no point in reviewing our advertising until Bronfman arrived. When he walked in, a bunch of guys fell over themselves trying to seat their leader. He plunked into the nearest chair and was ready to get on with the meeting, but someone blurted out, "No, *no,* Mister Sam—sit here at the *head* of the table."

"Young man," Bronfman deadpanned, "wherever I sit is the head of the table."

Later he fell asleep, snoring as his staff went ahead with the meeting. Some of the boys even talked directly to their snoring bossman, because Samuel Bronfman was the kind of emperor who could never be called naked. When his snoring got too loud they dumped a flipchart off its easel and the mighty Mister Sam returned from dreamland.

But he never dozed off when it came to art. Bronfman, whose Seagram Building is the most stunning office building in New York, had some original paintings and sculpture in his office which I had heard about but hadn't seen. He was a culture patron and was known to take great pride in his art collection. When he stopped me one day and asked, "Lois, have you ever seen my office?" I jumped at the invitation. "You're an *artist,*" he said. "Come on in. *You'll* understand." I was thrilled to my bones. At Music and Art High and at Pratt Institute my favorite courses were art history, and for years I've covered the Manhattan galleries on Saturday afternoons. I've always regarded painting and sculpture as the true story of man, without the distortions of historians. I knew I was in for a rare experience.

Samuel Bronfman's office was graced by several breathtaking works. I wanted him to know how fully I appreciated his collection by naming each piece. "That Sisley," I said, "a beautiful landscape." He was delighted that I knew the painting. "The best," he beamed. I pointed to another canvas and identified it correctly—artist, period, school. He was obviously delighted. "Fantastic work," he purred proudly. "I see you *know* these masterpieces." I especially knew the piece of sculpture that dominated his office. It rose from a pedestal and seemed to tower over us.

"I love what you have here," I said, "and that Rodin study of Balzac is really exciting. If I'm not mistaken there are only six or seven bronze casts of that Rodin."

Bronfman turned pale. "What did you say?"

"Only six bronze casts of that Rodin. You own one of the six."

"No, no. *That's* Rodin. *That's* the sculpture."

"I mean the bronze cast from the original . . . from the clay original."

"But *that's* the sculpture." He was growing confused and I was heading for trouble. The bronze sculpture loomed over us.

"Mister Sam, let me explain. That's a bronze cast made from the original clay sculpture. And what you have is called an original bronze cast. It's a terrific piece of sculpture, but I'm quite sure there are five or six other bronze casts just like this one." I was trying to soften the shock; actually it was one of several bronze casts from one of several studies Rodin did for the great piece of sculpture of Balzac at the Museum of Modern Art.

"No, no—you don't understand. This is the original. This is the *only* one."

There was no way out—I had to explain how bronze sculpture is made: "First the artist makes a clay sculpture—that comes first. Then he makes a plaster cast of the clay. After that, bronze is poured into the hollow of the plaster cast. Now, if the casting of the bronze is done while the sculptor is alive, chances are he personally supervised the filing and polishing and all the fine details of finishing. He can make one, two, three, four, five—in fact, as many casts as he wants. But he usually does just a few, and in many cases the original clay sculpture is destroyed. However, the bronze casts *are* considered originals. So what you have here, Mister Sam, *is* an original bronze." That was one of the rare occasions when I called him Mister Sam.

He sat down heavily behind his stunning Biedermeier desk. "Do I get this right?" he asked. "There are six of these . . . and this is not the original?"

"It's not the original clay, but it is an original bronze. And yes, there are probably about six of these." It hurt to make it that clear —and Bronfman was visibly pained. He shifted uneasily in his chair. His shoulders drooped.

"Awright," he finally said. "*Awright.*"

Someone had messed with my Massa Sam and I pitied the poor sonofabitch who gave me the sad chore of explaining sculpture to this sweet tyrant. But Massa Sam was a fine client who never diddled with our ads.

Edgar Bronfman was especially proud of PKL's work for Seagram. We had won over his formidable father to our irreverent style and we had catapulted Wolfschmidt into fame. Samuel Bronfman's black sheep vodka had finally made it as a real liquor.

Massa Sam, moreover, never treated me like one of his Madison Avenue darkies. "Lois, come here," he once said to me as he studied one of my ads.

"Comin', Massa Sam," I said, shuffling to his desk in my best yassaboss cadence from Fort Sam's stockade. He stared at me quizzically.

"Lois, tell me," he said, "what's your derivation?"

"Human bein', Massa Sam."

"Don't play games, I asked you something."

"I'm Greek, Massa Sam."

"Greek," he repeated. "Aha. *Awright.*"

Did he finally understand the meaning of Massa?

When Ron Holland pleaded with the Commandeur of the Confrérie des Chevaliers du Tastevin, better known as Joe Baum, to comment on our ads for his newest restaurant, the Commandeur finally said, "I don't care, run the shit."

Joe Baum of Restaurant Associates hated to praise anything. The approval of an ad or a salad for his growing network of restaurants might imply perfection. With Baum you could always do better and in his search for the ideal he found imperfections everywhere—usually with his incredible fingers, dangling like sausages from his runty hands, darting into the hearts of salads, plowing through the lettuce leaves to pluck out a flaw.

Restaurant Associates, which owned the Four Seasons, the Forum of the Twelve Caesars, the Brasserie, the Tower Suite, La Fonda del Sol and other eating joints still on blueprints, became a PKL client in 1961. Joseph H. Baum, RA's boss, was leading a personal crusade to convert eating into an experience. The Baum period of my life began at our first meeting. "I'll need photos of your key staff with each man's name and title," he said. "In each of our restaurants we'll post one set in the locker room, one in the back office and one at the director's stand. If anyone on my staff doesn't recognize your face or know your name, *I want to hear about it.*" He waggled a Corona like Edward G. Robinson playing Little Caesar. "But please do *not* go to the Forum until you've received my orientation. We'll plan on lunch. Allow four hours."

Our group arrived at the Forum of the Twelve Caesars at noon. We were escorted by Puerto Rican kids in Roman getups to a large table in a corner usually reserved for V.I.P.'s, surrounded by a ring of smaller tables that were stacked with chafing dishes, serving platters, pre-Christian silverware and every correct gadget for an eating orgy. We were joined by the staff of Restaurant Associates and served by three captains plus six waiters. Paying guests gawked as Joe Baum took over.

Every item on the poster-size dinner menu was prepared right there by Baum. As his new ad agency sampled each dish, he narrated. His sausage fingers waved a cutlet of wild boar (deviled in mustard seed and apple nuggets), stabbed an oyster in pink caviar (a "Lucullan Fantasy"), twirled the Neptune's bisque, pinched a ring-neck pheasant, squeezed one of Cleopatra's sautéed love apples and sunk his pinky into a Patrician Parfait as wines flowed to Baum's voice-over: "Marvelous but needs more aging . . . superb but not entirely . . . incomparable but might be better . . ." We started at noon and quit at 4:30. After that simple lunch the Forum's staff knew our names and faces. And I could never forget Joe Baum's fingers.

RA was the sort of account that scares off most advertising men. The work never ended and you never knocked out any full-page, portfolio-puffing ads. I relished RA because it needed gutsy work for a growing string of restaurants, each with a special personality. La Fonda del Sol in the Time-Life Building was a classic joint for Baum's sweeping vision. Its South American flavor was so real you could almost believe that Montezuma was the doorman. Unfortunately, Baum's Peruvian paintings and pre-Columbian sculpture scared away the droves of secretaries who swarmed through the neighborhood. Since La Fonda looked like a museum, they were sure its tab was for art collectors. We had to sell a restaurant that looked like a Lima gallery to typists from Hackensack.

One of Baum's imported folk treasures was a puppet's head with a pencil-line mustache. He became my ad symbol. I put him in a prone position and closed his eyelids to show him lying down on the job. He was then christened Stupido and the museum became a fun place. "No, no, Stupido," said our ad, "we said *Fiesta* at La Fonda del Sol, not *Siesta*." And certainly no gallery would say in its ad, "Will the lady who lost her composure during Fiesta at La Fonda del Sol please come back every Sunday?" Then, when New York's reservoirs were drying up we announced, "Water shortage or no, we'll turn the hoses on the next group of dowagers who break into a fandango during Sunday Fiesta."

Baum had brought Peru to West Fiftieth Street, and nothing would mar his showcase. When we lunched there one day I waited for his fingers to find a blemish. His shrimp salad arrived and Baum went to work. His fingers plunged immediately into the dressed lettuce. The director of La Fonda, Jim Tsighis, came quickly to our table. Baum sneered at him while his fingers crawled through the sliced tomatoes. "How much do we charge for this salad?" he asked his director. "A dollar eighty-five, Mr. Baum," said Tsighis. La Fonda's director was on his toes and self-assured, but Baum was Baum: "A dollar eighty-five for this salad? And we advertise to bring people across town to have lunch here? I wouldn't cross the street to have this salad *free*."

"What's the matter with it?" asked Tsighis calmly. "It's not attractive," said Baum, plopping a shrimp onto the mangled salad. He squirmed up his face like Edward G. Robinson with gas pains. "The tomatoes are not sliced properly, the lettuce is not laid down carefully, the shrimps are not placed evenly. My God, Tsighis, even if you had a kid who was sick in bed you would try to make his tray *attractive*." Tsighis, a proud Greek, wasn't ready to genuflect in full view of the restaurant. Rather smoothly he said, "Well Mr. Baum, I guess I just don't understand what you mean by *attractive*." He started to take off when Baum plugged him between the eyes: "Well, I don't mean it hasn't got big *tits*."

Tsighis removed Little Caesar's plate.

After several months with Baum it became obvious that our work would be exciting, challenging—and exasperating. He had impossible standards, a wild imagination and he never thought of an ad as something apart from how a restaurant was experienced. Each room of Baum was a universe of a thousand meshing elements. I worked on menus, interior decor, logotypes—also as interpreter of Baum's ramblings to his punch-drunk architects. His passion for detail was my meat and drink and we developed a bond that was called "symbiotic" by a food editor. "Mutual fascination" said it better because we both wanted a perfect moon. "When you point to the moon," someone once said, "it's the finger that counts, not the moon." With us it was the moon; Baum's fingers made it no contest.

He was a Renaissance man with clairvoyant taste. He personally transformed America's concept of a "restaurant," whatever its price or menu, into an exciting experience. He chose the main floor of the Seagram Building for his incomparable Four Seasons when the building was having trouble renting space. Later, when the Pan Am Building was going up, he created three restaurants for their main lobby: Trattoria for Italian food; Zum Zum, a Bavarian snack bar; and Charlie Brown's Ale & Chop House. Emory Roth & Sons, the architectural firm that executed the designs of Pan Am—designs that were supervised by the great Walter Gropius—watched over the graphic integrity of that grotesque erection. Any signs or designs for Joe Baum's restaurants had to fit in with the sterile, mortuary atmosphere of Pan Am's lobby. So they vetoed my designs for Trattoria, Zum Zum and Charlie Brown's; their lobby was not to be botched by bursts of color and dissimilar graphics. But I was convinced that each design was true to the flavor of Baum's new restaurants and we were given an audience with Emory Roth & Sons to plead our case.

My reverence for Gropius and my irreverence toward the Pan Am Building was summed up in a speech I gave at a designers' seminar in 1964: "If I were an architect or an industrial designer, I would owe everything to Gropius. Not only because he was the great educator, but also because he showed in actual work what could be done. He was a better architect as early as 1911—and certainly in 1925 when he did the Bauhaus Building in Dessau—than most are today. But I am not an architect. All I can do is sink to my knees to him. His leadership has directly and indirectly inspired teaching, industrial design, pottery, weaving, stage design, painting, typography, layout and, of course, architecture. *I forgive him the Pan Am Building.*"

But Emory Roth & Sons wouldn't forgive me my designs—not in keeping with their lobby. While Baum chewed on his Corona I blew my stack royally: "You guys have the nerve to talk about *taste* after putting up this monstrosity and fucking up the look of New York City for a hundred years to come? You have the *nerve* to sit there and criticize these designs?" I tore into the sculpture of the talented Richard Lippold in their Vanderbilt Avenue entrance, comparing it to his stunning work that hangs over the bar of the Four Seasons. "When a brilliant architect like Philip Johnson works with Lippold, a masterpiece shows up at the Seasons because Lippold is working with a man of taste—but when you guys work with him, he turns out crap." To be sure, the Roth firm wasn't about to take that kind of crap. They showed me the door, but I demanded to meet with Walter Gropius, who was in his seventies and probably not a very busy man. Mr. Gropius, they angrily insisted, was much too busy to see an advertising man about restaurant designs. Their irritated glances signaled Baum to remove his arrogant friend, and Joe hustled me out of their offices. I was disgusted to the core. But a few days later Baum was told that Gropius was shown the designs and *liked* them. The lights, colors and graphics came to life in Pan Am's antiseptic lobby, pulling in paying guests to Baum's new bistros.

Two years later I met Walter Gropius for the first time at an Art Directors Club reception in his honor. "Mr. Gropius," I said, shaking the great man's hand, "my name is George Lois." I said my name very slowly to trigger an association with my "forgiving him the Pan Am Building." He turned over my name in his mind, smiled in recognition and said, "Ah yes, yes—verry lovely, verry lovely—*Trrattoria* . . . *Zoom Zoom* . . . *Charrlie Brrown* . . ." The trace of a Bauhaus accent flavored that lovely moment.

There was action everywhere with Baum, but never a word of approval. As Ron Holland began to work with the Commandeur, a symbiosis hatched between them that turned explosive. At a meeting to review one of our campaigns, Baum and Holland went at each other's throats, cursing and screaming. Ron finally shouted at Baum, "Joe, *I hope you die!*"

"—a rich man," I added.

Baum rambled at meetings like Casey Stengel with words by Buckminster Fuller, thinking out loud in great circles of confusion. He expected that everyone would understand his meandering and agree with his final concept. At one meeting Ron disagreed with Baum. Joe lashed out at Holland, accusing him of trying to hurt Restaurant Associates. "He doesn't want to hurt us, Joe," said Dick Blumenthal, one of Baum's sharpest aides, "he just *disagrees* with you." Baum bit into his cigar and said, "I've never confused a mask of controlled hostility for loyalty." Later, disgusted with Joe's constant bitching, Ron told him bluntly, "Joe, you're absolutely paranoid." Baum answered calmly, "You would be too if everyone was persecuting you."

His love of perfection was contagious, and when he opened Charley O's our work was swept up in Little Caesar's passion. Before the greening of Charley O's Bar & Grill & Bar, a very Irish joint on the corner of Forty-eighth Street and Rockefeller Plaza, the swells ate at Baum's lush Forum while the slobs ate at Chock Full O' Nuts. The corner was occupied by Holland House (no relation to Ron), a dump. "Corner that corner," I begged Baum. "Between the Forum and Chock Full, America is starving." In 1966 Baum took over Holland House and converted it into one of the most charming spots in New York. "Every night around midnight I look around my lovely bar," said one of our first ads for Charley O's, "crowded with men and classy women and I think, if only Robert Benchley were here." The ad was signed by a mythical Charley O. "This is the kind of place I always wanted to open and finally did," said Charley O in another ad. The joint was *gemütlich* Irish, stylishly publike, *joyful*.

We covered the walls with large photos of booze-lovers, some famous, but many known only to their girlfriends and bookmakers. Each photo was captioned with a fragment of food lore or New York wit. The magisterial head of Julian Koenig sits on the west wall over his trademark line, "Eat, drink, and Brioschi." Koenig's first choice was turned down because it wasn't Irish enough: "The only heroes on the *Andrea Doria* were the sandwiches." Errol Flynn, one of the few celebrities on the walls of Charley O's, is credited with the bull's-eye description of its flavor: "Any guy who has more than ten grand left when he's dead is a failure."

Ron Holland, the Rhode Island Irishman, coined the name

Charley O's after losing out with two others: Ron Holland's (after Holland House, the dump); then P. J. Baum, vetoed modestly by Baum. Joe wanted Lovely Houlihan, but that was killed because anyone from St. John's parish would rip the place apart for calling micks fags. My choice was The Bloody Nose, with a fighter's fist as its trademark and ex-pugs like Tony Zale as the joint's maître d's. Baum tried hard to sell it to the management of Rockefeller Center, the landlord of his new restaurant, but they nixed it with a vengeance. "We'll have a Bloody Nose somewhere else," Baum promised me. We settled for Charley O's, very Irish.

But Ron managed to sneak a Holland into Baum's Irish restaurant. Before his grandmother passed away years before at a grand old age, she was lectured by a young priest on the sins of booze. "Reach your maker cold sober," he warned her. Grandma Holland, who looked like Grandma Moses, rose up from her bed and told the priest, "I'll keep drinking it as long as they keep making it." In the north alcove of Charley O's sits the twinkling face of Ron Holland's grandmother with that caption.

Baum's symbiosis with Holland was later interrupted for a year when Ron was transferred to PKL's London office in 1965. Baum was upset. He told Ron that no other copywriter could service RA. Ron recommended Dan Greenburg, then a copywriter at PKL and author-to-be of *How to Be a Jewish Mother*. Months later at 5:00 A.M London time Holland was awakened by his bedside phone. Baum's voice said, "Greenburg's better." Then Ron heard a fast click.

But lucky for Joe Baum that his Irish advertising man was back in New York when Charley O's was born with its authentic Gaelic charm. Ron told Joe to call it Charley O's Bar & Grill & *Bar* because any bum can build a bar (but it takes a genius-drunk to build two) —and it would enable Charley O's to sell sandwiches at one of them. Ron also told Joe to charge less for a dry martini because any jerk in an Irish bar who fouls up his gin with too much vermouth doesn't belong. "And best of all," said Ron, "we'll put my grandmother's picture on the wall, God rest her Irish soul."

On the eve of its opening a carload of pictures still waited to be hung. They had to be positioned exactly right, so I hung them myself into the wee hours. The next morning at 7:00 I returned to complete the picture hanging after a few hours of sleep. Charley

O's first customers would start arriving at noon. I covered every parcel of wall until I ended up in a corner of the restaurant, surrounded by mounds of wrappings and sweepings. I jumped off the ladder and scooped up two armfuls of litter but I couldn't find any garbage pail. "What do I do with this stuff?" I asked a passing waiter.

"Put it in the garbage pail," he said helpfully, and walked off. A second waiter came by, bustling about his chores—the hours immediately before a restaurant's opening, particularly a Baum restaurant, are frantic.

"What am I supposed to do with this stuff?" I asked the second waiter. He ignored me and scurried off. After being ignored a third time, while holding all that garbage in my arms, I blew a gasket at the third passerby. Bill Dickenson, the new restaurant's director, rushed over. "You can't ask our waiters to do that," he tried to explain. "Our maintenance people do the cleaning up." But I wasn't interested in union protocol—all I wanted was the courtesy of being informed where the garbage pail was located.

"Dickenson go fuck yourself," I shouted, dumping the wrappings at his feet. I went back to PKL and said screw the whole Baumshit. Ron was at RA when I got to my office. I called him there and told him I was going to resign the account. "Wait," said Ron, "don't do anything rash." But I wouldn't have changed my mind if they had changed the name of the joint to Alias George Reardon.

It turned out that Dickenson didn't know that I was suffering from lack of sleep while getting a hernia hanging Baum's pictures. Holland sized up the situation fast and sent one of our young kids from PKL's art bullpen to Charley O's with a Polaroid camera and secret instructions. Four hours later a large flat package was delivered to my office. I opened the wrappings to find a gold-framed photo of Dickenson with the caption "The same to you, George Lois." That framed blowup now hangs opposite the bar of Charley O's, caption intact.

"Let's go bust balls," said Baum one night, heading for the Four Seasons. His restaurants were all over town and he dropped by at all hours, usually unannounced. At the top of the Seasons' regal stairs he was greeted by the director. Baum promptly asked, with a growl, "What was wrong with the consommé tonight?" flicking ashes on the carpet of his finest restaurant. "Well Mr. Baum," said the director, "we had some difficulty with the blah so we added some va and now it's just right."

"Aha," said Baum, knowingly.

"Joe how did you *know?*" I asked as we sat down to dinner. "That was fantastic. You hadn't even *tasted* the consommé."

"George," he said, limbering up his fingers, "there's *always* something wrong with consommé."

Imperfections were everywhere—and money was no object if it could make his impossible dream come true. Commandeur Baum of the Confrérie des Chevaliers du Tastevin spent $10,000 to host a dinner for a hundred Chevaliers of his elite Confrérie at the Four Seasons. Its entire staff rehearsed the dinner the night before as Ron Holland and I watched in awe. Maestro Baum orchestrated with total authority, and the real event went off perfectly, even by Baum's standards. The Chevaliers, lifelong gourmets, were so overwhelmed that they passed an incredible resolution. The next morning Baum asked his publicity man, Roger Martin, for a report on what he was doing to publicize that wing-ding event.

"Well, at our press conference right after the meal," Roger said proudly, "they resolved unanimously that it was the finest meal ever served *in the history of the world.*" Baum listened intently and suddenly snarled, "Goddamit, that's not *enough!*"

Would Baum ever realize his impossible dream? In Miami, when we stopped for a bite during a trip to set up a Zum Zum in the Orange Bowl, the Commandeur ordered a sandwich. He peeled apart the slices, stripped the insides, waved the shavings of ham and prodded the cheese with his fingers. It wasn't there either.

At the bar of the Forum he once asked the bartender before sipping his Bloody Mary, "Is this the *best* Bloody Mary you can make?"

"Yes, Mr. Baum," the bartender answered with assurance. "Taste it," Baum ordered. The bartender sipped and reflected. "It's pretty good," he decided. "Can you make a better one?" asked Baum. The bartender mixed a new Bloody Mary. "Now taste it and tell me what you think," said Baum—his lips had not yet touched either drink. The bartender took a sip. "This is very good, Mr. Baum. It's *perfect.*" The magic word was finally dropped. "Then why didn't you make it that way the first time?" asked the Commandeur.

Baum's reputation began with the Newarker Restaurant at Newark Airport, where he added sparkling desserts to the menu. "People like to watch fires," he explained, "and the flames don't hurt the food." He was a malcontent and a genius who read *Du* and *Daedalus* and hung Ann Corio's pasties on his library wall. Because of Baum the United States is becoming a nation of exciting restaurants—in the style of the Commandeur.

Advertising was only one building block in the cultures of Baum. We began with an ad and soon reached for miracles. But as an ad agency client, Restaurant Associates flunked the cost-accounting test. We turned out twelve hundred ads a year, which takes a lot of handling. And a senior partner of PKL should not be hanging pictures in a restaurant. I was urged to resign the account. "Pencil pushing horseshit," I said. "Restaurant Associates is my relaxation." I resented the cold-turkey logic of cost accountants. Working on RA made life a little richer even if the agency may have become a trifle poorer. How often in one lifetime does a Baum come along?

I assigned a few restaurants to other art directors, but the work was treated without respect. Careers in advertising don't flower from twelve hunded tiny flower pots, but from eye-popping, full-page color ads. I took back all the projects for Restaurant Associates, from fifty-line ads for Trattoria to lapel buttons for Zum Zum waitresses. Ron Holland and I would do it all. We would continue to bring our work to Joe Baum, and when he would chew on his bootlegged Havanas, when he would glare at us with his Little Caesar puss, we'd wait for him to jab the air and say, "Run the shit."

Our first client in the world of politics was New York's Senator Jacob K. Javits in 1962, but as we went into gear for the incumbent Republican I thought we were working for his wife.

Javits was at the crest of his popularity when he ran for reelection that year against James B. Donovan, a political nobody. The odds were heavily in Javits' favor. Only one question remained: could we get his plurality to go over 500,000?

The senator's law firm was in the Seagram Building, where Julian and I met with Javits and his staff. We were card-carrying Democrats and made no bones about it, but Jake Javits was a sophisticated pro who wanted straightforward advertising with mass appeal. That was pre-historic 1962, when political advertising followed a pattern: candidate sits in a studio surrounded by a fake library of hollow books with bindings that prominently flaunt names like Plato and Aristotle; also, an American flag is a mandatory prop beside the candidate's desk as he talks to the TV camera with Barney Google eyes darting across the idiot cards.

But effective advertising for a politician must be truthful, natural, human—and believable. His "official photo" for handbills and platform flyers—and especially for his billboard—often sets the campaign's tone. And that first billboard can pack a tremendous psychological wallop *with the candidate*. If he sees his favorite face larger than life just a few days after we get started, he knows we're working. And once the campaign gets going, he rarely has the time to see himself on TV. I wanted an immediate photo of Javits to prepare that kickoff billboard. The minimum printing run was about twenty, and the cost was exorbitant, but I needed only *one* board to post along the senator's route from his home to his office. And the photo had to be right.

I shot the photo of Senator Javits with natural light to capture his Mount Rushmore strength without losing the warmth in his distinguished face. When the photo and the billboard layout were ready, our account man, Paul Keye, brought them to Javits' office and came back with a fast okay from the senator's staff. Javits himself hadn't seen the material, but I rushed ahead with the billboard. It would be posted on the East River Drive turnoff to the Seagram Building in a few days. The next day Keye told me that Javits saw the photo and liked it—but his wife hated it, so the picture was dead. Also the billboard.

Keye wanted to set a date for a new shot. I could have said what the hell, why tangle with the senator's lady, but this was going to be a campaign that would show the real Javits with all his warts, on film. It was a very simple shot and no big deal, but if I compromised at the start, I'd end up with his wife standing over the Movieola to okay each frame of TV footage of the really important stuff. I called Javits to explain why I felt it was so important to use *that* photo. "It's *you*, Senator," I said. "That picture has strength and warmth. It's very real and very honest—and that's what voters respond to. It may sound like nit-picking on my part to take up your time over a photo, but believe me, Senator, *that's* what your campaign is all about. It has to be *you* or it's razzle-dazzle. We want you to win big by being yourself without any cosmetic jobs or snow jobs."

Javits admitted that he liked the photo although Mrs. Javits *was* a little unhappy with it. Like a smart politician, he passed the buck to me, suggesting that I try to talk her into it. The senator gave me her unlisted phone number and I called Mrs. Javits. She turned out to be a strong-willed lulu. It was crystal clear that she detested the photo. "He looks old, he looks bald, he looks fat," she said with disgust.

I tried to explain that while the worst judge of a man's picture is the man himself, the second worst judge is his wife. It was my *profession*, I went on, to be objective about pictures; would she therefore please try to understand that if anyone was best qualified to choose the best shot of her husband, it was *me*. After a lot of hassling I was getting nowhere. She hated the picture, period. But I kept her on the phone, yakking at high speed to wear her out. I would never convince her, but I've dealt with tougher customers than the senator's lady. I knew I was getting there when she screamed at me, "I don't care what you say. He still looks old, he still looks bald, and he still looks fat."

"Mrs. Javits," I said, "I got news for you. Your husband *is* kind of bald, he *is* kind of old, and he *is* slightly fat." There was a slight pause, then she said, "Ohhhh . . . *do whatever you want*," and slammed the receiver. We used the photo. The senator beamed when he spotted our billboard—and its visual style set the tone for our campaign: lifelike and real. No cosmetics for Senator Jake.

Javits was a shoo-in, but I knew we could swell our client's plurality by showing his strengths and weaknesses. He projected a visible integrity, a perfect mix of strength and warmth. His only minus was voter doubts about his Republicanism. To many in his party he was a Democrat at heart. It was important that Javits explain why he was a Republican. We began with street-corner footage of the senator talking to people off-the-cuff. He answered questions, bearing down on the core issue of his Republicanism. Ten years ago most candidates used very little television, and the very idea of showing a candidate as a believable person was unheard of—it had never been done. But Jake Javits was ideal for this approach because he was tough, he was tender and he was probably America's best-informed senator. With the Javits campaign in 1962, *cinéma vérité* in political advertising was born.

When questions came from waitresses or plumbers, his answers were always gutsy and honest. And when we brought along a videotape crew to get footage of Javits in shopping centers, we made sure the senator told why he was a Republican—without his realizing why that question always came up. I went into the crowd, picked out a sour face and I said to the guy, "He's full of shit. He's a goddam liberal, not a Republican. Ask him if he's really a Republican and you'll knock him on his ass." I was dressed like a laborer. I mingled in the crowds without standing out like a Madison Avenue stiff—and it paid off. I was able to coax forth real feelings. Sourpuss picked up my cue, and the camera swung to his face as he asked, "Listen, Senator, you say you're a liberal, so how come you're a Republican?" Javits bristled. He pointed a finger at the crowd and answered with a tinge of rage, "I'll tell you why . . ." Out came a gem of a speech on "Why I am a Republican."

Our TV spots turned his one weakness into an asset by bringing out the real man. His integrity connected. He was the face from Mount Rushmore with an open collar and a believable honesty. He was also kind of old, definitely bald and maybe a few pounds too heavy. But he won by close to a million votes. Nelson Rockefeller ran for his second term as governor that year. He won by 550,000 against Robert Morgenthau, regarded by many as an even weaker candidate than Donovan. Whatever the circumstances, you can't knock a 550,000 plurality. But when the returns came in on victory night, Rocky looked like a fella who ate so many blintzes during the campaign they were backing up on him—Senator Jake had stolen the show with his whopping spread. There's no question that PKL's milestone advertising for Javits added to his incredible plurality.

A few perceptive insiders followed the Javits campaign and understood its unorthodox style. There was a man named Smith, for example. He was quite impressed. And in 1963 his brother-in-law, who worked in the White House, was impressed by the Volkswagen "Think Small" ad. He asked an assistant to check out the agency, which happened to be DDB. By then the ad's author, Julian Koenig, was president of PKL, the ad agency that worked for Javits. Smith came to the right place in 1964. He had a special problem on his hands when another brother-in-law decided to run for senator from New York. Steve Smith was managing the campaign for Robert Kennedy, and he knew that RFK was no shoo-in. Bobby had the Kennedy appeal plus lots of bucks to spend. But he was ruthless Bobby, the late President's hatchet man, an ambitious sonofabitch who was aiming for the Senate as a stepping-stone to the White House. RFK also had the lousy luck to be running against incumbent Senator Kenneth Keating, who looked so grandfatherly with his white hair. And Keating's image as a liberal was strengthened by his disavowal of Goldwater for President. Even being a Kennedy worked against Bobby. When comparing him to JFK, many saw a pushy Irish tough who would stop at nothing to reach the top. It boiled down to those two rib-crushing words: *ruthless* and *carpetbagger*.

When we first met RFK I thought of the phrase that described another Irishman, PKL's Bill Murphy. This clear-eyed Kennedy, with his feet on the desk and his collar open, with his sleeves bunched over his elbows and his hair flopping over his forehead, was completely "unbefouled by mannerism." As we looked at the ruthless carpetbagger I realized that if ever a state got the short end of Washington's stick, we were living in it. We *needed* a carpetbagger ruthless enough to twist arms for the sake of New York. So we told Steve Smith we could deflate the "carpetbagger" balloon by coming out at once, even though it was early September, with the theme "Let's put Robert Kennedy to work for New York." Smith knew it made sense, and he arranged a meeting with Kennedy. Bobby played devil's advocate—digging, probing, asking, challenging. We had ourselves one helluva "client."

I had remembered those familiar photos of RFK in the White House with his sleeves rolled up, an image that lingered when we shot our campaign photo of Bobby. "Stay the way you are," I suggested. "And if I were you I'd be seen as much as possible with my sleeves up." He glared at me, but he left his sleeves bunched above his elbows and during the entire campaign he rarely wore a jacket. We passed up the ego billboard with Bobby. Instead we plastered the state with "Let's put Robert Kennedy to work for New York"—a fast counterattack on his big liability. We held back on our TV blitz until October.

Television showed the real Kennedy. I worked the street corners with RFK, videotaping give-and-take with commuters on the Staten Island ferry, with housewives in shopping centers, with blacks in a Harlem housing project and in Bedford-Stuyvesant. He was asked tough questions and he reached deep inside to find the answers, often in visible agony to avoid a phony comeback. Javits was always totally informed, but Bobby went home to bone up on subjects that threw him off. We taped miles of Bobby taking-and-giving, all unrehearsed. It was edited down to TV spots that showed the real RFK, who could field the tough ones—even when his answers came out with pain. We were showing the real man.

In New Rochelle he was asked by a cocky young executive in a shopping center if he was running on his brother's coattails. Bobby told the punk he wasn't about to apologize for having been part of John Kennedy's administration. Like no ad agency could ever write for him, he said, "I was involved in the things we did in Washington—*both good and bad*—during the last three-and-a-half years." That made a great TV spot because the questioner was a classic stiff. Bobby's answer hit the screen with the pure power of deep conviction.

He loved to quote Aeschylus, but he was no slouch on Archimedes. "One thing I learned when working with President Kennedy," he would say, "is that one man can make a difference. And as Archimedes once said, 'Give me a lever and I can move the world.'" Then he would thrust a thumbs-up fist at the crowd. "How did Archimedes go over today?" he once asked me. "I like the line," I said, "especially since my ancestor wrote it. But it could bomb out if the audience ain't right." Later, in Bedford-Stuyvesant, he used it again—with his thumbs-up clincher. The street crowd stared at him blankly. I was standing among the blacks, the only white face he could see from the sound truck. He scanned the crowd for a knowing nod, his fist stuck out with his thumb up. But he got nothing. As he spotted my white grin he slowly turned his thumb down.

One of RFK's advisors, K. LeMoyne Billings, threw a tantrum when we held up the Staten Island ferry one morning. It was jammed with commuters on their way to work. When we got near the Statue of Liberty we asked the captain to stop for a minute so we could include the torch in the background while RFK talked with commuters. The captain was glad to oblige, but Billings was ready to piss. He thought the reporters would roast Bobby for stopping the ferry in order to get good TV footage. But the reporters were more interested in the verbal free-for-all between Bobby and the commuters about campaign issues. When the press saw the video cameras catching the man-to-man talk, they thought it might be a charade. "You don't understand," I said. "We're showing the real Bobby. If you find one plant asking questions I'll jump overboard." The reporters were finally convinced—and slightly amazed. K. LeMoyne Billings was the only guy on the ferry who was upset. When I heard he had been Jack Kennedy's roommate at prep school I wanted to take back my JFK vote. When I heard he was a wheel at Lennen & Newell I understood.

The first phase of RFK's campaign never mentioned sweet Senator Keating, but the polls showed a seesaw contest. In the race for President every pollster showed Lyndon Johnson swamping Goldwater by at least a million votes, but the polls showed a fat undecided vote in the Kennedy-Keating race. The shrewd door-to-door pulse-feeler, Sam Lubell, showed Keating actually ahead in mid-October, three weeks before the voting. Bobby could have made it a simple race by cozying up to LBJ, but he hated Johnson too fiercely to reach for his coattails.

Kennedy held back his okay of our commercials until the clan blessed them. From Hyannisport, Washington and wherever a Kennedy happened to be, they swarmed to the videotape studio on Manhattan's West Side. As we ran the reel of commercials they applauded. Cool strategist Bobby was suddenly the anxious kid among his fellow Kennedys, hungry for their approval. As we ran the reels they liked what they saw, and Bobby waved a happy thumbs-up to his PKL guys as Eunice said, "I like the way you answered that man in the Harlem schoolyard" or as Ethel said, "That was good, Bobby, a very honest answer in New Rochelle." He seemed most interested in Jacqueline Kennedy's reactions. She always impressed me as the shrewdest woman in the family.

The commercials began in October, while the polls were still fuzzy. In the middle of the month he went to Buffalo and campaigned with Lyndon. Bobby must have gulped hard; the *Times* reported on October 16: ". . . both seized the opportunity at every stop to heap effusive praise on the other. They appeared, to many observers, to be making a special effort to squash public reports of a rift between them." His staff had been urging him to kiss and make up with LBJ, at least in public. But only Steve Smith could have goosed the stubborn Irishman to share a podium in Buffalo with the man who had ruled him out as a vice presidential running

mate just a few months before. And it was Steve Smith who sold
RFK on our ad and poster: "Get on the Johnson-Humphrey-Ken-
nedy team." RFK gulped again, detesting that line. But after
Buffalo we added it to most of his TV spots. Every word counted
and I wanted this guy to win because he understood America. I
never respected a tougher Irishman than Robert Kennedy.

We had lots of important clients at PKL by 1964, but it seemed
so much more important to help Bobby than sell products. Freddie,
Julian and I devoted disproportionate energy to RFK's campaign.
Freddie became personally close to the Kennedy clan. We wondered if he would some day give up the ad agency business to become ambassador to France after RFK reached the White House.

When Keating began to attack RFK directly, our TV campaign
took the offensive with clips of Kennedy telling why he wanted to
be a senator. He attacked Keating for his votes against Medicare,
aid to education and housing legislation. Bobby now had the needed
opening to crack Keating's liberal following. It became a format
speech, but the style was pure Bobby: "I want to be a United States
senator like Senator Wagner was a United States senator. I want to
be a United States senator like Herbert Lehman was a United
States senator. Where would they have been when the education
bill came up in 1961?"—and on to a direct attack on Keating's
"liberal" voting record.

A winning momentum was in the air and we went to Columbia
University for a new give-and-take session. The best in Bobby
would come out as he dueled with the smart college kids. The students were sharp, Bobby was a wow and we caught every electric
minute with three videotape cameras. Suddenly a question came
about the assassination. Bobby's face stiffened and he left the stage.
The auditorium was stunned. There was an eerie silence. About a
minute went by, and he was still shaken when he came back to the
podium. The whole joint was absolutely choked up. "Next question," said the ruthless carpetbagger.

In the final days the polls showed him moving ahead of Keating.
The *Daily News* predicted a Kennedy plurality of 1,148,000, but
the *Times* said the *News* poll ignored the undecided vote. Kennedy's private polls showed a plurality of 490,000 but Keating
claimed an undecided block of 14 percent, with two thirds going

to him. And while Lubell concluded that Kennedy "should win," he still gave Keating "an underdog chance."

A few days earlier, reaching for a clincher, we came up with a twenty-second spot—just words against a dark screen in four successive frames: "Which of the candidates for the United States Senate . . . has the better chance of becoming . . . a great United States senator? . . . A *great* United States senator." The idea leaped out under the crazy pressure of the seesaw tension—and because anyone who knew him couldn't let Bobby lose. A voice was needed to reinforce the words on the screen. Time was short. Freddie Papert narrated, "When you're in the election booth, think about this. . . . Which of the candidates for the United States Senate . . . has the better chance of becoming a great United States senator? . . . A *great* United States senator." Freddie was never more persuasive. We pleaded with Steve Smith to rush over and look at it. He dropped what he was doing, came over to see it, then he got RFK to come over. Bobby okayed it fast. During the last week of the campaign we ran that twenty-second gem in every slot we could corner.

Kennedy won by 720,000, and Johnson beat Goldwater by 2,700,000. RFK's margin was 230,000 more than Steve Smith estimated, but his victory was the closest landslide in modern political history because we'll never know how many votes were swept in by Johnson's incredible win—*two million* more than Kennedy's plurality.

We showed the lovely Irishman for what he was and it must have helped. In 1965 a former *Herald Tribune* reporter, Terry Smith, who had covered RFK's campaign, analyzed PKL's advertising in detail for *Esquire*. His attitude was anti-advertising at the start, but he ended up admitting, "When I finished watching the reruns of the commercials, I was convinced they accounted for the size of the plurality." Then he spoke to other ad agency men who pooh-poohed PKL's work for RFK. But Smith still had to admit, ". . . unquestionably Kennedy's plurality would have been smaller without the boost he received from his advertising." At the New Rochelle shopping-lot taping, Smith thought at first that ringers were tossing the questions at Kennedy. "Convinced they either were shills hired by the agency or actors understandably out of work," he wrote, "I asked them if they had been rehearsed or were being paid. They were not." The only acting in Kennedy's campaign was done by Bobby himself when he forced a smile in Buffalo with Lyndon.

And that was how an art director helped elect a Mount Rushmore Republican and a ruthless Democrat to the United States Senate from the Empire State. One was a Jew and one was an Irishman. The art director was Greek.

Only in New York.

Shortly before Norman Grulich fired Ron Holland, the black-haired Irishman did some original research for a new client that made office copiers. The company was called Haloid-Xerox. Holland had a hunch that their name should be cut in half, but first he needed facts and figures. He drew up a list of ten brands like Thermofax and A.B. Dick, with Haloid-Xerox stuck in among the ten, and he showed the list to office managers who bought copiers. When he tallied up his answers he knew he finally had it made as an account man: only 3 percent had ever heard of Haloid-Xerox—a startling nugget to dig up.

Our client with the loony name was already a glamor stock among the investment boys, so you might be inclined to leave well enough alone. But Holland had his bull by the horns. He rushed up to Haloid-Xerox in Rochester to recommend an historic decision. "Gentlemen," he said, "our research has proved that Haloid-Xerox has minimum recognition. Our sample shows only 3 percent awareness among your key customers. We believe a major reason is your cumbersome name. We therefore recommend that you *cut it in half.*"

They nodded in agreement because they felt the same way, and Ron's research was fact-and-figure backup for their own plans. "That's very valuable input, Mr. Holland," they said. "And now that you have this excellent documentation, what's your recommendation?" Holland banged his fist against the table and shook the shit out of downtown Rochester as he said it crisp and clear: *"Haloid!"*

They sent Ron back to New York and changed their name to Xerox. "Schmuck," I said to Ron, "if you did your homework you'd have known that Xerox is short for Xerography which means dry writing and comes from *xeros*, a very Greek word which no Irishman could appreciate because it means *dry*. So if only to kiss *my* ass you should have told them to go with *Xerox*." But Carl Ally was sour on Ron for sucking around Julian, and Ron sincerely believed that Xerox was a godawful name. "No one can possibly pronounce it," he said. "They'll call it Ex-Rox, the famous Japanese laxative."

We got Xerox as a client in a roundabout way. Bill Bernbach's agency was their first choice, but DDB had Polaroid, a potential competitor in the duplicating field. So one of Bill's key men gave them my name, along with a ringing recommendation—and he wrung a promise out of me never to tell Bill. (I never told Bill.) Xerox wanted creative stuff, but their budget was small and they had fixed ideas about where their advertising should run. Moreover, most people hadn't even heard of their company. But they had this incredible new 914 copier that a child could operate in seconds without smudging a pinky. At our presentation to Joe Wilson in Rochester we told him to show his amazing product on television so that overnight his copier would become a household word. But Wilson was tough to sell. Like almost every new client in the early sixties, he looked at us like shysters trying to fleece him of his ad dollars in one quick binge on television. The men who founded Xerox, and especially its president, Joseph C. Wilson, had to be shocked out of their hangups.

"Schlocky," I said to Wilson, and his chair almost hit the window. "Most businessmen think of duplicating as a schlocky, sloppy mess,

with a slob in their back room splattering ink over his white socks." It was the only way to unsell Wilson on his belief in selling copiers to a few thousand purchasing agents with ads in trade magazines. We insisted to Wilson that only *television* could turn his miracle machine into a showroom product. We wanted millions of secretaries to see how the Xerox 914 worked so they would bug their bosses to get one fast.

Our media director, Bill Murphy, came up with six news specials on "CBS Reports." It was quite a trick to spread Wilson's thin budget of about $300,000 over six network shows. And while their audience was no match for "Gunsmoke," we were still reaching millions of people on a trade ad budget, a far cry from jerking off with a few thousand purchasing agents.

Before we left for Rochester, Freddie sent Ron, still an assistant account man, on an inspired mission to run off copies of our presentation, including the ad layouts, *on Xerox paper*. Their stock was climbing, but it was hard to find a 914 in most business offices, so Ron went to their sales office for his Xerox copies. I may have shocked Wilson with "schlocky," but when we pulled out our presentation on sheets of Xerox paper, that was the schmaltziest windup in Rochester since "Abie's Irish Rose." After they dried their eyes we went to work for our new client.

We made Xerox famous overnight by going on "CBS Reports." After that, when their salesmen made cold calls they were no longer mistaken for Zerex antifreeze or a Japanese laxative—people finally knew who they were. And suddenly business offices were including "Xerox rooms" in their floor plans. But after one of our first commercials on the 914 we got PKL and Xerox into hot water with the feds and CBS.

We showed a little girl, asked by her father to run off three copies of a letter on a 914. She skipped over to the Xerox, holding a rag doll under her arm. She placed the letter on the 914, pushed the buttons, waited for the clicks and out came the copies in seconds. Then she put her rag doll face down on the 914, pushed the buttons again and out came copies of her doll.

When that spot ran on "CBS Reports," a few duplicating companies thought it was a hoax. They screamed foul to CBS and the Federal Trade Commission, insisting that *no* duplicator could work the way we showed the 914. So we yanked the commercial off the air—and to show that we weren't playing with mirrors, we scheduled a new shooting for the CBS brass and the FTC bureaucrats who were checking out the complaint. But instead of using the little girl, I told our casting department to get me a monkey.

When the feds came to the studio I played it straight, except that the chimpanzee farted on the set, which showed where *he* was brought up. When the cameras began to roll, the chimp waddled to the 914, plunked the doll on its glass surface and jabbed the buttons.

He scratched his armpits while the 914 clicked out copies of the doll. The chimp picked up the Xerox copies, grabbed the doll and waddled back to me for a banana. PKL came out of that session with an even stronger commercial than our first. Now we were free to show on television that even a monkey could run a 914. The country went ape for Joe Wilson's machine—but the chimp spot wasn't loved by everyone.

After the chimp was shown on TV an angry letter was received at Xerox from an embarrassed secretary. She asked them to please discontinue that spot; the morning after it ran she brought some work to her company's Xerox machine—she was its operator—and found a banana waiting for her on the 914. Our client was shook up by that letter. They asked us if that TV spot lowered the status of Xerox operators. I had to be careful with our sensitive client so I struck a bowlegged stance, scratched my belly and grunted like Cheetah. We continued running the chimp.

Xerox was the *strangest* client I ever met because Joe Wilson's boys in Rochester were sitting on stock that made them millionaires. They evaluated the results of our work with one eye on the Wall Street tape. My farting chimp, to cite one example, may have added $200,000 to each man's net worth.

To deal with Xerox we needed someone with a fierce enthusiasm to help plan campaigns and sell our work. Carl Ally therefore became PKL's account supervisor, shuttling between New York and Rochester in our Beechcraft Bonanza. The plane was a four-seater and I wondered more than once how I ended up at six thousand feet in choppy weather with my life in the hands of a Turk. But I decided a Greek's chauffeur *should* be a Turk. On one of our trips when Ally was chauffeuring me to Xerox the plane bounced through a murderous front. My Turkish chauffeur looked confident enough behind the controls, but Carl was overweight and smoked a lot. I wondered what would happen if he ever had a heart attack in the air. "Does a Turk ever crap out at the controls?" I asked him. He smiled Turkishly and said, "Only when a Greek prick who can't fly is his co-pilot." We swooped out of the thick clouds, landed safely, waded through the snow and grabbed a cab to the bile-green buildings of downtown Rochester. We drank warm lemonade, a popular drink at Xerox; then we showed Joe Wilson's middle-management millionaires how to become richer—with Ally selling and planning like the most enthusiastic sonofabitch who ever hit the town.

But it was television that freed Xerox from the back room and made it more famous than famous—to a point where barely six months after we started their advertising, America was becoming known as the "Xerox culture." Particularly through Freddie's sophisticated direction of this account, we insisted that they sponsor prestigious TV shows, with a consistent emphasis on public service and cultural programs. Xerox thus became the sponsor of "Death of a Salesman" and "The Glass Menagerie" and "The Louvre." They also sponsored "The Kremlin"—the first time any Western TV crew was allowed there. And Xerox was literally catapulted from the schlocky backroom to become the company with the classiest image in American industry. Our advertising *made* them— virtually overnight.

When the name Xerox became a household word I needled Ron Holland about his Haloid proposal. But the ex-itinerant peddler was a copywriter now and was turning into the fastest gun on Madison Avenue. "How do you like Six-Up for a soft drink?" he asked. "Goes great with Ex-Rox."

We became the first ad agency to have our own Xerox room, a sure sign of our rising fortunes. But two incidents shook me up once our 914 was installed. One night after a late dinner I went back to the office around midnight to pick up some layouts for a client meeting early the next day. I heard the steady clicking of our 914 and went quickly to the Xerox room to pat the late worker on the back. The door was closed, but from the relentless, nonstop rhythm of the 914 I could sense that an urgent project was coming into being. I opened the door and was hit by a blast of sweltering heat from the overworked duplicator. I also found Dan Greenburg

—our star copywriter who took over with Joe Baum while Ron was in England—standing in his shorts. I suppose that was one way to keep cool, but I got plenty hot under the collar. Greenburg was surrounded by a dozen stacks of Xerox sheets, each about three feet high, or roughly 40,000 sheets at a nickel each, for a cost to PKL of about $2,000. Greenburg's physique with his pants on was no bargain; in his underwear he looked like distress merchandise. That was tough enough to look at, but when I peeked at those Xerox stacks I was shocked—they turned out to be copies of his manuscript, *How to Be a Jewish Mother*. He was embarrassed, but not enough to grab for his pants.

"What are you doing?" I asked, knowing what he was doing. Greenburg stared at me blandly with his droopy eyes. "Uh . . . making copies," he said, truthfully. The next day I finked to Julian that our ace copywriter had upped our overhead by about two grand because of his Jewish mother. But the kid was talented so we absorbed the cost. His book was published fast—he sure had enough manuscripts to show around—and it became a best-seller. But *I* never read it. The fact is, a Jewish mother happens to be a very minor league character compared to a Greek mother. And Greenburg never bothered to dedicate his masterpiece to our 914.

On another midnight check of the office I heard squealings and scuffling from the Xerox room. If that was Greenburg this time *with* his Jewish mother I was ready to fire the sonofabitch in front of his old lady. I rushed over to the door and flung it open. But it sure wasn't Greenburg's night. One of our account men was using our 914 in a way that Joe Wilson never intended. He had a sweet young doll perched on its deck, completely bare from the bellybutton down. Her legs were wrapped around his hairy back. I knew it was hairy because he was bare from the ribs down. In fact his pants were bunched over his shoes. In the middle of a very stylish standup bit he turned to me and smiled nicely. Without missing a stroke, he said, "Hi George, want seconds?" She sure wasn't the little girl in the Xerox commercial, but the account man was built just like the chimp. I was set to explode, but there was a lady present.

We were by then the first ad agency since 1929 to have gone public, and you just don't behave that way in a dignified corporation. Our decision to go public came about while watching the miracles of capitalism in Rochester, where men in their thirties became millionaires. Norman Grulich explored the idea. He told us it could be done even though none of the four thousand ad agencies in the United States were publicly held. In September 1962 we offered 85,000 shares of PKL stock to the public for $6.00 and it sold out fast. But right from the start we were damned by the advertising establishment. "I wouldn't want to be part of an agency that owed its primary obligation to stockholders," said the industry patriarch, Fairfax Cone, of Foote, Cone & Belding. But the following year FC&B went public, and according to *Forbes* (September 15, 1968): "Fairfax Cone, the executive committee chairman, and his wife sold 106,000 shares for $1.5 million." One respected advertising man who didn't scoff was David Ogilvy. In 1966 his agency went public and he walked away with a bigger bundle than Fairfax Cone—without having to eat words. By 1972 no less than seventeen ad agencies went public, including Doyle Dane Bernbach. I wondered if it might have happened had Koenig and Lois stayed at DDB. When Bill used to say "Stick with me, I'll make you rich," little did he realize that if I stuck with him *he* might not have become rich. In taking this radical step we were telling our industry that we're not lackeys to clients we *service*. In a 1964 speech I said, "The image of our business no longer has to be that of shufflers who make money because they have a slick line of talk. No pride, just talk." Which may explain my affection for Ally the Turk, who never shuffled.

After we went public I wanted to give Carl a piece of the PKL action. But we were now very respectable and I ran up against a brick wall by suggesting that we make a stockholder of a brash guy with flapping shirttails. Carl began to feel he was getting the shaft. One night he asked me what was going on, yes or no, and if no, why not? He was slightly tanked and I was slightly hopeful that I could still swing it. I told him it was still being considered, but Ally called me a lying sonofabitch and swung at me in a seething rage. I grabbed the lovable Turk but we both knew that he would be pulling out of PKL. Shortly after that the ad manager of Peugeot moved to Volvo and asked us to take over his $1 million account. This meant we would have to dump Peugeot, a much smaller account, but our charter client. Peugeot helped pay our bills when we hung out our shingle, and Victor Elmaleh didn't want to lose us. We stuck with Elmaleh and told Carl to take Volvo and start his own agency if that was what he wanted. That's what he did. When he left PKL to start Carl Ally, Inc., never was a Greek more shook up by the flight of a Turk.

Carl left, but Luke the Duke had arrived. In July 1962 my second son, Lukas George, was born. With the arrival of Luke we slipped a George back into the Lois line. Harry was four by then. Haralampos was sixty-six and still running the store. Nineteen-sixty-two was an eventful year—second son, booming business, gone public, sudden wealth, recognition in the industry. I was thirty-one, a millionaire, and our agency was the talk of the industry. Haralampos bought shares in PKL and dropped in at stockholders meetings. He never fully understood exactly what I did, but he knew that my *store* was prospering.

Freddie was chairman of the board, Julian was president, and I was secretary of the corporation. But now that we were solid businessmen, just like our clients, we weren't going to shuffle like service slobs. The big test came fast. Four months after we went public and exactly three years after we began, we added National Airlines of Miami, a $4 million client, our biggest to date, boosting us toward the $25 million mark. We were chosen after a pitch by Freddie to National's new president, Lewis (Bud) Maytag, Jr., a thirty-six-year-old former jet pilot, fresh from Frontier Airlines out of Dallas. Maytag wanted a Volkswagen-type campaign that would build his new airline.

At first we expected that Bud Maytag would call all the shots on National's advertising, but he quickly got caught up in other duties. The decisions on our new client's campaign passed to his Number Two man, J. Dan Brock, a tall, drawling southerner. Brock came to Miami from Frontier in Dallas when Maytag took over National. We gave Maytag his campaign, although Brock never pulled the cork from champagne bottles over our work. Our advertising for National led to frustration, fame, a $4 million phone call and a fantastic reversal of fate.

We began by searching for a theme that would say National runs their airline in a lively way—like dressing their stewardesses in outfits by Oleg Cassini, like coming out first with fan jets, like introducing special meals on certain flights—a theme that would actually *force* National into exciting innovations.

Papa

"Edwards and Hanly,
where were you when I needed you?"

The Pontiac Choir Boys

Braniff International
(When you got it, flaunt it)

Ford: *Don't you think a knuckleball is much harder to hit than a screwball?*
Dali: *Oh no, no, no, no Whitey.*

"I want my Maypo"

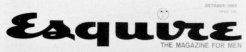

1962

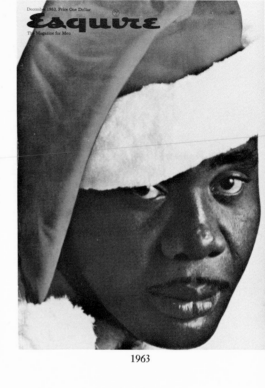

1963

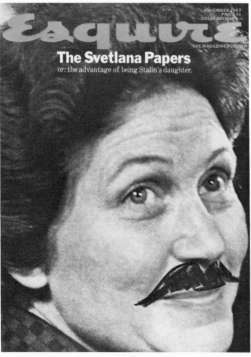

1967

1969

1966

1968

1970

Lewandowski Lois, 1967

Robert F. Kennedy, 1964

"I want to be a United States Senator like Senator Robert Wagner was a United States Senator."

Senator Warren G. Magnuson, 1968

Announcer:
"Senator Magnuson, once youth is gone, once dash is gone, what can you offer the voters of Washington?"

1961

1971

Papert   Koenig   Lois

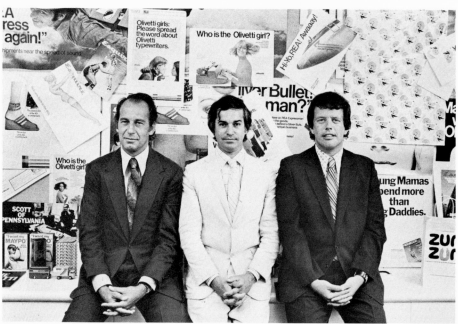

Lois   Holland   Callaway

I had a sea of layouts around me while Julian was scribbling. I lettered out a headline that I knew was right, but somehow off-key. "Something like this," I said to Julian: " '*Is this any way to run an airline? You're fuckin A.*' " The last part needed fixing; it flopped off, and the "A" was confusing. Otherwise it was a clean piece of advertising. "Asshole," said Julian. " 'Is this any way to run an airline? *You bet it is.*' " That *was* better.

Now that we had our theme we needed proof that National was an exciting airline. Being first with fan jets, for example, wasn't unusual enough for Jewish accountants from Forest Hills to choose National instead of Eastern during Passover vacations to Miami. The New York-Miami route was one of the biggest money-makers for National, and many passengers were circumcised.

But Dan Brock was transplanted to Miami from Texas, and his tough young boss had saddled him with an offbeat Noo Yawk ad agency. Suddenly he's stuck with a Jewish writer and a Greek art director who sounds more Jewish than most Jews. It was a delicate situation. I always had the feeling that Brock was overly self-conscious about the possibility that National might get to be stereotyped as a "Jewish airline." Julian once suggested that National serve matzohs on their New York-Miami flights during Passover. "*Maa*tzohs?" drawled Brock, almost incredulously, and nixed the idea. As a certified matzoh-freak I got so upset that I could barely finish my ham sandwich at the Miami airport while waiting for our flight back to New York. (Was this any way to run an airline?)

After a few meetings with Brock I decided to keep my distance unless something urgent came up. Meanwhile we had opened a PKL office in Miami to service National and we had a sizzling theme for our campaign. But as the months went by the theme got played down in our newspaper ads. There just wasn't enough about National to play up—but we kept trying.

Julian found out from our client that they had a Hialeah Flight. It left New York and arrived in Miami in time to catch the races. We carried the idea further by suggesting a *Gambling* Flight. We proposed that National route a flight fifteen miles beyond the offshore limits, gut the plane's interior and install gaming tables. Our TV spot would show a lovely stewardess saying, "Is this any way to run an airline? *You bet it is.*" Then she'd plunk a ten dollar bill on the table. Our lawyers and their lawyers said it was workable.

Yet the first flying crap game never got off the ground—possibly an image problem. But we still had our theme, and it kept National in the public eye because of Andrea on television.

We wanted a million dollar face with a lovely voice to be National's TV stewardess. Our casting department sent us a steady stream of models to look over but she wasn't among them. Then I saw her in the street. She had long blond hair, full round eyes and a willowy walk. I went up to her and said I really wasn't a wiseguy, but if she was interested in auditioning for a TV commercial would she please go to a taping session at an address I wrote for her on my business card. Her audition tape on PKL's Sony was breathtaking. I saw a captivating face—and as I listened to the sound of her voice I heard the enchanting tones of Jean Arthur. I had found our TV stewardess, Andrea Dromm.

Her assignment was a model's dream. She was on camera with those dozen words—"Is this any way to run an airline? *You bet it is!*"—with residual payments piling up every time Andrea came on the tube. She made a bundle. But I couldn't rate her as a dramatic whiz—a problem with most models.

We were working on a TV spot to push National's credit card. Andrea's line went like this: "Charge it all on National's credit card"—not exactly ringing with emotion, like "Is it vulgar to put more than one Dilly Bean in your mouth?" It came out very blah, so we told Andrea to hold up the credit card and try the line again. That didn't help either. Finally we told her to say the line, then *kiss* the card. Andrea complained that we were asking her to remember too much. But once on the screen she was unforgettable. She was spotted in a National commercial by Norman Jewison, the film director. He signed her up for a part in *The Russians Are Coming, the Russians Are Coming*, and movie star fame came to Andrea.

After the movie was completed I was having lunch at the Four Seasons, where I was introduced to Norman Jewison. "Are you George Lois . . . from *Papert, Koenig, Lois?*" he asked. "Uh huh," I said suavely. (Hot stuff for the Kingsbridge kid—my name had spread to *Hollywood*.) "So *you're* the schmuck," he barked at me in the debonair Seasons, and my head jerked back so hard I almost chucked up my mouthful of Baum's fiddleferns. "So you're the master talent scout of Madison Avenue," Jewison went on:

"the genius who discovered Andrea." She evidently wasn't the smoothest actress in his film, but she was still our million dollar stewardess. After I washed down the fiddleferns with a gulp of dry red, I was ready to take on Hollywood. "Well, uh, I'll tell you, pal," I said elegantly, "you make da fuckin movies, I'll make the ads."

We put 60 percent of National's budget in TV spots, a bold move in the early sixties—for political clients, for Xerox . . . and also for the airline industry. But our TV blitz caught hold with the public because exquisite Andrea was belting out her magic dozen.

To announce new routes in a catchy style, we used TV in our Noo Yawk, wiseguy ways. One of several PKL commercials in that style ran in the fall of 1963, around November. To promote a new National route from Miami to Dallas we had a cowboy shoot off his gun, blow the smoke off its barrel and tell the public, "Anyone who doesn't want to go to Dallas got to be plumb loco." It was running on TV around the time John Kennedy's open car was moving in front of the Book Depository Building.

As soon as we got over the initial shock after hearing the first reports from Dallas, we called all PKL clients to cancel their TV advertising. The President's condition was still unclear and the networks hadn't yet slapped a moratorium on advertising, but our clients agreed this was no time for business as usual. Our biggest account, National Airlines, was slower to come around. We wanted to yank their TV *and* print ads because of our ha-ha tone. One of our account men in New York called Dan Brock in Miami to get his okay, but Brock told him they would talk about it down there in Miami, whatever *that* meant. I got on the phone and said to Brock, "I'm sorry Dan, I guess you haven't heard, but the President's been *shot?*"

"I know he's been shot," said Brock. "He's *dead.*"

"Well look, Dan," I said, "we think it would be in *terrible* taste to run your stuff on the air, especially with its humorous tone."

What do you say to a $4 million client on November 22, 1963, when he tells you in a sweet drawl, "I think you boys in New York are blowing this out of all proportion"?

"Well do you think the story is going to be on page *twenty-two* tomorrow?" I asked—then I shouted at him, "Hey Dan, we're pulling *all* your stuff off the air and we don't give a damn what you think." We yanked everything, all of National's TV spots and newspaper ads. Later, when the President's death was confirmed, the networks blacked out all TV advertising during the official mourning period. During that terrible time, one newspaper ad for National somehow slipped by our staff. It ran in Washington, D.C. Our ad said, "Come on and spend this lovely weekend in Florida."

A week later National Airlines shifted their business from PKL to Kenyon & Eckhardt. My last words with Dan Brock probably dotted the *i* on a decision that may have been in the works by then. The trade sheets had been hinting that National would soon be dumping PKL, but the fact had to be faced that a public corporation with $29 million of billings by 1964 had suddenly lost $4 million. We never learned why we lost National. When Julian was asked at our stockholders meeting to explain, he gave them the straight stuff: "Frankly I don't know the reason. I suggest that you write to National Airlines and ask them why we no longer have the account. And when you find out please let us know."

But National's new ad agency kept running lots of our commercials, they stuck with our famous theme, and Andrea's lovely face kept popping up on the screen. Bud Maytag may have been nagged by second thoughts because a year and a half later he hired us back. When Maytag gave us back his account he said, "I'm a proud man, as you know," admitting that our work was right. There aren't many men in business who would publicly reverse themselves the way Maytag did.

I still don't know why National canned us after our first year, despite my words with Brock. I think what it finally comes down to is how far ahead you happen to be of accepted trends. I've always felt that my work should be thirteen weeks ahead of its time —the length of a television cycle. When you're *three years* ahead you're asking for the ax. Our work for National was prematurely on the button—by about three years. We took the airline industry out of timetable advertising into television, and long before Braniff dressed their girls in Pucci outfits we were pushing Cassini. Years before the stewardess became the industry's drawing card we hired Andrea. And long before exotic cuisine was served in planes, we pushed for matzohs to Miami. Someday even the flying crap game will get off the ground.

Maybe some client-romancing is good insurance against the risks of clairvoyant work. During our second stint with National, my wife, Rosie, who paints professionally under the classy name of Lewandowski Lois, did a canvas of a Boeing 727 cockpit after logging seven hours in a parked National plane at Kennedy Airport during an airline strike, doing preparatory sketches and snapping photos of the cockpit. Since 1957 Rosie has been painting all kinds of machines, always in their most intricate detail, in a superb realer-than-real style, from a nineteenth-century Underwood typewriter to a work entitled, *Detail of Analog Computer Simulating an Oil Refinery*. Her *Boeing 727 Cockpit* (Lewandowski Lois comes up with snappy titles) captured every knob and dial with the most breathtaking precision. I suppose I'll be accused, and rightly so, of bragging about my wife—but in 1967 art critic John Canaday of *The New York Times* thought enough of her work to write one of the longest reviews in the history of his distinguished column about a first one-man show. And as a result of that show, Freddie bought *Boeing 727 Cockpit* on behalf of PKL. He then flew Rosie's canvas down to Miami and presented it as a gift from the agency to Bud Maytag. "It's a family portrait," Freddie told our client.

I wondered at the time if I should have sent Dan Brock an autographed copy of my three-foot-high matzoh poster back in 1963. That way we would have gotten the biggest matzoh of them all on a National flight to Miami.

When you're the officer of a public corporation, I suppose you have to bend a little to hold a $4 million client. But we took our lumps and kept growing. My store was in good shape—the only store left in the Lois family. Around Easter of 1963 the flower shop of Haralampos was sold. My sisters had moved to the suburbs, my mother's condition had not improved and my father's work load was fierce. My parents had moved out of their Kingsbridge apartment a few years before and were living in Yonkers with Ricky and Captain Ernie. Haralampos commuted to the store from his new home and shopped the flower market as he did when I was a kid. I urged him to ease up, and after thirty years, the store that was meant for his son was sold—to a fellow Greek. An era ended for Haralampos, but a new era was in full swing for his son.

I was a big wheel in the first publicly owned ad agency. Our future was limitless—if only we watched our language, squashed the horseplay, muzzled our hotheads and turned the joint into a dignified place of commerce.

But being traded on the American Stock Exchange was no reason for an ad agency to become a store full of stiffs.

Our stockholders had no idea, but PKL became known as the only ad agency in the world that gave athletic scholarships.

Before we added a new man he was brought to my office for a final checkout. "George, I'd like you to meet this new account executive we're thinking of hiring," said the account supervisor as I reached into my table for a circular glass paperweight. "Hi," I said, chucking the paperweight at the new man. I watched his wrists and reflexes as he went for the weight. If he caught it with style he was hired, otherwise he was in trouble. "Good hands, hire him" became the recruiting slogan.

Ballplaying at PKL was very serious business. Our softball team had the highest paid infield in the history of professional baseball, all art directors. I played first base, Charlie Piccirillo played second, Stew Birbrower played shortstop, Sam Scali played third. At an average salary of $50,000, not counting stock options, the PKL infield earned more than the best of the championship Yankees.

Batting averages were posted daily on the company bulletin board. Our stock may have gone up a point, boosting my paper riches by $100,000, but it was more important to check my standing against art director Al Amato. Any error in the posted averages aroused fierce emotions. We *cared* about performance at public-PKL.

Clients were sometimes riled by the hijinks in our corridors, where we warmed up before big games with other ad agencies. Dave Hotz, a PKL account supervisor, caught hell one day from Restaurant Associates. Their ad manager bitched that his company's ads were getting short shrift because of our hangup with sports. Dave closed the door and reviewed our work for RA, reassuring his client that our ballplaying was just part of PKL's happy camaraderie. Hotz was biting the bullet because there *were* times when ball came before client, but he didn't want to embarrass the agency. RA's ad manager began to leave Dave's office, his doubts cleared—but as he stepped into the corridor he was almost beaned by a wild pitch. We kept the account. We also kept Joe Baum's cousin as a hostage; if RA canned us we'd hit Greenburg with a bill for $2,000.

PKL also produced one of the best basketball teams in the annals of advertising. But after putting away every ad agency team in sight, we were stopped dead by the Bank League champs, coached by Dick McGuire, soon to become coach of the Knicks. In fairness to PKL's court jocks, I must explain why our outside shots were off in the final championship game. We were thrown by a true story in the locker room from a PKL account man who was known to be having a hot affair with a voluptuous Hollywood actress. (We did a lot of traveling to the Coast, where New York advertising guys fitted in neatly between the silk sheets of celebrated, stunning, stacked broads.) The actress was so wild for this guy that whenever she came to town she called him from her hotel for a Manhattan matinee.

Well, as we were dressing for our big game, he tells us that she called him an hour before. That put him in quite a spot; he had to choose between two kinds of performance. She was checking out of her hotel in a few hours for a flight to Paris. He would have to drop everything if he hoped to drop his pants. But time was short and he decided he couldn't have it both ways. He told her there was this urgent appointment that couldn't be put off. "Are you stuck with a client?" she asked. "Well no," he blurted out, "I gotta play basketball." She seemed to gasp when he said it, so he decided to explain further or she might think he was ending the affair: "Listen sweetheart, you *gotta* believe me. We have this team at the agency and we're the Advertising League champs and in an hour we have to play the *Bank* League champs because the winner gets to play the *Industrial* League Champs." She still thought he was conning her. "Let me get this straight," she said. "You're gonna pass up fucking *me* to play with some *boys?*" If he hadn't told us that story we wouldn't have been distracted during the game and we would have gone forward to glory against the Industrial League!

Tony Palladino, another art director, was too short to play basketball but he placed tall bets on games. When he lost, he hated to pay off. The morning after I won a $100 bet from Tony on a World Series, I found a railroad spike driven through my wall. A hundred splayed bills were pierced by Tony's spike. It cost public-PKL $300 to repair the wall; with more winnings from Palladino our maintenance costs would have startled our shareholders. We shipped our sore loser to PKL's office in London, where he worked with Ron Holland on Players Tobacco. This account was headed by a Mr. Broadhead, known behind his back as Mr. Broadass. When our fine British client told Holland and Palladino he was going on vacation, Tony's tongue slipped. "*Mrs.* Broadass," he asked, "is she going too?" But we were safer with Palladino insulting our British clients than destroying our Manhattan walls.

While visiting our London office I went to lunch with Tony in a restaurant where the food and the service were disastrous. Tony refused to pay the bill. "We're leaving," he told the waiter, "and I will not pay for this meal. Apply the bill against what you still owe us for lend-lease." He walked right out of the restaurant, swinging his British umbrella.

It was wild and carefree at the first red-hot creative agency, but we did our jobs and we earned our fortunes. As we became rich cats Julian bought a string of race horses. He wanted to call them the Augean Stable but a Greek jockey bridled. One of Julian's nags was called Midnight. In a TV spot for National Airlines we included a Hialeah clip. Sportscaster Fred Capossela announced, "And Midnight is in the lead . . ." Although Midnight lost, we never told our stockholders that PKL's president could read a racing form quicker than an operating statement. Our breezy joint was unbefouled by mannerism, where people felt free to shoot back at each other, titles notwithstanding.

Ron Holland tangled with Julian like a parish brawler over his copy for an ad. Julian felt the copy missed and Holland blasted the president of public-PKL as freely as he took on Little Caesar Baum. Julian finally said, "Just *try* it my way." Holland thought about it and said, "All right, Julian, but in the words of Oliver Cromwell's great warning to Parliament, 'I adjure you by the bowels of Christ, you may be wrong.'" Julian shot back, "Well by the balls of Moses, *I* may be right."

People felt free to shoot back. But because we were a public corporation, *how* we shot back caught the industry's attention. We became tagged as "Stillman's East," after Manhattan's West Side gym for boxers. And since many of PKL's art directors were Italians from the Bronx and Brooklyn who loved some rough fun, we became known as Madison Avenue's "Graphic Mafia," with me tagged as the Don. Classic incident:

Art director Bob Fiore was a wiry little guy who boxed as a kid in the Golden Gloves. One day he showed up in a shirt with the ugliest floral design since the printing salesman's tie at Lennen & Newell. Lou Musachio, another art director (who owned the finest Renaissance name in advertising and had a manner of speaking like a three-sewer stickball hitter) needled Fiore about his ugly shirt. Sam Scali and Al Amato, stars of our great softball team, got in a few good licks too. They were all busting Fiore's balls to the point where Bob began to dart from office to office, bugging each art director for a favorable word. "Tell me you like this shirt," he pleaded. "Ugly," they all said. While Fiore was making the rounds, Tony Palladino popped into my office. "What do you think of Fiore's shirt?" he asked me. "Ugliest shirt in the history of the world," I said. "I can't stand it either," said Tony. "Let's do something about it."

We rounded up a gang of art directors and ambushed Fiore in the corridor. Each guy grabbed at his shirt around the shoulders and we shredded it down in flapping strips over Fiore's pants. It was all handled very tastefully—while his sleeves were also stripped off, nobody touched his collar or tie. The former Golden Glover stood there in semi-shock, his hairy chest fully bared, his shirt hanging in long shreds from his belt. But he still sported his attractive tie, neatly knotted against his buttoned collar.

Myths are made by advertising men, but when the myths are made about their own kind, beware—particularly when the myths are based on kernels of truth. Fiore, for example, was known to swing at anyone who called him a wop, the ethical way to react. And Tony Palladino added to the myth of the "Graphic Mafia" because of his antic ways—resulting in a notorious rumor that PKL kept a gun on its premises. It all added up: New York's street dagos were taking over Madison Avenue. Let me tell you about tough dago Palladino and the gun:

Tony, whom I've known since Music and Art where we first met as fellow students, was an accomplished Pop artist twenty years before it became a respectable art form. His work has been exhibited at the Museum of Modern Art—and I especially treasure a framed Venetian blind in my apartment, an original Palladino that hangs on my living-room wall. From a distance it looks like a perfect American flag. Close up you can see that he painted the flag on its horizontal slats—and when you pull the drawstring it switches into a Greek flag. (His spike in my wall was more the work of a Dadaist than the act of a sorehead.) Well, one afternoon in 1963 Tony came into my office after a shopping jaunt at lunch and plunked a World War II army carbine on my drawing table. "On sale at the Army-Navy store," he said. "Two bucks. What a *thing* I could make with this mother—the *symbolism*, George." Tony's gun was the same model carbine I had used in Korea. I shut my eyes and stripped it apart. "Can you put it back together with your eyes closed?" he asked. "Wanna bet?" I said. But Tony wasn't in a betting mood this time. Instead he called in some of the other art directors and said to me, "Okay, George—you got an audience now." I reassembled the carbine with my eyes closed, the guys thought that was hot stuff, and Tony shoved the gun in his drawer. There were no bullets; the gun would probably end up as a striped barber pole or whatever Pop artist Palladino would eventually concoct. But on November 25, the Monday after the assassination, Palladino brought in the carbine and dumped it on my drawing table. "Strip it for me," he said. He was carrying an empty shopping bag. As I stripped the gun apart he shoved each piece into the shopping bag. Then he rolled it up, went to the art bullpen and jammed the bag into the bottom of the huge trash barrel. But more than three years later there was still talk about the "Graphic Mafia" packing a rod at PKL.

One incident, however, actually raised a welt. One morning the agency was buzzing with lurid stories about a fight the previous night between John Cholakis and account man Burt Sugar, another PKL ex-Golden Glover. I heard that Sugar had clipped Cholakis in the mouth during a full-scale donnybrook. Concerned about our image as a public corporation, but more concerned about John's teeth, I called in Cholakis for a detailed report. "What the fuck happened?" I asked him. His lip was slightly swollen, otherwise he looked as Olympian as ever.

"Well George," he said, "we all had a splendid lunch yesterday."

"Yeah . . ."

"And when we got back to the agency one of the account guys told me to call off a Piel's Beer shoot at Aqueduct. I guess he had his reasons, but I already had five grand tied up in a film crew out there and I saw all that dough going down the drain. One word led to another and before I knew what was happening I was in a wrestling match with the account man."

"Yeah . . ."

"And pretty soon I'm locked in an iron grip and I can't break loose."

"So far, John, a Jim Londos you ain't. And on top of it you end up with a fat lip. Cholakis, you have besmirched the glory that was Greece."

"Wait, George, wait. A few of the guys moved in to break it up, and the second I got loose I turned around and threw a punch —I was that steamed up, let me tell you. But much to my surprise I belted the wrong guy."

"Sugar?"

"Right. Big mistake. Instinctively he countered with a fast right and he caught me on the chin."

"Terrific, John. You get into a wrestling match and end up in a hammer lock. The other guys break it up and you swing at PKL's star light heavyweight. Then you take a right to the mouth and land on your ass."

"Landed on my *ass?* You got it all wrong. I never went down.

I took Burt's punch and kept my feet. So I ain't no Londos, but we *Hellenes* can take a punch from the best of 'em. In fact, after that we all repaired to Manny Wolf's bar and everyone had a big laugh about the whole incident. And that's the whole story."

That *was* the whole story, as I learned from one of the other PKLers who was there. But a fistfight on Madison Avenue is always a hot topic over cocktails, and a few years later *The Wall Street Journal* quoted a "Papert-Koenig alumnus" who said "'It took an hour to mop up the blood.'" Well, any ad agency that could be so bloody should staff up with anemics. Nevertheless, since most of the jocks were hired by me, I came to be known as the "wild man" and the "crazy man." My episode with Casey didn't help.

There was this Madison Avenue pro, Bill Casey. He joined PKL as a vice president and copy supervisor on National Airlines. Casey was very talented, and when he joined our agency he was already something of a legend. Until he came on the PKL scene I didn't know Casey from Adam, although I had heard his name mentioned often. Well, one night I was at a Copywriters Awards dinner, and during a trip to the men's room I ended up at a urinal next to a chubby guy who was bitching up a storm, talking to nobody in particular. Suddenly he looked up at me, realizing for the first time that someone was standing beside him. He stared at me, looking pissed and surprised, and grunted, "Screw you too." He began to zip his fly as I reached over and twisted his nose.

"Who's that chubby guy?" I asked Julian back at our table, pointing to my urinal-neighbor, massaging his nose. "That's the Mighty Casey," said Julian. "Holy smokes," I said, "I just roughed him up."

Not too long after that Julian told me he planned to hire Casey and asked me if I had any objections. Julian said Casey would work under his supervision, I said I had no objections—and Bill Casey came to PKL. We greeted each other like old buddies, and not a sour look passed between us for months. Then one day I got an urgent phone call.

Lou Musachio was at an impasse with Casey over a headline for a Trommers Beer ad. Musachio, the art director, felt that Casey, the copy supervisor, was saddling him with a lousy headline. Lou asked me to come to the TV conference room before someone ex-

ploded. I dropped what I was doing and dashed downstairs to find
these two guys all steamed up. The disputed ad was pinned on the
wall at the far end of the room near the edge of our enormous
conference table, about twelve feet long and six feet wide. The
mood was tense, so I kept my voice low and calm like a cool corporate officer of a public company. This time I would be *very*
careful.

As I said, Casey was a pro, and his headline was a talented piece
of writing. But I felt it wasn't appropriate to the marketing problem. I tried to explain why I thought his concept was off, speaking very gently. As I went on with my explanation Casey moved
to the other side of the table, near the door. And just when I
thought I had him convinced, out of nowhere his voice shot out,
"Why you no-good, crooked-nose Greek sonofabitch."

It was like the first left that caught my nose in the parish when
I was keeping my eye on the kid's right hand, like being called
"greaseball" again after all those years. The adrenalin must have
spurted. I vaulted the table on my fingertips and charged after
Casey, but he was already out the door and running down the
corridor. When he looked over his shoulder and saw that I would
be on his back in two more lunges he suddenly heeled, turned
toward me, sunk his chubby head into his shoulders, and gave me
a little-boy look, sticking out his hand to shake and make peace.
That stopped me dead in my tracks. I shook my head and said,
"Someday you're gonna insult the wrong guy." That seemed to end
it, especially when Casey followed me back into the conference
room, and said to me with an impish grin, "If you ever hit me,
I'll call a cop." With a toothy grin I said to Casey, "If I ever hit
you, you'll call a dentist." Then we worked out the ad, complete
with handshakes, apologies and all the kiss-and-make-up crap. But
the story didn't end there after all because the incident became
prime grist for Madison Avenue's rumor mills—"wild man Lois"
had, after all, vaulted a table in the heat of a Greek passion and had
almost clobbered one of the most talked about personalities in the
ad world.

So about four years later the table-vaulting incident cropped up
in the oddest context: it was included by my fellow Madison Avenue crazy man, Jerry Della Femina, in a war book he wrote about
Pearl Harbor. His facts were incredibly fucked up—for one thing,

he never spoke to Lou Musachio or to me—but it was a hot paragraph, and lots of people who like to read about Japs now know there's a wild Greek running roughshod over Manhattan.

But in fairness to Jerry, not everything in his book was inaccurate. For instance, here's a *totally* accurate passage chosen at random: "There are literally hundreds of George Lois stories around town. George is a big husky Greek guy who has a hell of a temper, plus the fact that he's very, very creative and a hell of a good art director. All of these factors rolled into one tend to make things very exciting when George is around."

But Jerry Della Femina wasn't the only one to write about my Casey encounter, and by the time he got to it, the incident had been given wide currency and had ballooned to bravura size. Months after Casey left our agency (well after our episode), *Ad Age* ran a story about his breakup with PKL. My table-vault was brought up, also an alleged attack on Casey by Bob Fiore, plus the Cholakis-Sugar incident. *Ad Age* mentioned that "Agency watchers along Madison Ave., who have been hearing the rumors of one-punch altercations for some time, noted that PKL seemed to be oriented toward an interest in the manly art."

Heavens to Betsy!

And the following year *The Wall Street Journal* wrote a detailed story about PKL in which a choice nugget popped off the page. Casey was quoted as saying about Bob Fiore and me: "If I see either of them on the street I will run to the nearest cop."

I walked around in disguise for months, and Bob (a very bald guy) wore a wig.

We sure had our hijinks at loosey-goosey PKL, adding more emphasis to my image as "wild man Lois." Because of stories like this (and my earlier shenanigans) I've been accused of swinging at guys all over town. It's absolutely not true—anyone who would say such a thing about me has got to be punchy.

Even so, the talk didn't bother me as long as our public corporation stayed nice and carefree. Lois was my name and making ads was my game—my favorite game.

With the money that came to me as the principal of the first public ad agency I bought Greek vases, Tiffany lamps, Oceanic art, Indian masks and African sculpture. The living room of my West Twelfth Street apartment became a jungle of primitive sculpture and ancient statuary. On weekends I gave Harry a glove and a baseball. He pegged pitches at me in a clearing between my precious relics. If one throw went wild a priceless amphora would be demolished. But the kid never threw a single pitch outside the strike zone. He was developing great hands. I realized then that my paperweight test wasn't all that silly—if the Mighty Casey had taken the test I might have known right off to forget his hands and watch his mouth.

As a fast ball whizzed across our living room, Rosie covered her eyes. "George, *George* . . . be careful," she said with a shudder. I signaled Harry to try a curve.

"Take my word for it, Harold, even though there ain't a book-maker in Las Vegas who gives a million-to-one odds, his chances of keeping the title are one in a million because when those sledge-hammer hands connect, he'll land flat on his ass. So what we oughtta show is a black guy in the champ's trunks lying cold-cocked on the canvas, but in an *empty* arena. It may *look* as though we're calling the fight, and even if that's the intention, which it ain't, everyone knows how it'll end. But when you show a black heavyweight left for *dead*, you get a mood on the cover that makes people stop at every newsstand in America and say, 'What the fuck goes on? Is that Patterson? Is *Esquire* saying that Liston's gonna knock him out? But how come the whole goddam place is empty? There's something going on here that I don't understand, so I'll buy the magazine and find out.' A cover, in other words, has to be ballsy, but not completely literal—you gotta raise a big question after you get attention. The fight's on September 25 and you'll hit the stands a week before, so you can be sure that some people are gonna bitch because they'll say you're calling the fight, which ain't very cricket for a national magazine. But if you want to grab people's interest you have to go for the guts, and when they holler you just say, 'Listen, if you don't like what's on my cover you can always buy *Vogue*, sweetheart.' "

In 1962 *Esquire* asked my advice on their covers—they knew something was needed to juice up the magazine's face, something powerful to jack up newsstand sales. After expressing myself on the special relationship between covers and contents, I was asked to do their October cover. Harold T. P. Hayes, one of *Esquire's* editors, sent me all the articles slated for that issue and gave me carte blanche. He had no idea what I might come up with. When I saw a short piece on the upcoming Patterson-Liston fight I told Hayes I wanted to show a flattened black fighter in an empty arena. "Can you find out the color of Patterson's trunks?" I asked him. Harold Hayes was a midtown Mark Twain from North Carolina, stylishly decked out in a white suit when the weather was warm, and usually waggling a handsome stogie, not the Little Caesar gorillas that Baum chomped, but slender beauties in keeping with his white getup and poker-player eyes. He fingered his stogie and told me to do the cover. But he couldn't find out the color of Patterson's trunks because that was traditionally the champ's option; if his manager leaked it before a fight that might put a whammy on the champ.

So I took a black model built like Floyd Patterson to empty St. Nicholas Arena with *two* pairs of Everlasts and we shot him on the canvas twice—in black trunks with white stripes and vice versa. St. Nick's was set to be razed a few weeks after our shot. The empty joint was like a vast funeral parlor, especially with our model lying there like a corpse, the last stiff to hit the canvas in that historic arena—and with its smallest gate: one photographer and a Greek art director.

"Run the shot with the black trunks," I told Hayes when the photos were done. "*Surreal*," said Harold, looking at the tiny figure of the flattened black man surrounded by tiers of empty seats. We went with the black trunks. A few days after that issue came out, Liston put away Patterson in the first round to become the new champ. But calling Patterson's trunks on a million covers of *Esquire* was tougher than calling the fight. He wore the black Everlasts, which convinced lots of people that we *were* predicting the outcome. Some insiders may have felt that we even put the whammy on Patterson, but I was really showing how fast the world runs from losers. The reams of bullshit about heavyweight bouts don't matter for a minute because performance is the only word that counts and no amount of talk can hide the fact that someone landed on the canvas and suddenly he's dead meat.

Esquire's publisher saw it as a prediction. "Sly editorializing," said Arnold Gingrich, but with a wry smile to his words because newsstand sales went up as his magazine became an eyestopper. With that first cover I began a decade of visual editorials for *Esquire*.

A year later Liston, the ex-con ghetto *nigger*, was still king of the ring, with a media-made image as the meanest man in the world. For the 1963 Christmas cover I told Hayes that Sonny Liston would make a fine Santa. Harold was a southerner and many advertisers don't like to buy ad pages from niggerlovers. That may have stacked the odds against doing Santa Liston, but *Esquire*'s editor saw its jolting symbolism at a time when America was being rocked by the black revolution. Hayes leaned across our table at the Four Seasons, where we often discussed each month's cover, lined up his fine Carolinian nose against my crooked schnozz and said he would put his Dixie neck on the chopping block if I could pull Liston away from the crap tables in Las Vegas long enough to pose as Santa without winging his thirteen-inch fist at an artist prick who was fool enough to interrupt his favorite fun. I told Harold if I couldn't get Liston to pose I knew someone who could.

Sonny Liston was living in Las Vegas, where he loved to gamble, and while the "mean man" image was mostly hoked up, he was one of the roughest mothers who ever wore the heavyweight crown. Liston's arrival in the national limelight by decking the *Negro* Floyd Patterson, a devout Catholic who was hated by many *blacks* for being an Uncle Tom, belted America like a rabbit punch. There were freedom rides then and Martin Luther King was making black waves in the big white sea. Liston had served time for armed robbery and was hardly a white man's black man. But he idolized one of the finest human beings of the century. "Name your inter-

mediary," said Hayes. I rubbed my gorgeous nose and said, "Joe
Louis." Hayes leaned away, dragged on his stogie and said, "This
meal's on me."

When I called Joe Louis in Las Vegas to tell him I wanted to
shoot a black Santa Claus, he said, "That'll be the day." But he
promised to help and I headed west with Carl Fischer, the photographer who has worked with me on most of my *Esquire* covers.
Joe Louis was Sonny's idol, advisor and big brother. In our Las
Vegas hotel room Carl set up his equipment and Joe Louis brought
in the biggest, blackest, meanest-looking sonofabitch I ever saw.
And Sonny Liston was plenty pissed-off as he plopped into a camp
chair under Carl's lights. I placed a Santa cap over his enormous
head, dipping the white fleece over his black forehead while Joe
Louis sized up his boy and told Liston that if he didn't go through
with the shooting he would get his ass kicked. Then Joe left us
to our work as Carl clicked out Polaroid test shots.

"Sensational," I whispered to Carl, "but move fast—he's getting
ready to bust heads." Carl quickly switched cameras while I adjusted the fleece and whispered to Liston, "Great shot, Champ,
we'll be done in five minutes." He was turning beautifully fierce.
"*Now!*" I shouted to Carl, but as he was focusing, Sonny bolted
from his chair and flung off Santa's cap. "Had me enough of this
motherfuckin crap," he muttered, lumbering back to the crap
tables. Instead of blocking the door, Fischer ran to the lounge,
where he spotted Joe Louis and told him what happened. As Liston
blew on the dice for a new roll, Joe grabbed his collar, twirled
him around and pointed him toward the elevator. "Git," he
whispered in Sonny's ear, "git, *git!*" We returned to the room and
Fischer clicked the meanest, blackest Santa of them all.

Liston, I later found out, was the twenty-fourth of twenty-five
children. He described his mother as "helpless" and his father
"didn't care about any of us." I found that out in 1971 in his
obituary, after he was found dead in Las Vegas, with narcotics in
his room. "A nice thoughtful man," was the way his wife described
him. She always called him "Charles." Five years after I shot
Charles Sonny Liston as Santa Claus in Las Vegas he did a great
TV commercial for me with Andy Warhol, one of the best pieces
of advertising I ever did (which also helped me lose the biggest
account of my career), but there was something awesome in watch-

ing this black, brooding mountain of a man under the white fleece. I was looking into the eyes of a changing America, and I was showing what was coming *before* it became the most agonizing change in our history since Lincoln freed Sonny's ancestors.

After that issue went on sale a Hunter College professor of art history described Santa Liston in a letter to *Esquire* as "one of the greatest social statements of the plastic arts since Picasso's *Guernica*." But a few advertisers said shove it and yanked their ads out of *Esquire*. "Rude raspberry," was Hayes' buzzword for Santa Liston. Six months later Arnold Gingrich wrote in his monthly column, ". . . you'd never believe the number of hours we devoted to long and earnest exchanges of correspondence with people who kept asking why we ran that particular cover." John Kennedy was killed a few days before that issue was released. When black Santa showed his face I wasn't sorry about the coincidence.

The big reason *Esquire's* covers succeeded when they did was Mark Twain Hayes' hands-off attitude toward my work. Two months before each issue he told me all he knew of its contents, and I called my own shots. The Liston cover was inspired by a minor item on his terrible ferocity in *Esquire's* fattest edition ever, their thirtieth anniversary issue, with articles by the top literary bananas of the era. I went for Santa Claus because I was free to come up with the rudest of raspberries. But a beautiful lemon was bound to hit the newsstands on other occasions when I thought I was thinking big.

A few months later a story was due on the American Indian, reason enough to tell Harold Hayes the time was ripe for a gem of Americana. I suggested a photo-portrait of the same redman who posed for the Indian-head nickel. But first I called the Washington bureau in charge of Indian Affairs to find out who the Indian was —and if he were still alive. I was astonished to hear the Washington official stammer on the phone after he had dug into his records, "Chief Johnny Big Tree . . . think he's still alive . . . the Onondaga Reservation . . . outside of Syracuse."

He had posed for the nickel in the early 1900s when he was in his thirties. I called my Syracuse father-in-law, Joe Lewandowski, and asked him to drive out to the reservation to find out if the chief was indeed still alive—and if so, to see if he was willing and able to pose, because he would have to be about ninety. Carl and I would then go to the reservation for the shot.

Joe Lewandowski drove out to the reservation, where he located a ramshackle cabin without electricity. A few minutes later Chief Johnny Big Tree walked in, toting a bundle of twigs. He was eighty-seven years old and stood six feet two. I had given my father-in-law detailed instructions to work out the most convenient arrangements for a sitting at the reservation because if the chief was sick or senile I wanted him to be treated like a piece of fragile ancient pottery. If this relic of America's bloody past was indeed alive, I was sure he shouldn't come to Manhattan Island even if it cost *Esquire* more than $24.

My kid Harry, who was five by then, answered the phone that evening while watching a TV western. "It's Grandpa," he shouted to me. "Haralampos or Lewandowski?" I asked him. "Grandpa Joe," he said. "He says the redskins are coming." I grabbed the phone from Harry. "Get a room at the Beekman," said Joe, "and meet him at LaGuardia because he likes to fly and he wants to come to New York. The Beekman is his favorite hotel. He's in great shape, but there's something about the old guy that's not all there." I was so thrilled to hear the original nickel-Indian was on his way that I shouted at my father-in-law, "Joe, for God's sake, if he's senile or absent-minded and needs help, get somebody to fly down with him and we'll pick up the tab."

"George, George, calm down. All he needs is a new set of teeth. And listen—you know the Indian on the Pontiac? That's him too. Terrific old man. His father's name was Twenty Canoes. You'll love him."

In 1912 the sculptor James Earl Fraser spotted Chief John Big Tree in a Wild West show on Coney Island and asked him to pose for the Indian-head nickel. The chief was a Seneca, a descendant of the Iroquois Confederacy, dating back to the 1500s. When he arrived at Carl Fischer's studio he wore a business suit and a butch haircut. Makeup man Eddie Senz dressed him in a black wig and built up his toothless mouth with cotton wads. We were about to start clicking when the chief yanked out the cotton and waved his hand. "Nickel is only me to the bottom of my nose. I pose for forehead and nose. Other chiefs, a Sioux and a Cheyenne, they pose for chin and hair." But Chief John with a cotton mouthful looked fine and we shot his historic profile. Then he flew back to Syracuse on Mohawk Airlines.

When the majestic face of Chief Johnny Big Tree hit the newsstands a half century after he posed for the Indian nickel I was more proud of that cover than any I had ever done for *Esquire*. It was pure Americana. But I found out that Indians don't sell magazines. "Not a rude raspberry this time," said Harold Hayes when he saw the newsstand sales of that issue. "A red lemon," I had to admit. "This meal's on you, Lois. Any pemmican on the menu?" asked Hayes, lighting a stogie.

Four years later, when I did a cover on the martyrdom of Muhammad Ali, I found out what was missing from the portrait of Chief John. Ali was out on bail at the time, waiting for his draft evasion appeal to reach the Supreme Court. Meanwhile he was getting the shaft while hanging in limbo. *Esquire* was planning an article on the agony of his exile from the ring. I decided to show Ali as St. Sebastian, the Roman soldier who survived execution by arrows for converting to Christianity, and was then clubbed to death.

I got a postcard miniature of Castagno's painting at the Metropolitan Museum and described the pose to Ali on the phone—a full photo of his body in a Crucifixion agony, pierced by arrows. He ran off at the mouth whenever I said *martyr*, but he seemed to understand what I had in mind, and agreed to pose. We went ahead and made arrows in pads of plastic blood, suspended by wires, to be glued against Ali's body, exactly like Castagno's Sebastian, a distinctly Christlike pose. When he arrived at Carl's studio I asked him again, "Muhammad, you're sure you know what we're trying to say with this cover?" Black Prince Ali was a complex kid, and while I was sure he knew what a martyr was, I was afraid he might have misunderstood the pose that I described in words. He hauled off again with a ten-minute spiel on how and where he was screwed, naming every place and date of his martyrdom. When I showed him the Castagno miniature he studied it closely and pointed out a serious contradiction: the painting was very *Christian*.

Sebastian looked like a suffering Christ, and Ali reminded me that he refused to be drafted because of his religious beliefs as a Muslim minister. He phoned his manager, Herbert Muhammad, in Chicago. After a long explanation of Castagno's painting by this semi-literate kid who played the fool to build his gates, Ali told us it was okay to pose. He changed into his Everlasts, we fixed the arrows to his body and he struck the stance of St. Sebastian better than a professional model.

After defeating Liston in 1964, the champion who was then known as Cassius Marcellus Clay announced to the world that he had become a Muslim and changed his name. "I don't have to be what you want me to be," said the new champ who now called himself Ali. "I'm free to be who I want." As I watched him pose, quiet and relaxed in the martyr's stance, I saw a completely free man.

Carl Fischer fell in love with that photo, framed a color blowup and hung it in the entrance to his studio. He wanted to come out with poster blowups, but no publisher would touch it. Carl printed it privately and ended up with a large inventory of unsold posters. Even in ghetto stores it fizzled. The photo showed Ali's suffering as an authentic black martyr too clearly. It was also chancy as a magazine cover, yet *Esquire* took the risk. And in arousing concern about the abuse of a black man who said screw you Charlie, I'll be black *my* way, "The Martyrdom of Muhammad Ali" drew attention to a terrible wrong that was righted in 1971 by the Supreme Court. But his four martyred years won't be brought back. All he has is a picture of those years.

After the Black Muslim Muhammad Ali, formerly a Baptist, posed as a martyr after the white Christian St. Sebastian, formerly a pagan, based on the painting by the Italian Catholic Castagno, directed by Greek Orthodox Lois, photographed by Carl Fischer, Jewish, the issue appeared on the newsstands of Syracuse and my Polish father-in-law called me. "If Chief Johnny were still alive," he said, "I could have brought you some great arrows."

At the Four Seasons with Harold Hayes I leaned across the table while he lit his pencil stogie to beat him to the buzzword. "*Ecumenical*," I said. "What's that?" he asked, scanning the poster-size menu. "The Ali cover," I said. He exhaled a billow of fine smoke, shaking his head. "Wrong," said Harold T. P. Hayes. "Pictorial Zola. I'll start with the consommé."

"The consommé's lousy tonight, Harold."

"How do you know? You haven't tasted it."

"Mr. Hayes," I said, clearing the smoke, "we artists are clairvoyant." Across the room a guy came in who looked like Edward G. Robinson imitating Little Caesar, chewing on a bigger stogie than Harold T. P. Hayes', flicking ashes on the carpet. His face was meant for an *Esquire* cover.

I began to count the months of my life by these covers. Each one became a labor of love. I was paid $600 a month, and donated the money to a fund for Greek orphans. When the Colonels took over I stopped the donations. But as the turbulent decade raced on, I was given greater latitude than I ever thought possible from a mass periodical. In many ways it was more exciting than creating advertising. My cover messages were uncensored commentaries on serious issues in my own style. I was doing my hawk-nosed Columbus and Mussolini-the-fat-man on one of the biggest blackboards of America. They outraged the mighty, they angered advertisers and they irritated readers—but they visualized America's changes and needled our hypocracies. And nobody ever diddled with my work. The ruder the raspberry, the happier was Hayes.

In the late sixties we hit the torrid issues of race, war and politics. We blasted the silly hangups of pop culture and deflated the synthetic images of celebrities. I showed Andy Warhol drowning in a giant can of Campbell's tomato soup for an issue headlined "The final decline and total collapse of the American avant-garde." I created a notorious cover with poolside shots of a man who looked like Howard Hughes and a dame just like his wife, Jean Peters. The Hughes cover deceived a lot of people, but it was a tongue-in-cheek hoax. I showed four deliberately out-of-focus snapshots of an actor in a bathrobe playing Hughes. He spots a photographer hiding in the bushes and orders a bodyguard to get rid of him. Then the model who plays Hughes' wife pops out of the pool looking startled. Above the snapshots, all very authentic-looking, we said, "Howard Hughes: We see you! We see you!"

When that cover came out everyone thought it was the real thing. The issue sold like hotcakes because the "invisible" Hughes was finally "discovered," but *Time* magazine found out it was an elaborate put-on. When the press swarmed over Harold Hayes, he summed up the silly hoohah over the mystery celebrity: "What we're doing is an attempt to satirize the whole obsession with Mr.

Hughes' anonymity—his idea that people are constantly pursuing him when they're not trying to pursue him." That was fully three years before the Clifford Irving affair.

A cover that never ran on black militancy would have been the rudest raspberry of them all. Brace yourself: I took the lovable Aunt Jemima trademark and superimposed a photo of her black hand, wielding a meat cleaver. When Hayes saw the layout he thought I was working a pun. *"Eldridge,"* he said. I hadn't thought of that, and it certainly fit, but the cover was replaced at the last minute by a bigger subject that came up suddenly. In almost a decade that was the only cover killed by Harold after I shot it. A great line to go with the symbol would have been "Aunt Jemima . . . what took you so long?"

During the Svetlana Stalin binge, *Esquire* ran a story on her weird hangups with assorted religions. It analyzed how she was taken in hand by the smart boys in publishing and international relations when she came to the United States with her hot manuscript about Life with Father Josef. By then all the women's magazines had gone ape with cover pictures of Stalin's little girl. "Ya father's mustache," I muttered as the *Esquire* deadline was drawing close; with all those pictures of Svetlana stuck on my wall, I couldn't see how one more cover would possibly stand out. Then it hit me: I grabbed a grease pencil and drew a graffiti mustache on Svetlana's face. It was incredible—she looked just like her old man; she was completely transformed into Joe Stalin with long hair.

But like Chief Johnny Big Tree, it was one of my best covers and one of *Esquire*'s worst sellers. I think the world had had its full serving of St. Svetlana by then. But what probably hurt newsstand sales most was the realistic grease-pencil mustache against the photo of Svetlana. It was pure graffiti, as though some kid went by the newsstand and drew a mustache on each cover. People don't like to shell out a buck for a marked-up magazine. Edmund Wilson complained that it was disgraceful, so Harold Hayes got a photo of Wilson, put a mustache on him, and ran it as a one-page feature within the magazine. He looked okay with a mustache, but Svetlana looked more like the real Joe.

In early 1968, before Nixon was nominated, when he was thought of as a loser, I did a composite shot of our next President being made up before a TV appearance. In the wire service archives I found a good profile photo of Nixon snoozing. Then I had a separate photo taken by Carl Fischer of four hands working on the profile: one with an aerosol spray can to set his hair, a second with a makeup brush to paint out lines under his eyes, a third with a powder puff to dull the light bounce off his nose—while a fourth hand moved in with a tube of lipstick to give his mouth definition. The four hands were lighted with surgical care to match the perspective and lighting on the Nixon profile photo. It showed a routine makeup job prior to a TV appearance. But I got a call from some guy on his staff, bitching about that cover; he said it was an attack on Nixon's masculinity. I explained that it was a satirical comment on the 1960 TV debates when his man lost to JFK by a shadow because he looked like hell in front of the cameras. In fact, the cover's title was "Nixon's last chance. This time he'd better look right!"

I was amazed at the gripe. I've been working with makeup people ever since I've been in advertising. If I could use lipstick on Joe Louis, Joe Namath, Mickey Mantle and Johnny Unitas before a TV shoot, you can be sure it's not regarded as fag stuff. "That wasn't intended at all," I said. "I was simply carrying an idea to its very edge. If you're put out because Mr. Nixon might appear vain, that's a justifiable knock and I accept that, but the *masculinity* stuff—you must be kidding." Well, these birds in Nixon's corner don't laugh too easily. He called me a sonofabitch and hung up. But Richard Nixon sure looked better on TV in 1968 than in 1960. I wonder if he used lipstick.

The fact is, I was much, much rougher on the man Nixon ran against. In 1966 I had a ventriloquist's dummy constructed to look like Hubert Humphrey. The cover showed him sitting on someone's knee. The HHH-dummy said, "I have known for sixteen years his courage, his wisdom, his tact, his persuasion, his judgment, and his leadership." Pretty rough on the Vice President, no? But the cover didn't end there. It continued as a foldout, springing Lyndon Johnson as the ventriloquist holding Hubert on his knee. "*You tell 'em, Hubert*," said Lyndon the ventriloquist. There's a case where I carried an idea to the very edge of a President's knee at the expense of the Vice President. But nobody called me to chew me out. And two years later when I was in the Vice President's office for a meeting on political advertising, there it was, hanging on the wall of an anteroom. I told the Vice President that I was the wiseass who did it. "You no good sonofabitch," he told me straight out. He looked very miffed, but professional politicians like to collect stuff about themselves, the good and the bad; it wouldn't have been in his office if he felt it went *too* far. "Well then why do you have it hanging there?" I asked the Vice President. "Because," he said, "it's a wonderful cover."

The rude raspberries played no favorites. After Chappaquiddick I showed Teddy Kennedy in a Santa cap for an article on the "Re-shaping of Teddy's Image." When Roy Cohn told his side of the Army-McCarthy hearings in *Esquire* I propped a gold halo behind his head and showed him like the angel that he claimed to be. I showed Aristotle Onassis, the man who had everything, with the one thing he lacked—youth; I superimposed his head against a muscleman body. I later superimposed a movie marquee featuring *Easy Rider* against St. Patrick's Cathedral for an article on the impact of our new youth culture. But among the rude raspberries we planted a sweet grape—a cover that knocked nobody. It led to an unusual gathering one afternoon in Carl Fischer's studio.

In the front of the group sat Norman Thomas, by then a very old man with a painful spinal paralysis that had spread across his shoulders and up through his neck. Joe Louis stood directly behind Norman Thomas. Marianne Moore was at his right, a link between the two great fighters. She clasped one hand of Joe Louis and one hand of Norman Thomas—who needed all the support he could get. In a grouping around them were Helen Hayes, Jimmy Durante, Kate Smith, Eddie Bracken and John Cameron Swayze. They were "The Unknockables," eight Americans for a 1966 cover. The headline explained why these eight men and women were looking up at the camera: "In a time when everybody hates somebody, nobody hates The Unknockables."

Carl Fischer was on a balcony above, asking them to look up at his camera. But Norman Thomas was having an agonizing time trying to look up because of his paralysis. Carl leaned over the balcony and asked him very softly, "Mr. Thomas, could you just lift your head up a *little* more?" The old Socialist strained from the guts just to look up at Carl. Without moving his head more than an inch, he said, "I . . . don't think . . . I can."

Joe Louis, who was standing behind the frail Thomas, leaned

over very gently and said, "Oh, Mr. Thomas, *you* never had trouble sticking your neck out before." Tears welled up in Norman Thomas's eyes. He looked up and we shot the cover.

Vietnam, the biggest issue of the 1960s, became an obsessional subject with me from the war's earliest days. By the summer of 1963 we had lost a total of eighty-one Americans since its official start in December 1961—small stuff, just about the number of deaths in one bad plane crash. In the fall of 1963 I suggested to Harold Hayes that we run a full-face photo on the cover, life-size, of our hundredth casualty, with the simple epitaph: "The 100th American killed in Vietnam." The cover never ran because in those days it was a small war. There was talk of a truce each Christmas that might end the shooting. The hundredth GI was never shown and I did a more conventional cover for the holiday season: our first black Santa Claus.

Three years later 350,000 Americans were in Vietnam and six thousand GI's had died there. *Esquire* assigned the writer John Sack to report on the fate of an infantry company, from training in Fort Dix through its combat cycle in Vietnam. Sack's first article came out in October 1966. In his account of a search-and-destroy mission, he reported a GI's reaction when he found the body of a dead Vietnamese child. I put the GI's words on the cover of that issue, with no illustration and no visual—just the stark white words on a solid black page: "*Oh my God—we hit a little girl.*" Even the masthead was muted to give each word the power of a thousand pictures.

That was years before we became concerned about the civilian population of Vietnam. The world later heard about Mylai, and a lieutenant named Calley became the focal point for America's feelings about the war, pro and con. John Sack was writing Calley's story as a book. Harold Hayes ran a pre-publication excerpt from the book while Calley was awaiting trial. The lead article in *Esquire*'s November 1970 issue was the excerpt from Sack's book, "The Confessions of Lieutenant Calley."

"Tough subject for a cover," said Hayes at the Seasons. "He's innocent until the army decides. Think about it." I didn't think it was that difficult. "Can you get Calley to Carl's place for a sitting?" I asked Harold. "Sack probably can," he said, "but it depends on what you have in mind." I explained the shot: "We'll show him with a bunch of oriental kids. No guns or anything that suggests killing. Just Calley and the kids—happy, smiling, oriental kids. Those who think he's innocent will say *that* proves it. Those who think he's guilty will say that *proves* it." After Hayes got off the floor he went to call John Sack.

Sack came to Carl's place with the lieutenant. Calley came in civvies and changed into his uniform at the studio. He was edgy, almost suspicious; but the presence of this young nobody who suddenly caught the attention of the world and put a magnifying glass on the war gave the place an eerie feeling. It was like being on the inside of something terrible and momentous.

I took him aside before the shooting to calm him down. He had that shifty look as though he expected to get a royal screwing by the big media. Meanwhile four oriental kids were horsing around in the studio—two little girls nicely dressed in checkered dresses, a cute little boy in a white shirt, and a baby in a jumper. Carl had lined them up through a casting agency. Their mothers were with them, cooing over how the kids looked. The women were terribly excited about having their kids on a magazine cover.

I told Calley that I had seen action in Korea, and that I knew what it meant to protect men in combat. Then I explained the shooting: "Lieutenant, this picture will show that you're not afraid as far as your guilt is concerned. People can read that into the picture if they want to, or they'll refuse to see it there if they don't see you as guilty. The picture will say, 'Here I am with these children you're accusing me of killing. Whether you believe I'm guilty or innocent, at least read about my background and motivations.'"

The kids were fine at the shooting. The baby sat on Calley's knee while two kids leaned on his shoulder. The fourth kid leaned against the lieutenant's right arm. There were no props; not even the chair was seen. Only Calley's combat infantryman's badge was visible. The kids looked just a trifle tired, but Calley snapped out of his edgy mood long enough to grin from ear to ear. And we completed the shooting. The mothers were gaga about their kids appearing on the cover of a national magazine. They knew who Calley was, but they seemed to be unconcerned about the famous event for which the lieutenant was standing trial.

When I sent the finished shot to Harold Hayes he called to let me know that the office was plenty shook up. "Some detest it and some love it," he said.

"You going to chicken out?"

"Nope. It's your most outrageous work since Santa Claus."

The cover ran. Those who thought Calley was innocent said *that* proves it, and those who thought he was guilty said that *proves* it. But many who thought he was guilty detested it with a vengeance, although on one of Harold's campus lectures he asked for reactions to the Calley cover, and one student called it the statement of the century. Just one.

It was just a simple portrait of a young American lieutenant from Miami with four Asian children, and the shooting went off without a hitch, except for the mothers, who yakked a little.

This was the cover that replaced Aunt Jemima with her cleaver.

(Too bad Lieutenant Calley killed Aunt Jemima.)

I looked up from my marble drawing table and saw this great big fat kid in a tightass Madison Avenue suit. He was no more than about twenty-seven, his hair was slicked back with pomade, his face was strong and he weighed close to three hundred pounds. I whipped the glass paperweight at the kid and his hands moved like a bird. "He's a football player," said the account supervisor. "Played for Missouri and just came from Benton & Bowles."

The kid had good hands, but PKL wasn't in any football league, and while it's okay to come from the Missouri sticks, what bothered me most was this mob from Benton & Bowles invading my agency. What I didn't know when I met the kid in February of 1965 was that he came to PKL to escape B&B, as I later found out when I got the full story of Jim Callaway.

By the time he was eighteen his family had moved forty-three times, which can make a kid fast on his feet even if he weighs a ton, and Callaway was always fast and fat. "I collected enough letters playing football to write my name," the kid told me at lunch, "and I was always overweight. I was not only always the new kid in school, but also the new *fat* kid in school." His old man was always in and out of business ventures, and he either hit colossal paydirt or he bombed out like nobody before him. But he always saw the bright side, and his ventures made life exciting for Jim. During World War II he patented a battery charger for airplane starters on aircraft carriers, which isn't ho-hum stuff—we might have lost the Battle of Midway if not for Jack Callaway's chargers. After the war he developed a spectacular screw for the car-makers called Threadlock, which couldn't shake out after threaded in with a special torque wrench. Chrysler and Ford were Jack Callaway's customers, and that's no ho-hum stuff by any means. Then he hit the jackpot when he sold his screws to General Motors, twenty-seven for every GM car, which could have brought in enough bread to *buy* Benton & Bowles for his fat kid. Everything was humming along, when someone adjusted the torque wrenches wrong and they sheared off all twenty-seven bolts on every car. As a result, General Motors shut down just about all their worldwide plants for a whole week. "That was about the last we heard of the screw business," said Jim. His pop also developed the Autronic Eye on Cadillacs that dims lights automatically. Then he went into the fur-lining business, raised chinchillas and also became the first man in history to invent infrared sandwich machines. "He was always into something unexpected, and occasionally it ended up in disaster" said Jim, "so we moved a lot, quite often late at night." When the kid from B&B was a sophomore at the University of Missouri and living in St. Louis with his family, they all moved to California that summer because Jim's old man was also an amateur songwriter and decided to hit it big in Hollywood. So out to the Coast went all six Callaways—Jim's folks and their four kids, Jim being the oldest. By then he was plenty ballsy himself, having learned more about making his way in life than most jokers in their forties. "I sold shoes to support my family during the summer," said Jim, "while Dad tried to sell songs, none of which he sold." When it was time to go back to school he kissed his folks good-bye at the Los Angeles airport and boarded a DC-6 to St. Louis, stopping at Kansas City. Jim called home from Kansas City to ask what's new, but the Callaway phone was dead—his family had al-

ready moved. "By the time I got to Kansas City my father had gotten another job in Phoenix and they'd moved to Arizona while I
was in the air. No more song writing."

In 1959 he graduated from Missouri—Big Eight football hero,
Phi Beta Kappa, IQ of about 160 and weighing in at 285. He came
to New York to hit the big time and began as a trainee at Benton &
Bowles, not knowing what an ad agency was. But B&B was smart
enough to see that this kid was a pistol and he moved up fast to
become the chief account executive at twenty-five on the $20 mil-
lion Post Cereals account of General Foods, supervising seven account execs under him and pissing off B&B's brass with his maverick ways. "When I did anything the creative people thought was
good, the management of B&B thought it was bad, so I didn't see
much of a future for myself there. I decided it was time to get myself a new job."

He decided to try PKL because we were known as the red-hot
creative agency. He leaked word that he was available and our
account group went after him. They doubled his $11,000 B&B
salary to $22,000, assigned him to Quaker Oats and brought him to
my office for the glass paperweight test.

"How much do you weigh?" I asked him. "Two eight-five . . .
two ninety . . . around there," he said. "Too heavy," I told the
Missouri kid. "Lose a hundred pounds." He looked startled. "I
haven't been down to one ninety since I was seven years old," said
Callaway. "Stick with me kid," I said to our new account man,
"and I'll make you thin."

I've gone into all this about Callaway's background because he's
a classic example of that special kind of guy you occasionally bump
into on Madison Avenue who doesn't fit a mold and makes life
more exciting when you have the good luck to be with him. People
like Callaway are always alive with ideas, they have bull's-eye instincts that push them into chancy alleys—and they're never dull.
I may knock the J. Walter Thompsons a lot because the world's
biggest ad agencies carry a lot of bureaucratic fat, but if you picked
out all the talented people at J. Walter and matched them up against
the best minds of a corporation as big as Westinghouse, for example, you'd find that J. Walter has it all over Westinghouse, you can
be sure. Ron Holland, a former Good Humor man, wrote better
copy and sold more products with his wit and instincts than the

world's best salesmen. And a kid like Callaway was a born maverick with a nose for results and the brains to find the formula. Holland and Callaway were great advertising men because they could reach fast and free from the guts for the right answers. These were no stiffs who fake out the world with double-talk or run from risks with three reasons why. That's why advertising can be the most stimulating profession—it attracts the most exciting people.

Callaway began to work with Ron Holland on Puss 'n Boots cat food, owned by Quaker Oats in Chicago. After Jim's first trip to present a marketing plan, I asked Ron how it went. "First time I ever saw the entire room pay attention without one man dozing off when an account man opened his mouth," Holland reported. "In fact they were actually taking notes. His knowledge of their business was encyclopedic." Ron also mentioned that on the plane back from Chicago they cozied up and talked politics. "If Mayor Daley were running against Abraham Lincoln," Callaway told Holland, "I'd vote for Daley. That's the kind of Democrat I happen to be." Good hands, good mind, good politics—if I could knock a hundred pounds off the kid he'd become a sure winner. His maverick ways were my cup of tea and his instincts for product-pushing advertising had him coming to my office like a process-server.

We were working on Aunt Jemima together, another Quaker product. When we wondered how come they didn't have a syrup while everyone knew their famous pancakes, PKL quickly whipped out a plan for Quaker to market a syrup. But this time we struck out, possibly because Quaker was edgy about the sugar field, a tricky category for food companies. Now we could have quit on syrup at that point; instead we came up with a sweet, simple, clincher: Callaway worked on a brief questionnaire with our research man, a pro named Art Wilkins, one of the few research guys I've met who's no crap artist. They asked a few hundred housewives to pick out the syrup they used most recently from a list of the top brands like Vermont Maid and Log Cabin. Aunt Jemima was included, and even though there was no such animal, about 25 percent of the women said they used Aunt Jemima syrup. So we went back to Quaker, pulled out our research and told them if they put Aunt Jemima syrup on the shelf when one out of every four women thinks she's already bought it, the product couldn't miss.

That did the trick and Aunt Jemima syrup was born. Then, to put it across without shouting "new" and "now," the theme line for our ad campaign was the simple question, "Aunt Jemima . . . what took you so long?"

Callaway aimed for results, for *sales*, because he understood that advertising was worthless if the product didn't move. When he didn't like a campaign that came from our staff, even at the first red-hot creative agency, he dropped by my office the night before a client meeting, dumped the ads on my table and said, "Look at this shit. Can you fix it?" His instincts were right and he sure knew how to reach a guy who loved to make ads. I looked at the dull stuff and looked up at this smart kid with all that heavy freight on his body—and I realized there were *two* problems staring me in the eye. "First of all," I told him, "these ads *are* shit. But second of all, you're too fuckin overweight. In fact, you're crowding my room, for chrissakes."

I turned out a new campaign and soon it became so routine that a few of our creative boys began to get miffed at the smartass account man who was always sucking around his admaking machine. But Callaway's batting average with clients was so good that he was promoted four times in almost no time until he was obviously one of the top account managers in the agency. Then I cut him down to size.

I went to California with Callaway and Holland for two weeks to shoot a batch of Puss 'n Boots TV spots. During all fourteen days Callaway put away pizzas-for-ten and giant pitchers of beer at topless joints without ever looking up from his calories. He was turning obese in front of my eyes. At a motel near our location shooting we had to stuff him into the stall shower. On the flight back to New York, while Callaway was scooping off the leftover food from our trays, I laid it on the line to the kid from Missouri: "I don't mind working with a wiseass, and I have to admit it's fun to be with a smartass. Now you happen to be both a wiseass and a smartass without being a stiffass. So far so good, Callaway. But I won't put up working with a fatass."

When we got back to the office he weighed 290 and I finally put Callaway on a diet to knock off a full 100 pounds. It was a simple weight-loss strategy: every day Ron Holland and I took him to the Four Seasons for lunch. We spent $20,000 over eight months on a drinking man's diet, and Callaway's weight began to drop away. When he hit 230 we dangled a classy carrot in front of his face to keep him off the carbohydrates: we promised Callaway that on the day he hit 190 we would buy him a $500 tailor-made Meledandri suit. When the Missouri kid pictured himself spiffed up like a richass swell in the niftiest clothes on Madison Avenue, his weight kept going down until the scale in his office showed him at 192. In eight months the fatass kid had lost 98 pounds.

But if he lost just two more pounds, Holland and I would each have to shell out $250 for the Meledandri getup. I didn't mind a $20,000 tab in Joe Baum's joint, but that goddam *suit* was carrying friendship too far. So every morning we sent up lip-smacking breakfasts to Callaway, with fancy Danish and globs of butter. When he opened his desk an Oh Henry popped out and at lunch we slid beers under his nose. But he was no amateur at dieting; he estimated that during his lifetime he had lost 2,000 pounds. Well, by this time Callaway's will power was plenty tough. He managed to lose one more pound but he never went below 191—so I saved $250 on the Meledandri and ended up with a fine-looking, loosey-goosey advertising man to the bargain.

Skinny Jimmy Callaway and ramrod Ron Holland went with me to a presentation for the Coty cosmetic people on a new eye makeup product. It was great getting into a cab with the two Irishmen because now I could sit next to Callaway without his Big-Eight shoulders and his former lardass shoving me through the door. We were also headed for an unpredictable meeting. Our advertising campaign was the reverse of what Coty's president, Meredith Hough, probably had in mind to sell his new product. Most cosmetic companies go for advertising with a "fashion" tone that shows models with concentration-camp faces and wispy voices—a dreamy sell that could work if the product isn't all that unusual. But Coty had a special gimmick in their new eye makeup: it was shaped like a pen. We therefore developed a straight-on, no-nonsense, product-pushing campaign on the product's functional advantages.

Before the meeting Ron said to me, "George, do be careful—Meredith Hough recoils from rough language." I knew that Ron was absolutely right, and I sure wasn't gonna fuck up our presentation by hitting a wrong note, so I let Ron and Jim carry the ball.

There were over a dozen people in the conference room, including several women—and Meredith Hough. I sat back and watched as Skinny Jim stood up straight and lean and wham-banged through his razor-sharp marketing concept as the gang took notes and nobody dozed. Ron then delivered a boffo explanation of our ad solution, stressing the pen shape and how the new product was as easy to handle as a ballpoint. But Meredith Hough was sold solid on the fashion route, and he just wasn't buying our functional strategy no matter who said what. We seemed to be beating a dead horse. But I also knew we were right and our client was wrong.

There was a lot of cross-jabber going on about other approaches, but I couldn't walk out sucking my thumb and promising to come back with cutesy-pie fashion garbage because I knew that would never sell the product. The real problem seemed to be that Meredith Hough didn't *understand* our functional strategy. I decided to reach him—somehow.

"Hold it—wait, wait," I finally butted in, "stop, stop, it's easy, it's easy. You don't want to do all that fashion stuff. It's functional, it's simple—eye makeup in pens, eye makeup in pens—it doesn't suck, it doesn't fuck, shove it up your ass and it blows your balls off."

The room was quiet for about ten seconds, then the girls exploded into screaming, hysterical laughter. But most of the men said hardly a thing. One or two squirmed in their chairs and seemed to be playing frantic pocket-pool. Meredith Hough, however, blushed crimson—and not long after that we parted company with Coty, for a loss of about a million bucks. They went to a new agency and introduced their eye makeup pen with a fashion campaign. It bombed out. To be right may have been costly, but going down in style is also worth something—shit yes.

By then PKL was on its way toward the $40 million level. As we moved up the dollar ladder we lost an account here and there, like Coty, but we picked up new accounts and we kept going toward the $40 million rung. Any ad agency headed for that kind of volume isn't exactly at a welfare-case level. But the old PKL that I cherished seemed to be losing its lovely carefree ways once it passed $30 million. For example, while I was on vacation in 1965 we added Salvo detergent tablets from Procter & Gamble, a million dollar hunk from the biggest advertiser of them all—hot stuff for upstart PKL. *Ad Age* called it ". . . a move tantamount to the Beatles being honored by Queen Elizabeth." *Very* hot stuff—but I wanted us to keep away from P&G and I had started talking to Lever Brothers. I kept saying that any agency with P&G as a client runs the risk of losing its soul. "It serves to place in perspective the PKL image," said *Ad Age*, "which has been as somewhat non-conformist, despite the agency's window on Wall St. through public stock ownership." The next year we got over $5 million more from P&G, and our stock went up a full point on the American Exchange. But we sure began to watch our p's and q's with the biggest mother of them all as our client. Some of us began to wonder about who we were, staring self-consciously at our bellybuttons. The endless talk at our board of directors meetings about sprucing up our image drove me up the wall. "We should be a combination of Doyle Dane Bernbach and Norman, Craig & Kummel," was one refrain. I began to feel like the agency jerk when I asked, "Why can't we be just PKL?" Later the ideal image became Doyle Dane plus Benton & Bowles. Again I asked, "Why can't we be just PKL?" I was so hung up on keeping our old flavor that I became the chief bitcher and moaner of PKL, a temperamental old fart art director with no sense of "business." And we were beginning to turn out *good* work—worlds apart from *great* work. That was impossible for me to live with indefinitely.

At $40 million we were still very profitable and still the miracle ad agency of the decade. But we couldn't break through to the next plateau—to $75 million, then to the magic $100 million. Growth is surely one name of the advertising game, but I felt we could grow *only* if our ads were bold and if our standards were not compromised. Our advertising was no longer breakthrough work, no longer exciting enough to make the agency my joyful home. By all outward appearances, I had the world in the palm of my hand: six figure salary, major stockholder, great future and all that jazz. But the fun was going, going, gone. We were laying down bunts instead of swinging for a homer.

Haralampos dropped by the agency from time to time, always unannounced. He thrilled at my "importance" and he reveled in our luxurious setting. We had moved twice since our early days in the Seagram Building. Prosperous PKL was now spread over five floors in a new building at 777 Third Avenue. When I was told my father was visiting I stopped whatever I was doing and went to greet him. We kissed in the corridor and I brought him to my spacious office, with its spiral staircase winding up to my office from the floor below. He purred with pride in a leather Zographos chair, watching me, chatting softly. When my secretary came in with a message, interrupting our small talk, he raised his hand and said, "Work first." In his quiet presence I went about my busy routine—phoning clients, giving instructions to our staff, correcting imperfections—playing the part of a big-wheel executive. He was the proud father of a hugely successful son. Papa repeated my phone conversations to Rosie and he clipped each article about me that appeared in the *Times* advertising column. He carried the articles with him, flaunting them among the wholesalers at the flower market. There was never a doubt in Haralampos' mind that I was not only prosperous but that I loved my work. He thought of me less as a businessman than as an *artist*. ("Art isn't all nudes," said Dr. Callahan, and Haralampos remembered.) But the aura of my position visibly thrilled him—while in my heart, the life force of my career was losing its joy. I missed the exhilaration of reaching for great work in a carefree way. The *climate* at PKL had changed.

I came to feel like a stranger in the house I built except when I was working with the two Irishmen. But Ron Holland was beginning to feel that his days at PKL were coming to an end when our board decided to bring in a hotshot creative director and beef up our staff with new talent. Ron had always worked directly with Julian, Freddie and me; but now he would have to report to a new creative director. He was also asked to interview new writers at forty grand when he was pulling down nineteen and was ten times more talented. "The agency is looking for a Jesus," said Ron. "Being at PKL has always been for me a personal, warm, rewarding life, but we're becoming impersonal. Do we distrust the very things that made us great?" Holland told Julian he planned to look around, but I told him to hang in—there might still be a way to keep the old flavor alive despite the corporate juggling.

Callaway wasn't bothered by the new turn of events at PKL because he wasn't shy about stepping on toes to get the best work for his clients, so he kept dumping our "good" work on my table, and I gave him new campaigns while he waited, usually at ten o'clock at night.

PKL's climate became even more impersonal when our accounts were assigned to three group heads. We also added new people to the point where I was saying hello to a sea of unfamiliar faces for twenty minutes every morning before I could get to my room. As an act of self-preservation I was hoping to create an oasis for myself in the growing bureaucracy. One day I took Callaway to the bar of the Four Seasons after work. With a sly grin and feeling slightly finky, I said, "You, Ron and I could always start an agency *within* PKL"—and Callaway ran out of the Seasons to Charley O's, where Holland was adding to Baum's receipts for the night. The two wiseasses, it turned out, had been thinking along the same lines. We therefore came up with a plan to set up an autonomous creative unit at PKL, to be called AF-1, short for Agency of the Future Number One—a three-man nucleus of art director, writer and account man. We would operate *physically* outside of PKL, free to seek out new business while drawing on parent-PKL's media and administrative support. As AF-1 became a profitable venture, PKL could set up a second nucleus, AF-2, and so forth, until we had groups of lean trios who did great advertising—all part of PKL. It was a plan to kick the curse of bigness by bringing the business back to its first purpose: making great ads. In effect, we wanted PKL to become a holding company for a growing network of small, tight, productive, creative teams. The plan would have provided a ready-made umbrella for those creative talents in other agencies who were itching to start a business but didn't know quite how to pull it off. The program was turned down cold by our board, and when Freddie saw the plan he told Jim, "You guys are crazy. You don't have a businessman with you. Do you know what a convertible debenture is?" Callaway didn't know, but he didn't think Freddie knew either.

I couldn't stay on. But when I told Holland and Callaway I was ready to make the break, they didn't believe it would happen, even when we put a binder on office space in the Squibb Building near the Plaza hotel. We were still working at PKL and it became a hairy situation while waiting for our new space to be ready by October 1, 1967. In mid-September I told Ron I was ready to give the story to Phil Dougherty, who writes the ad column for *The New York Times*. "He'll be in my office in the morning," I said. "Tell Skinny." Ron ran down to Callaway's office and shouted,

"We're gonna do it, we're gonna do it—*right now!*" But there was still a *but* in their minds; in exchange for an exclusive on our new agency, Dougherty (whom I trusted implicitly because he's an Irish kid from the Bronx) promised to hold the story until I felt the timing was right to avoid making waves at PKL while we waited for our new space. In the meantime we had a news photo taken of a smiling black-haired sonofabitch who didn't look at all like a former ice-cream hustler; a thin twenty-nine-year-old kid with a grin as big as the pizzas-for-ten he used to put away when he was a hundred pounds heavier; and an old fart Greek art director, age thirty-six, with a toothy grin and a handsome nose.

Callaway was commuting from Greenwich in those days, and on the morning of our meeting with Dougherty his train stalled in the north Bronx. He jumped onto the tracks, climbed a concrete wall, scaled a fence—and couldn't get a cab. "So I took a subway into Manhattan," said my new partner, as though an Irishman in the Bronx didn't belong in the transit system. After we gave the story to Dougherty I told Ron and Jim it's definite now—and I'd call him in a few days to run it. Even then I don't think they believed I would go through with it.

Before the story was released Freddie tried to talk me into stay-ing. But as his words flowed out with his infectious sweet-selling charm, I thought of his crazy chart of seven years before, and those visits to my office at Bill Bernbach's agency when I told him, "Listen, don't bullshit a bullshitter"—but I was leaving PKL for the same reason he wanted to start it when he was thirty-three. "Freddie," I said, "I'm too young to die." He reminded me about my responsibilities as a corporate officer. "George, be careful," he said. "You're our major stockholder. A move like this could have adverse effects on PKL and on the value of your stock." But I was too young to die.

The day I left Doyle Dane Bernbach, Koenig and I told Helmut Krone that if he wanted to come with us we would bring him in and the agency would be called Papert, Koenig, Krone & Lois— PKKL—but Helmut thought we were nuts. Seven years later, when I told Julian I was leaving the agency we had built, I said, "I'll ask *you* what we asked Helmut the day we left Doyle Dane—do you want to come with me?" He was still the greatest copywriter of them all, but Julian wasn't willing to move in my direction.

When Ron Holland told Julian how sorry he was to be leaving him and PKL, Ron said, "I'll try to remember everything you taught me, Julian, because when I came here I knew nothing, and so much of what I've learned has been from you." Julian asked Ron, "What do you think is the most valuable thing you're taking from here?" and the fastest gun on Madison Avenue said, "It's George Lois." Ron later said, "Julian didn't laugh—too loud."

Ron and Jim suggested George Lois Associates as the name of our new agency. But I decided on Lois Holland Callaway Inc. because I felt the relationship would be healthier from the start with all our names on the masthead.

On Thursday morning of that week, two weeks before we could move into LHC's new space, I told Ron and Jim that *this* was the day. Even then they didn't fully believe it would happen. "Wait for me in the lobby," I said. "We'll all meet there. Then I'll call Phil Dougherty to tell him the story can run." They rushed to the lobby and waited, watching the console lights on the elevator panel; but I had a few calls to make and I was longer than I expected. Freddie suddenly walked into the building and asked Ron and Jim, "Where's George?"—realizing at that moment that I *was* leaving. He went into the elevator as my new partners got the fidgets, convinced that Freddie would grab me before I could leave and sweet-talk me into staying.

They watched the panel lights and held their breaths as the gold dot of Freddie's elevator moved toward the thirty-sixth floor while the light on the adjacent elevator, the one I would be taking down, stayed dark. "I can't believe it," said Callaway. "My whole life is hanging in the balance and George is up there pitching a glass paperweight to the guy who's replacing me." Just as Freddie's light reached the floor another light went on and flickered down the panel. When the elevator doors opened in the lobby, a Greek walked out to receive the warmest hugs of his life from two Irishmen.

I called Phil Dougherty from the perfect joint to tell him he could release the story about my teaming up with the Irish to start a new agency—from a phone in Charley O's. Then we drank champagne at the Forum, walked around Manhattan in a happy daze until it was time for dinner, and we drank more champagne at the Seasons. At ten in the evening we went to the pressroom of the *Times* for the first edition with Phil Dougherty's article. It turned out to be a helluva spread, headlined: "Lois to Create His Own Shop," complete with the toothy photo of our trio. (A few weeks later, Joe Louis told us he had seen the photo. "Looked like a toothpick ad," he said.) But Callaway almost collapsed when he saw that our new agency's name under the photo was called Lois Holland *Company*. He rushed upstairs and hassled with the rewrite men until the correction was made while Holland and I laughed our chops off. Then we all went to Sardi's to see the corrected story in the *Times* later edition, and we drank more champagne.

Reardon Holland Callaway Inc. started with the longest blast of my life. "Eat, drink, and Brioschi," especially the Brioschi, was a line from Julian that saved my life after a day and night on the town with J. Ronald Holland and James T. Callaway. My second store, with two mick partners.

What would Uncle Costas Thanasoulis say now?

Holland went to a party and fell in love.

"She was very attractive, very articulate and very funny," he told us the next morning in our one-room office of Lois Holland Callaway. "She was also a grandmother. At first I didn't catch her name, but she said something I'll never forget. Someone mentioned that he was trying to get into his own house and didn't have the key, so he slipped a piece of plastic through the door to open the lock just as a police car drove by. When the cop asked him what he was doing, the guy said he got so rattled he didn't know what to say. At this point the grandmotherly lady said, and I quote, gentlemen, 'You should have told him to go fuck himself.' Then she said, 'You have no *idea* how much trouble you can save yourself in this life by telling people to go fuck themselves.' I was so impressed that I asked her if she would be willing to appear in one of our commercials, and she agreed to do it. I tell you, she's *fantastic*."

"Fantastic, *fantastic!*" I said. "A swinging grandmother for our first campaign. What's her name?"

"Sally Rand."

A week after we started we were on our way to a spectacular winner with our first client, a company very few people had heard of. But our new account didn't come to us on bended knees, pleading with us to handle their advertising.

After the Dougherty story appeared, Callaway thought the phone would be ringing from hungry advertisers, ready to dump their agencies for us, but the only call for Callaway was from a former secretary to wish him good luck. He also received a stack of postcards addressed to "Jim Company" from the wiseacres at PKL who heard about the pressroom goof. By the end of the day he thought we were wiped out.

We were truly starting from scratch—and it was understood we would keep away from PKL's clients, including Restaurant Associates, even though PKL wasn't happy about doing twelve hundred tiny ads a year for Joe Baum. Leaving one ad agency to start another can throw the old joint into paranoid jitters, but all I took from PKL was the chair I sat in for seven years. When Joe Baum heard the news he was ready to hand us his business. I held him off. He called PKL and they told Joe they were glad to unload the account. I told Joe that still wasn't kosher enough—there were such things as employment contracts and I didn't want to be accused of stealing a paper clip. "If you stole the whole agency it would be yours," said Joe, but I held him off until our lawyers got every conceivable release. "They're out to get you," said the Commandeur. But after a month we got the Commandeur. We asked Joe for a monthly fee of $5,000. "Absolutely not," he said. "Your fee is $5,500." Meanwhile, we were onto another Dilly Beans.

I told Callaway we needed just one account to score big, and it needn't be a heavy spender, but it would have to be a New York City advertiser so our work would be seen. I warned him that no phone would ring until *after* we demonstrated by our advertising that we were a creative force—we had to re-earn the right to be known as a creative trio without leaning on past achievements. And we needed a client where an ad vacuum existed—in an industry where great advertising was a rarity. If we started with a $2 million cigarette account we'd obviously pay the rent, but you can't get famous with cigarette ads because they're all the same—with an occasional striking exception like the Benson & Hedges 100 millimeter campaign by Wells, Rich, Greene. This brilliantly creative agency, founded by Mary Wells, became famous overnight because Mary talked about the *disadvantages* of a long cigarette, and her work drew instant attention.

Now, in 1967, there was a great bull market on Wall Street, but you hardly saw much advertising for brokerage houses. Years back Bill Bernbach's agency made the Dreyfus Fund famous by showing a lion on TV. An investment house named Shearson-Hammill was running an arty-farty campaign with scenes on Wall Street, which wasn't creating mob scenes at their offices. The ad vacuum was definitely on Wall Street. My link was a ballplayer. A handsome black Irishman.

Dick Lynch, who quit playing pro football for the New York Giants when his ankle gave out, was now a "limited partner" in an investment house with a seat on the New York Stock Exchange. Its name wasn't tough to say, like Haloid-Xerox, but no research was needed to prove that Edwards & Hanly was an unknown company while a bull market was in full stampede.

I had known Dick Lynch since PKL days when I used him in a TV spot for Puss 'n Boots. I told him I was starting all over again —with two smart Irishmen—and asked if he could arrange for us to meet his two bosses, Mr. Edwards and Mr. Hanly. Lynch set up a meeting with Bert Edwards and his two key men, Dick Gillman and Bob Zoellner. (Mr. Hanly no longer worked there.) Edwards turned out to be a dapper Walter Matthau—silver-blond hair, diamond ring, good cigar—and his two associates were brainy, fast-moving New York types. If ever I saw a maverick outfit in stocks and bonds it would have to be Edwards & Hanly. And best of all, they were hardly known.

Bert Edwards was willing enough to see what we might do for E&H if we came back with some ideas. But he warned us that if he gave us his account, our work would have to be done right and proper—especially since we were talking about coming on strong over *television*. I promised him we would stick to the rules and still make Edwards & Hanly famous. Before we left I asked Edwards to sum up his business for us. He said, "Baby needs a new pair of shoes." You bet, Bert.

Over the weekend we piled into my summer shack on Fire Island and by Monday morning Ron and I had completed thirty TV storyboards. When we showed our stuff to Edwards, Gillman and Zoellner, they knew they were looking at advertising that was different from *anything* they had ever seen. They realized it *could* make them famous. But before we could shoot the commercials or see any E&H dollars go into our empty kitty, we had to get every comma okayed by the New York Stock Exchange. What you say in ads about securities has to be very antiseptic, which may explain why most Wall Street ads are literally called "tombstone"; they're usually in newspapers, rarely on TV, and dishwater dull.

The members of the advertising department that cleared investment ads were well-bred Ivy League WASPs. They went over our copy with a jeweler's glass. There were no objections to our emphasis on television; in fact, they felt it was beneficial to the Exchange. We put on a genteel dog and pony show that charmed the Brooks Brothers pants off these very cautious gents, but they sure kayoed a few of our spots—like the one that showed E&H brokers at the end of a productive day, drinking beer in the Yale Club to the Whiffenpoof song with "sell" lyrics about investing through their firm. (That was understandable—you don't want to suggest that brokers are lushes; if the market slips, investors might blame a customer's man on the sauce.) About fifteen commercials were, however, okayed for shooting.

It was a busy scene at the shoot. At one point I walked through the dressing room without knocking because there were lots of people to film in one day. I couldn't waste a minute. Joe Louis was scheduled; also Jimmy Breslin and Dick Lynch; plus three kids, professional actors and our grandmother in the dressing room. Sally Rand was preparing for her commercial. I should have knocked, but she didn't seem to mind when I barged in. She was standing in the raw. "Hi honey," said the nicest built grandma *I* ever met. She went ahead with her makeup. Then she brought her fans in front of the camera and delivered her lines like the pro that she was: "I'm Sally Rand. *The* Sally Rand. I take my dancing seriously. And I take my investments seriously too. But I enjoy the stock market *so* much more since I switched to Edwards & Hanly." Then a voice-over announcer said, "Edwards & Hanly—*fan*-tastic brokers!"

Joe Louis said only ten words: "Edwards & Hanly—where were you when I *needed* you?" I had him look straight at the camera and we shot a tight closeup of his majestic face.

Dick Lynch said, "I'm a halfback for the New York Giants, *ree-tired*. Thanks, Edwards & Hanly." The three kids were a smash. The first said, "My daddy's an astronaut!" The next said, "My daddy's a fireman!" The third said, "*My* daddy works for Edwards & Hanly!" Then the first two went, "*Wow!*"

Jimmy Breslin played a scared investor dialing his broker. "Frankly, the stock market used to intimidate me," he said, "but now I have no compunction about picking up the phone and talking to Edwards & Hanly." Then Breslin suddenly turned nervous as he got his number, and stammered, "H-h-h-hello, Edwards & *Hanly?*"

Another spot had a broker telling a meek customer, "You can plan to retire in twenty years with a total estate of $225,000, plus substantial annual withdrawals on your capital sum. Now that's provided you begin to invest $3,000 a month for a total investment of $136,000." The customer squirmed and said, "But I've only got $500." The broker lunged at him and said, "*I'll take it.*"

The next day I chose the best takes from the rushes and gave the film editor instructions on how to cut it together. The result was the usual kind of rough-cut that professionals readily understand—individual takes with grease pencil markings. But this rough version of any commercial could easily throw off anyone who hasn't worked around films. As soon as the reel was ready we showed it to Bert Edwards and his partners over a Movieola. We met at the raunchy West Side editing room and asked them to look at the rough-cut, with its cross-marked splices jumping out. The pictures they saw were rougher than 8-millimeter home movies, and the sound came from an audio reel that ran parallel to the film. The mind had to force a connection between the sound and picture. And our clients were from Wall Street, not Hollywood.

Those commercials must have come across as the weirdest spots anyone in their business ever saw. If our first client decided to dump us at that point I would have understood. But I couldn't let them get away. Since we were a new agency and they were a new advertiser, it was agreed that after seeing the rough-cuts they would write us a check for $183,000, the full cost of their campaign for the first few months. "Terrific," said Bert Edwards after seeing the spots—looking slightly uncertain. And he wrote out the check to Lois Holland Callaway Inc. for $183,000. Callaway handled our financial affairs. He didn't know what a convertible debenture was, but he stashed away the $183,000 check as deftly as a pickpocket. We thanked Bert Edwards and his partners, and kept our fingers crossed as they left the editor's room. They looked more and more uncertain as they headed back to Wall Street.

The minute they left, the three of us charged into the elevator, laughing insanely, mostly out of relief that we had come this far with our first wild campaign for the stuffiest industry of them all without getting stiffed by a frightened client. We ran through the Manhattan crowds like three stoned kids, laughing and whooping all the way to the bank on Fifth Avenue, a hefty spread from the West Side studio. We were near collapse by the time we reached the bank to deposit the check before someone changed his mind. "Where'd I *put* it?" said Callaway. We had enough horseplay and I wanted to get back to the office—but Callaway wasn't playing games. He was going through his pockets like a crazy man. When Ron and I saw what was happening we plunged in, six hands on Fifth Avenue plowing through every lining and pocket in Callaway's clothes. I had his fly zipped down and was jamming his pants off to search his underwear when suddenly he said, "Stop, stop. It's here, it's here. It doesn't fly, it doesn't lie. Stick it in the bank before it blows my balls off." The check had slipped between some of those "Jim Company" cards he was carrying in his back pocket. "Callaway you schmuck," I shouted after him as he went into the bank, "forget about convertible debentures and find out what a *wallet* is."

Our last hurdle was the Ivy League gang of the advertising department. To help us put over the campaign, we spliced on a sequence at the end with Sally Rand doing a bump and grind immediately after her "*fan*-tastic" commercial. As that beautiful bump connected, Sally said, "How do you like *them* apples, Mr. *Fun*-ston?" (Keith Funston was president of the Exchange.) We were edgy about showing the reel with that windup, but I guess it didn't hurt us. All our commercials were okayed. They began to run in New York starting in November for eight weeks. And about six weeks later some curious events took place on Wall Street and Madison Avenue.

Edwards & Hanly, remember, was a nobody on the Exchange. But by mid-December they were literally *famous*. Everyone was noticing their advertising, including some very big brass on the Exchange who hadn't seen the commercials when we were sweating out approvals with the ad department guys—a lower-level group than we assumed. Also, when they legal-eagled our storyboards, they couldn't quite connect the copy, which was innocent enough, with the people's faces or the pictures. Even when they reviewed the films they had little experience with commercials; and nobody had ever sprung so many at one screening. But when the upstairs brass saw the spot where the customer says "I've only got $500" and the E&H man says *"I'll take it,"* we were hauled before the advertising department and told to cease and desist from running it further. It depicted the stockbroker, we were told, as a hungry sonofabitch. Not very proper. Sally Rand also had to be yanked because her spot was considered a testimonial, clearly against NYSE rules. There wasn't much we could say about that except to tell Miss Rand that *we* liked them apples but this was *one* time when telling people to go fuck themselves would have gotten us and our client into deep trouble.

And they kayoed Joe Louis.

The spot was ten seconds long: "Edwards & Hanly—where were you when I *needed* you?" he asked. It was also prepared as a full-page newspaper ad with Joe's beautiful puss, sad and deep and spectacular. It was one of our first pieces of advertising and by far the most noticed, remembered, talked about, written about message of the entire E&H campaign. Larry Merchant, the New York *Post* sportswriter, wrote a column on that piece of advertising and called it "The Knockout." *The New York Times* magazine, in a roundup of memorable TV commercials, said an award should go to E&H for our spots on Joe *and* Sally. The Art Directors Club gave it a Distinctive Merit Award. The E&H campaign was written about by sportswriters, gossip columnists, financial writers and mass culture buffs—and when a picture was used, they showed the face of honest Joe. The entire campaign, and especially Joe's ten seconds, were just too strong for Wall Street to take. So we were told to kayo Joe. But that one was too great to kill, and we stood up for Joe against the Exchange. Unfortunately, we were up against an establishment that had made up its mind. The campaign was too persuasive and its strongest spot would have to be pulled. Callaway had to be restrained from busting loose. Some of his impatience might have been due to the way the press kept screwing up his name every time our agency was mentioned when they wrote about the campaign. Larry Merchant called us Lois, Holland & Cunningham. A trade newsletter referred to Neal Calloway. In *The Washington Post* he became Galloway. But we could have outmavericked our client right off the Exchange, and I got the three of us out of there fast. "George, do you realize what was going on in there?" said Neal Cunningham after we took our lumps. "Two micks and a Greek were arguing about a TV spot starring a *schvaatza* in front of a bunch of WASP's." I had to point out to the Missouri mick that his use of *schvaatza* was disgusting. "It's *schvarrtsa*, schmuck."

We lost Joe and Sally, but the campaign kept socking home Edwards & Hanly, with the two kids going "*Wow*" after the third said, "MY father works for Edwards & Hanly." In the Borscht circuit a standup comic saved his act by telling his audience, "Be nice to me. My father works for Edwards & Hanly." Their thirteen offices in the New York area opened 3,300 accounts in November and December. They showed a bigger profit in the first quarter of 1968 than in the whole previous year. And a 1968 awareness survey showed that E&H was the third best-known investment house in New York after Merrill Lynch and Bache & Co.

They became so famous we quit saying what they did for a living. We showed Whistler's Mother in a TV spot, with nothing going on until she picked up a phone and said, "Hello, Edwards & Hanly?"—one more spot in the E&H series chosen as one of the hundred best TV campaigns of 1968 by *Ad Age*. As a result of that campaign, lots of big agencies began scouting for new clients in Wall Street, normally considered tombstone territory. Finally we decided to make *ourselves* famous. We ran a commercial in which the first guy said, "I'm Lois," the second said, "I'm Holland," and the third said, "I'm Callaway." Ron said, "And we do the advertising for Edwards & Hanly." Then the kids' chorus went

"*Wow!*" Jim wanted our names to appear on the screen as we introduced ourselves. "If I could be sure Callaway would be spelled right," said Galloway, "I'd go right back to the Exchange and *insist* on it. As you know, they tremble in my presence." Edwards & Hanly (without an e) were the only names that were seen.

The campaign gave E&H the momentum to get through the 1969–70 recession, when bigger brokerage houses were folding like dominoes. And the $183,000 capitalized us at the start of LHC when we needed it, while advertisers we never knew were watching the E&H campaign.

Gaston deHavenon may have seen the LHC campaign, but he became our second client for a different reason: he collected African sculpture. Gaston also owned the Ann Haviland Perfume Company. They had a new product called Perhaps. Collectors of African art are more clannish than Greeks, and if you speak their language, a special trust develops because you're into the same mysteries that fascinated Picasso, Derain and Vlaminck. "It is late in the season for introducing Perhaps," said Gaston in December, "however, George, since you know that the antelope contours of my Bambara headdress are in honor of Chi Wara, the Babala's mythical founder of agriculture, I say to you, *pas mal Monsieur Lois*—and I ask you, are we *trop tard* to advertise Perhaps?" He was a debonair aristocrat, with white hair and a Parisian accent. "Hey Gaston," I said, "with a name like Perhaps we'll murder Revlon. How many bucks you got to spend?" His budget was only $16,000, less than we spent to slim down Callaway, but enough to do a job for Perhaps, and I don't mean maybe. It was too late to get into magazines and too little to buy TV time, but time enough to get the salesgirls in Fifth Avenue stores to push Perhaps. We ran small ads aimed at the big Fifth Avenue stores and last-minute Christmas shoppers. The day after the Metropolitan Museum announced that one of its archeological relics was a fake, we said, "If you bought her a copy of that fake Greek Horse, can you still save face? *Perhaps.*" For the mass market: "Does she wear *anything* under her Pucci? *Perhaps.*" We plastered signs against the sides of Fifth Avenue buses: "Quick. Sit next to her. Sooner or later she'll say *Perhaps.*" Our bus signs even pointed to a specific seat in the bus to sit next to "her." (If "her" turned out to be a dirty old man, it added to the fun.) Revlon was selling Intimate and spending a mint, but we gave them a scare with Perhaps in two wild weeks on a petty cash budget.

One morning we received Gaston's check for $16,000. We stopped everything and had a champagne party. None of us drew salaries for six months—and when we first moved into the Squibb Building we waited a long time for the telephone company to install our phones. I ran down to the public booths in our building with a roll of dimes to make calls, doing layouts with the receiver cocked against my chin.

We had an unknown brokerage house and an unknown perfume. But Charley O's was making it big, and Ron tackled the tough assignment of making a successful client more so. He came up with an ad for a publication that Greenburg overlooked when Ron was in England. Ron's copy was devout: "I hope you get to Heaven five minutes before the Devil realizes you died." He took the ad to St. Patrick's Cathedral, a few blocks from Charley O's, and showed it to the bishop who handled the weekly church bulletin. Ron decided it's a good way to get Sunday brunch business for Baum's Irish joint, but he was warned by Baum, who knew Peru better than St. Patrick's, that the ad would never be accepted. When the bishop saw the ad he asked, "Are you going to pay for the space?" Ron said of course. "Then we'll run it," said the bishop.

We started in one big room on the eighteenth floor of the Squibb Building with a staff of four: Jim's secretary, Beth Duffy; our production manager, Ed Rohan, originally from St. Peter and Paul parish; also my secretary, Marlene McGinnis, originally from South Africa. McGinnis is a beautiful Chinese girl who speaks with an Oxford accent, but her married name was hardly out of place in my Irish cell. If not for my assistant, Denny Mazzella (now a hotshot art director), I would have put a neon shamrock in our window. After a month we moved to larger quarters on the twenty-eighth floor, with a terrace and a sauna, a panoramic view of glorious Central Park, and a beautiful closeup of the ugly General Motors Building.

At Christmas we decided to give everyone on our staff a crisp $1,000 bill as a bonus. "You're crazy," said our accountants. "You can hardly pay the rent." I said, "Fuck it—that's the way things should be," and Jim went to the bank to get the bills. He was suspected of being not only crazy but possibly a criminal. He covered sixteen banks before he got the bills. He had to sign so many papers and show so much identification you'd never know that he was just a Missouri country boy ending the year in style. And not *one* $1,000 bill was lost when he got back from the bank.

During one of our first days in the eighteenth-floor room, Haralampos dropped in—an impromptu visit, as usual. I had told him I was starting a new agency, and he had clipped *The New York Times* article with pride and great expectations. Now he had come down to case my new setup, anticipating a working environment at least as luxurious as my former agency.

Papa's mental image of his son at work was firmly fixed by his visits to PKL's lush quarters, with its 60,000 square feet spread over five floors, staffed by 250 people. Visitors were invariably struck by its startling decor and architectural strength. It was always terribly important to me to live and work in a physical environment of beauty, in an atmosphere that accurately reflected one's own deep-down tastes. "My Edifice Complex" was the way I titled an article I wrote for a trade magazine about the importance of physical environment in a man's working life. It was that kind of lovingly designed interior that Papa could understand so well when he dropped in at PKL, even if he wasn't at all familiar with its subtle details. It was as though he walked into a palace—and if I was not around when he came by, our secretaries ordered up lunch and treated him like a visiting eminence, like royalty.

He walked into LHC's one small room in the Squibb Building and was stunned. Seven of us were tripping over each other in that crowded space. The floor was uncarpeted and our voices buckled the walls with a hollow, jarring sound. Marlene McGinnis received him very graciously—and scrambled about to find a chair. Haralampos sat in obvious shock. His son's second store was an unbelievable scene. After a few minutes he got up to leave. We kissed at the elevator and he left in a state of massive confusion.

He went directly to my apartment to see Rosie. After some small talk, his feelings bubbled out: "I went to see George today. Tell me, Rosie—*why did George do it?*"

"Because he wasn't really happy at the other agency," said Rosie.

"He didn't have the *atmosphere* that means so much to him, Papa. He didn't feel right . . . things weren't *perfect* enough for George."

"Yes, Rosie, yes. But his other business was so *successful*. It's hard for me to understand."

"Papa, listen. When George is at work he's just like you used to be when you had the store. When you wired flowers, wasn't that the most important thing in the world to you? Why did Toscanini come to *you*, Papa, instead of the Riverdale florists? Because your work was *perfect*. Do you understand, Papa? George wasn't happy with the work. You see the way he moves around here in the house . . . the way he's always straightening out things and picking up the tiniest specks? That's his nature, Papa, you know that. George has to feel that things are *perfect*. He didn't feel right at the other agency. He didn't have the *atmosphere* that keeps him happy. So he decided he would really be happier by starting all over again. Do you understand now, Papa?"

"Yes," said Haralampos, "I think I understand, Rosie. Yes, yes . . . I understand . . . I *really* understand." Then he leaned toward her and whispered, "I hope Mama doesn't find out."

The phones began to ring after Edwards & Hanly, but my image problem was one step behind each new client.

When I left PKL, here's the way my name popped up in *Ad Age*: "George Lois, 1st vp and self-styled 'crazy man' of Papert, Koenig, Lois has set up a new agency with two PKL colleagues as partners." That "crazy man" tag made Levathes edgy and it caused McCarthy's vice president to ask me, "Is it true that you once pissed on a client's rug?" First I'll cover the Levathes story, then I'll get to McCarthy's vice president. I prefer to save the Irish for last. Levathes, moreover, is a majestic Greek name.

Peter G. Levathes was a big vice president at the Lorillard Corporation. They marketed several cigarette brands, including Kent and a turkey called Century 100's. Lorillard also owned Tabby Cat Food. Levathes was a highbrow patrician Greek, formerly a right-hand man to the Greek-American tycoon Spyros Skouras at 20th Century-Fox. Originally a lawyer, he was always a serious student of Greek culture; at one time he was sought out by a major university in Greece to become its dean. He was a tasteful, cultured aristocrat—a good-looking Victor Jory, tough but also sweet. Levathes was highly regarded as a "creative executive" in the communications business. And he was very "mentorish" toward the mountain *Hellene*, yours truly.

Levathes had been with Young & Rubicam awhile back and we knew each other over the years, but not real well. Much of what he knew about me came from the trades, where I was hailed as a creative star but nailed as a wild man. Levathes the cultivated Hellenophile was proud of my maverick work. He was also concerned about my "crazy man" image.

My new agency was invited to make a pitch for Tabby Cat Food's advertising. Before our meeting with Lorillard's board of directors, Levathes took me under his wing to "mentor" me on proper behavior. He told me in his fatherly way to keep down the cursing. And he hoped I would not disgrace my fellow *Hellene* with any mountain-bred volatile Greek outbursts. "Peter, I promise you," I said, "I won't say one fuckin word to disgrace you." Before the meeting he checked my clothes in the kitchen off Lorillard's boardroom to see that I passed muster. "Now remember what I told you," said Levathes. "Watch your behavior, George. Be careful."

"*Ccchyessa* Pete," I told my mentor.

As it turned out, Lorillard's board chairman was no Meredith Hough. I couldn't tell whether Manny Yellen enjoyed our irreverent horseplay in his boardroom more than our ad campaign, but this tall, relaxed, warm-looking corporation head sure loved the idea of a television campaign for a cat food with Betty Grable, Jane Russell, Casey Stengel and Jack Dempsey.

Using celebrities in commercials is old hat. But we used famous people who had dropped out of the headlines. We had a double-grabber working: people are always interested in seeing how celebrities look *now* versus how they remember them. And our celebrities spoke about Tabby in their natural style. Jack Dempsey said, "I like cats better than dogs," ending up with, "I hope my boxer didn't hear this commercial." Jane Russell stroked a cat and said, "He eats Tabby day and night." Then she looked into its eyes and asked suspiciously, "By the way, where *were* you last night?"

We went through a wing-ding pitch, flooding over with story-boards and ads. Holland did a perfect imitation of Stengel, which was very confusing. I tackled Betty Grable and had her down pat, except for her legs. And Manny Yellen never stopped laughing. Levathes looked relieved—I had preserved our Grecian dignity. Ron and I looked even more relieved when Callaway talked about our media plan. That could have been a sensitive issue because we had no media department. All the TV time we bought at LHC was done by Callaway on the phone, with all of our small staff handling the paperwork. But Jim whipped through all the media jargon about network positions, audience reach, gross rating points —and while we sounded like the most creative trio alive, which we were, we also came across like the agency with the biggest media staff of them all, which was Callaway.

When we were done, Lorillard's board of directors applauded and Manny Yellen said, "Wonderful job, fellas. We're taking Tabby out of Lennen & Newell and we're giving it to you. Great job." Everyone shook hands. As the meeting broke up I went up to Manny Yellen and told him, "We'll blow the fuckin balls off Purina!" Manny slapped me on the back, and I saw that we had a sweetheart client. "Oh by the way," he said just before the whole gang was headed for the door, "How *is* your media department?" Ron Holland beat me to the draw as Callaway blew his nose. "Oh, Jim's fine," he said. "He had a cold last week, but he's okay now." Two million clams for the LHC kitty without a blemish on the glory of Greece.

The commercials were shot by Timothy Galfas, formerly of Atlanta, the only *Hellene* I've ever met with a southern accent. His father changed the family's name from Galiphopoulis, one mean mouthful in Dixie. Someone on the set asked him, "How the fuck did you get an Irish first name?"—which led to the Galfas Oration, always delivered at a raging pitch: "Irish? Irish? Timothy is a corruption of the glorious Grecian name *Timotheus*, friend of God. We Greeks had the greatest civilization in the history of the world when you Irish were still monkeys, swinging from the *trees*. Now get yoah freckled ass off mah set."

The studio was crawling with cats. Casey Stengel needed a few takes to get his lines straight. The real Stengel is like his media image: "Professional, in a wonderful, awkward way," from Ron

Holland's polite description to *Sports Illustrated*. He was the most rambling man I ever worked with, but he made an interesting point about the animals: "A great bunch of cats, except none of 'em can go to their left." Ron was working in front of the cameras with Betty Grable when he got a phone call from a friend who directs off-Broadway plays and regards advertising men as sold-out stiffs. "Can't talk to you now," said Holland. "I'm right in the middle of directing Betty Grable." Ron's friend said, "Oh," and hung up after a long pause. Jane Russell was an absolute professional on the set. We needed no more than fifteen minutes to complete her spot. She even improved our copy, a remarkable feat.

It was fun on the set, working with pros for an enthusiastic client. LHC was off and running. And after our work on Tabby, Peter Levathes let me be my folksy self. The "crazy man" tag with McCarthy's vice president was another story:

After we made the scene with our Edwards & Hanly campaign, Callaway finally got a phone call from a prospective new client. But now that an advertiser had actually called us, Callaway didn't seem to get too excited. "Lestoil," he said. "They're choosing agencies to look over, but God knows how many. First they're gonna interview, then they're gonna narrow their choices down to finalists—God knows how many—then the finalists are gonna make pitches to their management. *Then* they're gonna decide. Sounds like one of those awful deals where they cover forty shops for eight months. I couldn't get too much information on billings, but they were willing to tell me that their boss is a guy called McCarthy and he was made president on St. Patrick's Day."

I looked around the room at Callaway, Duffy, Rohan, McGinnis —and grabbed for my St. George medals. "Jim, you're absolutely full of shit."

"Well *somebody's* coming up to see us next Tuesday at ten."

"Mrs. McGinnis," I shouted. "Be sure Ron ain't at St. Patrick's on Tuesday placing ads with the bishop."

On Tuesday at ten, two men arrived from Holyoke, Massachusetts. They were from Standard Household Products. Their product, Lestoil, was the first household detergent of them all. Our visitors were Gerry Frazier, a huge, affable, "God love ya" Irishman, and Fred Murphy. I believe Murphy was also Irish. Frazier was marketing vice president, Murphy was his sales manager. They came without McCarthy, but the room that morning was occupied by more micks than a Kingsbridge saloon.

When Lestoil was the only detergent in the supermarket—going back about ten years—it sold like hotcakes. But when the big boys got wind of Lestoil's incredible success, the famous bald eunuch, Mr. Clean, was born. After that, Ajax came along, followed by a few others. With all that competition, Lestoil sales slowly began to slide.

They wanted to turn things around. Lestoil used some marketing consultants who told them to link up with a creative ad agency. Frazier asked for a bunch of names. One of the consultants told him, "If you want the best guy in the business, there's an art director named Lois who opened a new agency a few months ago. His shop did the Joe Louis commercial for Edwards & Hanly, which you may not be familiar with because you're up there in New England." Frazier had seen the spot in his Manhattan hotel room the night before—and a date was set for Tuesday at ten. We told Frazier and Murphy about all the work we had done—which was Edwards & Hanly—and they invited us to Holyoke a week later for a formal presentation. There were two other finalists.

They had a mini-auditorium, ideal for full-scale dog-and-pony shows. One of the agencies that followed us, we later learned, came up with a carload of visual projection equipment and brochures. They rearranged the room so that everyone could see their slides and films and charts while reading their brochures.

We brought our reel of Edwards & Hanly spots. But in addition, Callaway wore the longest hair ever to hit Holyoke, and Ron Holland sported the first wide tie ever to be seen in Massachusetts. There were fifteen men there, including Charlie McCarthy. He was a trim, terrier Irishman. He sure enough *was* made president on St. Patrick's Day, as we found out directly from McCarthy a few minutes after we walked in. The audience was loaded with names like McCarthy, Frazier, Murphy, Harford. Their national accounts manager was named R. Timothy Queenan. Even the names that sounded Scottish or English were owned by Irish faces. So I told them how to sell a Nazi car in a Jewish town, and we ran our reel of Sally Rand and Joe Louis. We said we could do a turn-around job for Lestoil because their work wouldn't be delegated to amateurs. "You're looking at our ad agency," said Ron. We were coming across, but all we had to show was our E&H reel and Holland's tie, while the other "finalists" were bringing charts and slides. "How do I know you can deliver?" asked McCarthy toward the end of our meeting. "You *can't*," said Ron. "All you can do is look us in the eye and ask yourself whether or not we're all bullshit." They looked us in the eye. Ron out-stared McCarthy. He worked hard at it because Callaway couldn't stare at anyone—his eyes were hidden behind his hair.

After we left, they took a vote. We got the account by 14 to 1. The one holdout wasn't Frazier; he was sold on us, although he had a nagging doubt. Toward the end of a four-hour dinner at the Seasons a few nights later he said to me, "Hey George, can I ask you a personal question—is it true that you once pissed on a client's rug?" I went through my whole career, beginning with the Lennen & Newell desk episode and ending with Casey. Then I went to the men's room to take a leak. I made sure to take Frazier with me.

Lestoil was squeaking along on a dated image. Our first job was to make it *tomorrow's* product. Our campaign showed a beautiful model in a space helmet—to jolt Lestoil's image out of the past by the most extreme change of setting. "In the year 2000," said the lovely dish behind her plastic visor, "I'm considered an old coot. But one thing has remained the same. Tomorrow's Lestoil is still tomorrow's Lestoil." The turnaround was underway.

Our new billings put a strain on LHC's media department, but Callaway's cold was all gone. With a million Lestoil ad bucks he personally bought all the TV spots he could get on ninety stations, all *preemptable*—spots at the cheapest rate. If someone offered the station a higher rate we could be preempted two minutes before airtime. In the words of the most famous kid in America, "What, me worry?"—and Alfred E. Neuman Callaway wasn't worried if one or two stations bumped us. As he locked up the last buy, he had every right to be proud—but not too long before airtime *all* the stations called to say we're sorry, Mr. Garroway, but you've been preempted. Jim and Ron and our small staff got on all the phones that worked to order make-good time. We concluded that Callaway was a better account man than a media director, and we decided to get a professional media department—but not as part of our agency. We went to Dick Gershon, who was media director at Benton & Bowles and one of the most brilliant media men in our business. Dick had been thinking of starting his own media service. We told him that if he made the move we would be his first account—which led to the formation of Independent Media Services. The paper barrages were eliminated, we went back to making ads, and we've been doing business with Gershon ever since.

In a roundup article on LHC at the end of 1967 the trade weekly *ANNY (Advertising News of New York)* said, "The archetype of the non-organization man, George Lois, finally broke out of the confines of Papert, Koenig, Lois, Inc. to set up a shop more to his liking. Early reports were the agency might dispense with memos in triplicate, time sheets, conference reports and other basic necessities of advertising life. But since they're still in business—and growing—odds are *someone* is handling those chores." The truth is *nobody* handled those chores. We were making ads not memos. The only memo I sent that year was to announce our Christmas party at the Four Seasons—to celebrate our growth in less than four months from zero to $8 million. We were the hottest new agency of 1967.

But the hottest new ad agency in town soon found itself in a strange and ticklish corner. Manny Yellen and Peter Levathes were straddled with their prize Lorillard turkey, Century 100's. This 100 millimeter cigarette was well on its way to disaster. It had all the earmarks of a classic debacle in modern marketing. One ad agency had struck out trying to move it, and a second agency was doing no better than the first. Century 100's violated a basic "must" in selling cigarettes: you gotta have a *name* for the weed. Marlboro is a classic, sensational success story; when a guy pulls out a pack he's a Marlboro Man, tattooed or not. But Lorillard introduced Century in 1967 after the 100 millimeter field was glutted—because of Mary Wells' great campaign for Benson & Hedges. It was a tough act to follow, and most of the new 100's never came close to Benson & Hedges. Century suddenly joined the herd with a real cutesy-pie gimmick: its name was printed on the cellophane wrap *only*. When the wrap was torn off all you saw was a silver-striped pack. No more name. Bad enough to dump one more 100 millimeter brand into a crowded market; without a name it was a stillbirth.

The first ad agency to handle Century introduced it by saying, "You'll never forget new Whatchamacallits." After about six months Lorillard moved Century to a second agency. They tried to save it by saying, "Everyone's dropping our name." A few months later the brand was still going nowhere.

This doomed Century needed a Jesus.

Whenever we came by to talk Tabby, we tried like hell to keep Century out of the conversation or Manny Yellen just might get the notion that maybe LHC could revive the stillbirth in which Lorillard had sunk a bundle. It was a tricky situation because we wanted a crack at Kent. Good old Kent had a lot going for it, including a budget of about $14 million. We Kented all over the joint every time we met with Manny, but because our Tabby campaign was selling a lot of cat food, we were becoming a sure mark for the Century shaft. When the subject of cigarettes came up we Kented with a fury, but Manny smiled and changed the subject. Sample conversation at Lorillard:

"Listen—how would you guys like to take a crack at Century?"

"Oy, Manny—why not give us a crack at Kent instead? We'll do such a great job you'll more than make up for the bath you must be taking with Century. Besides, if we give you a campaign for Century you'll love it, you'll buy it, you'll spend a lot of money, they won't sell any better than now, then you'll get pissed at us, we'll lose a terrific friend—and you'll never give us Kent."

"But you guys are the best *creative p*eople we ever worked with."

"Right, Manny, you're absolutely right. Now if you gave us Kent—"

"And you guys happen to be the very best *advertising* people we ever worked with."

"Right, Manny. Then why don't you give us Kent?"

When Manny Yellen and Peter Levathes finally concluded that Century was becoming the Edsel of Lorillard, they decided to make one last bold move to save it from the graveyard. In early May of 1968 they told us to take the damn cigarette and do something miraculous with it: "We're going to try just *one* more time to make it a success and we'll spend one million dollars *just* in New York City—so even if it still bombs out cold, you'll earn your $150,000 commissions."

"Okay, okay. We accept the million dollar budget. We accept the $150,000 commissions. But we don't think we can sell it."

"Well, do something sensational. After all, you guys *are* the best creative advertising men we ever worked with." So they handed us a million bucks on a platter and we went away miffed.

But once back at the Squibb Building we came up with an awareness campaign to end them all—to put across the *name. Maybe* we could implant the name of Century 100's in smokers' minds— to get them to *try* the brand even though the name would vanish when they ripped off the wrap. We came back to Lorillard with a batch of TV boards and ads, all based on testimonials from historical tyrants of past centuries, all smoking Century 100's: lovable types like Genghis Khan, Ivan the Terrible, Catherine the Great and Henry VIII. Sample spot as delivered by Catherine while puffing on a you-know-what: "Hi. I'm Catherine the Great. In the 1700s we introduced science into the Eastern world and still found time to carry on a little bit. Not bad. But let me tell you of a really *marvelous* century."

It was straight never-never land. Then she held up the pack as the announcer's voice said, "You won't taste a cigarette as good as Century if you look for a hundred years."

They loved the campaign when we presented it to Lorillard. And I got to love it myself. It was one of the smartest ad efforts possible for a dumb, impossible product. But I wasn't fool enough to think it would turn a miracle. Lorillard told us to run it, but before we left the meeting I said, "Look—we want to let you know *again* that you're *not* gonna sell these cigarettes. Your research will show that people will say these are their favorite commercials, but there ain't no reason to buy this cigarette, and we can't manufacture the reason." We spent the million bucks, we earned our $150,000 commissions—and just as we said, it didn't sell one more pack. But we got bitten by the same bug that bit Manny Yellen; we began to believe that with one more push we *might* make a success of this stupid brand with its nameless pack.

We put together a follow-up campaign and met with Lorillard's board of directors. But by then it made no difference what I said, how I said it or who I insulted—Peter Levathes was looking at the bottom line. "But George," he said, "we spent a million dollars, and as far as we can determine, we didn't sell one more pack. Now if we can determine that we *had* sold one more pack, we'd spend another million dollars and sell another pack. But we can't, so we're going to phase out the product."

Lorillard took a long look at its cigarette lineup and shifted its Kent business, about $14 million, out of Grey Advertising into Benton & Bowles—plus whatever was left for Century's funeral.

Meanwhile we were beginning to blow the balls off Purina with our Tabby work by signing up a 365-pound gentleman named Milan Greer as a consultant to Tabby and as the star of our new TV campaign. Milan Greer is one of the world's famous cat breeders, whose clients include Elizabeth Taylor. When one of her pussycats catches a cold, big Milan catches a plane and nurses it back to health. New York City is always crawling with alley cats, but when Milan Greer breeds a litter he gets as much as $500 for each kitty. We called him the Cat Man and brought him on the screen like Alfred Hitchcock. Then he spoke about cats like Bill Bernbach talking about advertising.

We brought on Milan Greer shortly after we lost Century. When you lose an account from a corporation with several products, the grapevine begins to buzz with rumors that you're in the doghouse with their cat food because you struck out with their watchamacallits. But we had a sweetheart client in Manny Yellen. He loved us for telling him he had a turkey that could never be a swan. When Century finally bombed out, Manny respected us more. The trade weekly *ANNY* called me to see if we were shaky with Lorillard. I gave them an unprintable statement which came out like this: "Lois mentioned the campaign [The Cat Man] to back up his point that Lorillard is 'one of the best clients I've ever had . . . Manny Yellen is a smart --- -- - -----.' " He was also a *sweet* sonofabitch. I wanted Manny to know how much I liked the guy. And I wanted Pete Levathes to understand that a little bit of the wild man was still in me. "If I go down with Century," Manny said when we argued against our own campaign, "I'm going to go down with this great advertising." You won't find a client as good as Yellen if you look for a hundred years.

But there are some events that play hell with an advertising man's life—like corporate mergers. At the end of 1968 Loew's Theatres, Inc., took over Lorillard. A fellow named Preston Robert Tisch became president of the whole shebang, and before long Manny Yellen and Peter Levathes were out of Lorillard for keeps. Tabby was then sold to the company that owns Lipton's Tea, and out went the Cat Man, the wild man and the Irishmen. I don't mind taking my lumps—even after having done such great work for Tabby, and even if it's caused by a merger. But when the head takeover guy is named *Preston*, after I busted balls in P.S. 7 to defend my first Preston, the nebbish, against the Kingsbridge micks—someone's got his whammies tangled.

First we lost Tabby after a merger, then Lestoil was sold to the Noxell Corporation and we took another lump. But after falling between two stools once, your can gets hard enough to fall again without hollering ouch. Shortly after the sale we got a call from Bates Hall, Noxell's ad manager. "We just bought Lestoil, as you know," he said, "and we'd like to drop by and have you tell us anything you know about the business. Our agencies are William Esty and Sullivan Stauffer. We intend to give Lestoil to one of them, but anything you know about the business we'd like to know. And I'd like to bring along Bill Hunt, our marketing manager." We said come on up and we'll tell you anything you want to know. Mergers can be cold turkey happenings. It was refreshing to talk turkey even if the merger axe already chopped our heads off. We told everything we knew to Hall and Hunt. Then we all went to lunch. We wished them luck and they thanked us for our helpful orientation.

When we got back to the office Bates Hall called to say they had decided to give the Lestoil account to LHC—plus several other Noxell products. I realize, of course, that many advertising guys reading this will say yeah yeah yeah, that's pure Lois bullshit—when the fast-talking Greek and his two smartass partners get the whiff of a million dollar account they'll sell like there's no tomorrow—and with the three of them yakking at once it ain't no "helpful orientation." Therefore, to any of my advertising colleagues who regard the Noxell story as bullshit, I can only repeat: I never bullshit a bullshitter.

Moreover, after Noxell took over Lestoil and assigned us the account, this "problem" product has become a big winner.

Shortly after I opened my second store, *ANNY* started its year-end roundup on LHC with this intro: "These days if you tell someone you work for Lois Holland Callaway, you're very likely to hear that person react with a 'W-o-w-w-w-w!' . . . Then the conversation will pick up with questions: 'Didn't you just get such-and-such account?' . . . 'Aren't you up for this-or-that account?'

. . . and, 'What's George Lois really like?' Perhaps that is what shoots an agency into the so-called 'hot' stratosphere. The questions."

There was no question about the health of the Lois store. But questions arose about the luck of the Lois clan.

1968 began in sorrow.

Mama died.

Vasilike Thanasoulis Lois succumbed to her final stroke in February of 1968. We kissed Mama for the last time as she lay in her coffin at the funeral service. Her treasured icon was placed on the sealed casket as family and friends filed by for their last respects before she was buried in a Westchester County cemetery. From the mountain hamlet of Perista, the proud sister of Costas the Staten Island farmer, bartered over while the faucet ran, raised three children in Harlem and Kingsbridge and left six grandchildren. And while she was an invalid for seventeen years since her first stroke in Greece shackled her furious energy, the Greek matriarch's death was a shattering event. The lady of our Kingsbridge incense and Orthodoxy was gone. Before her casket was lowered in the earth I took her cherished icon. The sacred symbol of Mama's Orthodoxy now hangs in my home.

The gods seemed to conspire that year against the family of

Haralampos. A series of mishaps, one almost fatal, followed Mama's death. First I severed my Achilles tendon playing basketball, and after an operation I hobbled around on crutches while working at the agency. Our business was booming. In 1968 we were headed toward the $20 million level, less than a year after we started. But the Evil Eye was on the Lois family. After Mama, we almost lost Papa. It happened casually.

Until my mother passed away, she and Haralampos had lived in a wing that was built on the home of Ricky and Captain Ernie Tracosas in suburban Ardsley. Ernie was in the contracting business. Haralampos the widower, now seventy-two, divided his time among his three children. When he came to our apartment he slept in Rosie's large studio room, surrounded by her massive canvases.

We were in the lobby of our apartment building during one of Papa's stays with us, waiting for the elevator. Papa suddenly realized he had forgotten to buy his Greek newspaper. He turned to head out for the foreign-language newsstand on nearby Fourteenth Street and walked into the floor-to-ceiling glass door. (His vision was bad because of previous operations to remove cataracts from his eyes.) The glass shattered and Haralampos fell to the floor, spurting blood. His nose seemed sheared off at the bridge and his forehead was severely gashed. I threw away my crutches, wrapped my jacket around his blood-drenched head, lifted him up and hopped with him on my one good leg to Dr. Benjamin Singer, a few houses away. Instinctively I knew I needed someone strong to help me through this. Papa was obviously in awful shape, and with my severed tendon I was of limited help. While at Dr. Singer's office I called a friend, George Kokines, to help. Kokines is a powerful ex-ballplayer, formerly a star guard on Bradley's basketball team, now a corporate executive. He's also a Greek.

"Very, very serious," said Dr. Singer. He got on the phone and dialed frantically. He spoke very quickly, then he hung up and told me to take Haralampos immediately to another doctor a few blocks away. "He's an internist," said Dr. Singer, "but he specializes in war wounds and he happened to be in Israel during the Six Day War, so if anyone can help your father, this man can." I hobbled up the steep stairs from Dr. Singer's basement office with Haralampos, his head wrapped in heavy toweling, and just as I reached the sidewalk George Kokines came charging down the street toward us. Helped by two Georges, Papa made it into a cab and we rushed him to the internist's office. A main artery had been cut—Haralampos was minutes from death when we arrived. He was stitched together and given a shot of whiskey. Within an hour he seemed well enough to come home. I asked the cabbie to stop on Fourteenth Street on the way back to pick up Papa's Greek newspaper—he seemed completely recovered. As Kokines stepped out of the cab, I said, "Hey George, be careful. An hour ago Papa almost got killed doing that."

I picked up my crutches in the lobby and brought Haralampos, stitched and bandaged, to his bed among Rosie's paintings.

The Evil Eye was over the Tracosas family as well. Ricky by then was the mother of three boys. Jon Tracosas, the first Lois grandson, was a high school football star; he later went on to become Cornell's star linebacker. Jon was okay, but Ricky's thirteen-year-old Harry, another football player, injured his knee and had his leg in a cast after the removal of a cartilage. A few months earlier, nine-year-old Billy Tracosas broke his hand. Then Hariclea broke an ankle. Three members of the Tracosas family were walking around simultaneously in casts.

And I was on crutches.

And Papa was almost killed.

And Mama had died.

Voula and Bill Chirgotis were living in Dobbs Ferry, where they operated a luncheonette. They had one child, a twelve-year-old daughter, Stamatiko. (Voula never had a son—we could never hide that from Mama.) There were no mishaps in Voula's family, but the rash of misfortunes, particularly Mama's death, troubled my older sister deeply. Several months after Mama died, while Papa was recuperating with us from his accident, Voula called Rosie. "What have we done wrong?" she asked. "Why is God punishing us this way? Rosie, *what did we do?*" Rosie said it was one of those series of coincidences that happens to many families, but Voula was still troubled—and like a young Vasilike she decided to *do* something.

When I came home from work that night on my crutches, I asked Rosie with a cocky feeling if any new disaster had struck the clan. My spirits lifted whenever I entered my home. Our apartment was the realization of my father's Easter chant, but in a style of my own. By then I had accumulated a collection of primitive art that dominated our spacious living room—fertility dolls, shaman's rattles, tribal masks, stone pipes, ivory fetishes, flaring headdresses, cult objects, reliquary heads, ceremonial staffs—a gallery of exotic works. Primitive statuary was starkly silhouetted against the changing light in our east-to-west rectangular room. The Orthodox icons of Kingsbridge were replaced by totems from pagan cultures. Mama's icon hung in our bedroom.

I basked in the voodoo aura, graced by Tiffany lamps and beautifully crafted Art Nouveau and early American antiques. I had followed the four priorities of Haralampos in its deepest sense. My store was flourishing, my home was a sanctuary, my family life was a source of rich fulfillment after seventeen years of marriage, and my sons were developing into manly, sensitive boys; Harry was ten and swarthy, Luke was six and blond—one Greek-Pole, one Polish-Greek.

"George," Rosie asked me, "would you have any objections if a priest came here—to our apartment?"

"*Here?* What for? What do we need a *priest* for?"

"For Papa, George. It seems that there's a curse hanging over your family. At least Papa believes that, George, and he wants a priest to exorcise it."

"A priest in *my* home? An Evil Eye over *my* family? Are you serious, Rosie? You're gonna have a goddam priest in here to sing *Kerie Eléieson*, surrounded by my pagan collection? Not a chance."

"Well Voula and Papa already spoke to him and they'd like him to come—tomorrow afternoon. It's very important to Papa. Since Mama died, and with all the accidents in your family, Papa needs *something* to hold onto . . . to purge his feelings. The priest has already gone to both your sisters' houses, but Papa doesn't think that's enough. He doesn't really think it's your primitive art that's putting an Evil Eye on everybody—he just wants the whole job done. And besides, George, I think Papa really needs a priest."

"Okay, okay," I finally said. "But just be sure the guy doesn't knock over my Uli. If his *Papathos* hat hits my sacred pagan Uli while he's rocking back and forth with his hocus-pocus, there goes a $25,000 treasure."

"Well won't *you* be here?"

"Rosie, my sweet Polish Roman Catholic—the priest's service at Mama's funeral was Greek Orthodoxy at its finest. I'll remember the passion in his prayers for Mama until the day I die. But I can't take more than one priest a year."

"Well it's the same priest who conducted Mama's service. That's why it means so much to Papa."

"Okay, okay—if it makes Papa feel better, have the guy over. But if I have to stand here in *my* house and watch, I just may piss in my pants. I warn you, it's gonna be one *incredible* scene. Just make sure he doesn't bump against my Uli."

My Uli is a rarity of Oceanic art from the Pacific island of New Ireland, a wooden male god, four feet high. It stands in the center of our living room on a two-foot black pedestal so that its pagan Halloween eyes are at human eye level. The Uli has large breasts, considered very manly. It also has an erect penis. In tribal societies they were kept in men's longhouses—communal shelters—so that no woman could see them. They were painted and pigmented over generations and centuries, producing a magical luster. When Christian missionaries came to civilize the Oceanic islanders they were quick to destroy the Ulis. Mine is one of the six great Ulis left in the world. But even after centuries of surfacing, the awesome luster of its penis can be penetrated by water—and the penis of my precious Uli is its most magnificently pigmented surface. Its erection is silhouetted with breathtaking clarity and its deep hues change very subtly as the light arcs across the windows of our living room.

The following evening I came home to my purged apartment. Papa seemed at peace with life as he sat at the table reading his Greek newspaper, sipping Metaxa from a brandy glass.

"How do you feel, Papa?" I asked him.

"Good, George. Good, good."

"Was the *Papathos* here?"

"Oh yes. I'm happy he came. Maybe now we'll have no more bad luck. A beautiful visit."

Harry tugged me aside so that Papa couldn't hear. "Ask Ma about the Uli," he said with a snicker. I glanced at my precious Uli. It stood in the evening light, beautifully erect. I went over to inspect it carefully. It looked unharmed. Then Rosie told me about the priest's visit:

He arrived in his floor-length black vestments, decked out in his seventeen-inch hat and his veil. He came equipped with incense and holy water. An assistant came with him. Voula accompanied them. In the apartment the priest poured his holy water into a metal cup suspended from silver-linked chains. His assistant carried the smoking incense. The two priests began their Gregorian prayers, joined by Papa and Voula. The head priest led a procession through the apartment. His assistant walked behind him, then Papa, then Voula. And Harry followed Voula, his eyes popping at the pageantry in his apartment. Meanwhile, Rosie kept an alert eye on Harry.

As the ritual proceeded, the priest followed a winding path around my reliquary heads and fertility dolls, chanting his Orthodox prayers with Gregorian bravura. His assistant chanted behind him as they moved through the apartment. Haralampos prayed with them and wept, Voula moaned and Harry picked up the rear with a grin, a happy kid latching onto a snake dance. *"Kerie Eléieson,"* chanted the priest, the Orthodox "Lord have mercy." The priest blessed everything in his path, from Tiffany lamps to shaman's rattles, finally stopping in front of my pedestaled Uli, eye to eye with my pagan god, chanting *"Kerie Eléieson"* at the crescendo of his liturgical ritual. As he dipped his hands into the holy water, Harry turned to Rosie and giggled. She looked over his shoulder, horrified—the priest was sprinkling holy water on my Uli's vulnerable erection. It was pointed at the cleric's black-robed groin. They were eyeball-to-eyeball and penis-to-penis. Rosie grabbed a terry cloth, and as the corrosive holy water sprayed the Uli's pigmented erection, Rosie smiled at the priest with Roman Catholic piety and quickly wiped the water off my precious penis. As the priest left my Uli he lifted his hands and spread his fingers into stigmata position, index fingers pointing to heaven, to the ceiling of our Twelfth Street apartment.

Papa released the tears of his loneliness and Voula sobbed from her Grecian heart for our dead Vasilike, for Mama.

A few days later we took Papa to a one-man show of Rosie's paintings. "They didn't look like that when I slept with them," said Haralampos.

A sadness had been exorcised.

Shortly after the Uli was sanctified a message was handed to me at a recording session:

Mr. Lois: Your secretary wants you to call immediately.

She said H.L. tried to reach you. She said it's urgent.

Haralampos Lois? More bad luck? Was the Evil Eye back in business? Did the *Papathos* strike out? Did the Almighty welch on us after all that holy water? I ran to the phone and called my South African Chinese secretary, Marlene McGinnis. Her Oxford accent was more spectacular than usual. "He called, Mr. Lois. He wants you to contact him at once. Oh Mr. Lois, we're all so terribly *excited!* Mr. Callaway has placed a tentative order for champagne."

In August 1968 the hot question on Madison Avenue was "Who's gonna get Braniff?" Our agency was less than a year old and our billings were up to $20 million—colossal for us, tiny to a major airline, but the grapevine reported that Braniff had been asking around about us. Was it possible? I called Braniff's president, Harding Lawrence.

He said he was interviewing a few ad agencies and wanted to meet with us in Los Angeles—but *fast*, because he planned to make a quick decision. I said I was quite sure I could rearrange my schedule. I grabbed Ron and Jim and we hopped on the first plane west.

"Why do you think he's got us on his list?" asked Jimmy.

"Well," I said, "maybe Harding Lawrence is getting a crush on me."

More than ten years before, my unused ads for American Airlines at Lennen & Newell were noticed by that bright young copywriter Bunny Wells. In 1959 our paths crossed again at Doyle Dane Bernbach, where Mary, no longer Bunny, liked my ads again. In 1964 while Mary was with Jack Tinker & Partners, a creative "think tank," she liked my PKL ads. In 1965 Harding Lawrence was made boss of Braniff and fired his ad agency. He switched his account to Tinker, where Mary was a senior partner and one of the top talents in advertising. She made Braniff famous by dressing their stewardesses in Pucci outfits and by painting their planes in pastel colors. In 1966 Mary started her own agency, Wells, Rich, Greene. Her first client was Braniff. In August 1967 the Texas conglomerate Ling-Temco-Vought got control of Braniff. Meanwhile Harding Lawrence fell in love with Mary Wells. In November 1967, just as our campaign for Edwards & Hanly was breaking, Harding married Mary. In August 1968 Mary Wells Lawrence resigned Braniff and picked up TWA—what with Braniff's boss married to the boss of his ad agency, LTV (headed by the Texas millionaire Jimmy Ling) was worried about a possible conflict of interest.

Harding Lawrence was hiding out in a bungalow at the Beverly Hills Hotel. We walked in, found it empty and waited. Then this handsome demon with bushy brows over bristling cat eyes walked in. He sized up us three hotshots with his fierce eyes and got right down to business.

With his $8 million account resigned by Mary, Harding Lawrence had taken off for the Coast to escape the barrage of calls from agencies out for his business. He was playing it smart. His callers were the brass of big agencies, with big payrolls to fill seats on Braniff flights. Lawrence was concerned about offending his callers by having to tell them that he had already narrowed down his choices to five agencies—including LHC. He wanted to meet us and size us up personally before sending his advertising honchos to check us out. He told us that Mary had mentioned my name to him as someone who might do a good job for Braniff.

Braniff's boss was a tiger, driving in close for exact answers to every question. Some were left-field ballbusters, like asking Callaway, "What's your *name*, again?" He seemed so intent on a wall-shaking answer that a cool bird like Callaway would stammer, "Uh . . . ummm . . . mmm . . . Callaway, yeah *Callaway!*"

Harding wore an open silk shirt and his hand was always rubbing his chest. When he spoke he shoved his nose under your eyes, and ended most questions with, "Huh? Huh?" It was easy to fall in love with Harding Lawrence.

Our meeting lasted four hours. When we left the bungalow I felt there was no question left for Harding to ask. But there was no question about his advertising sophistication, having worked with sharp outfits like Tinker and Mary's agency, where the word "creative" was the ballgame. He was probing, checking us out from nose to toe. His only decision was that we checked out for the next checkout. He had a Braniff team looking over Lennen & Newell; Foote, Cone & Belding (the agency that lost TWA's $15 million account to Mary's agency); Jack Tinker's shop; Ogilvy & Mather; and us three mavericks. He told us he would send his guys to meet with us since they were the ones who decided, not Harding Lawrence.

When we got back to New York we met with Ed Acker, John Leer and Tom King, who were making the rounds of the five shops. After four hours with Harding Lawrence in a bungalow, we were milked dry. But that was Phase One. When we met with Acker, Leer and King in New York, we were put through a team interrogation that lasted three hours. Harding's honchos had a thorough boss, and they squeezed us for more, more and still more. After logging seven hours with Braniff I was sure they had enough to decide yes or no. But that was Phase Two. "Okay," they said, "we'd like you to come to Dallas." I thought they meant to start work, that we had the account. When we got to Dallas we walked into a jammed conference room. "Okay," they said, "talk."

We talked for a few more hours. By then the choice had narrowed down to us or Lennen & Newell. Here the conglomerate wires could have tripped us. L&N was already involved with Braniff through their Dallas agency, which handled the corporate advertising for Ling-Temco-Vought; and LTV controlled Greatamerica Corporation, the outfit that had a controlling interest in Braniff. Sounds complicated, but it all boiled down to who should work on the account. I reeled off the usual promises of a big agency when it gets its hook in the mouth of a big fish: "I bet they're promising to put the agency's five greatest creative teams on the account. Hell, there aren't five great creative teams in the whole country. All we can promise you is brains, talent and hustle. If you like us, fine. If not, we go quietly." That was the end of Phase Three. The next day they awarded us their $8 million account. We opened champagne and shot a full day's work. It all happened at LHC less than a year after we started, and our billings were almost as much as PKL's. But we almost lost Braniff as soon as we got it.

After a few days of nuts-and-bolts orientation in Dallas we came back to start work. Suddenly one of Braniff's key men showed up at the agency, dumped a pile of magazine ads on my table and asked for my opinion. It was interim work that Mary's agency had done to tide over Braniff until its new agency's campaign was ready. I got the impression that *nobody* in Dallas liked the stuff—but that they wanted my reaction before deciding. A quick decision was needed because of the long lead time for magazines. About $300,000 of advertising was involved. I could have said it was fine, and collected $45,000 commissions for having done nothing. But I thought it was a weak campaign and the Braniff guy nodded in agreement. Then he asked us to come on down to Dallas and evaluate the campaign for Harding so the matter could be settled once and for all.

Callaway had to go to Lima, Peru, where Mary's agency had an office with twenty-nine people. It was a costly operation, but Braniff had a lot of routes to South America. It was understood that we would take over Mary's Lima office from our first day with Braniff. After his last gulp of champagne, Callaway took off for Peru to look over Mary's old branch office while Ron and I went to Dallas to talk over Mary's last campaign.

I laid the ads out on the table as Harding joined us. Then I explained why I wasn't happy about the theme, suggesting they scrap the campaign and save the money for the new campaign we were readying. I wasn't coy about my objections to the ads, nor was I at all nasty. I felt I had given them a frank and professional evaluation of its weaknesses—when out of nowhere Harding Lawrence suddenly lost his cookies. "We're not paying you to tell us what's wrong with other people's advertising," he shouted. "We *made* that decision and this campaign is going to run."

I was in a cute spot. I didn't want to shaft Harding's man by explaining that I was asked to give a fair and square evaluation—and that I was under the clear impression Harding wanted my opinion before he ran it. I felt the creative concept was dull compared to what I thought we could do. But when I pointed out that some route ads in the campaign were outdated, Harding flew into his ballbusting rage. He apparently thought they had been brought up to date with his current schedules. He called Mary in New York right there and then and laced into her with a fury. I was very embarrassed for myself—but even more embarrassed for Mary. Then Harding told *me* to explain the situation to Mary. To my surprise, she was very calm and asked me very coolly what was going on down there. "Mary," I said, "I never saw anything like this in my life. I criticized your advertising and Harding's going wild with rage." Mary was very sweet about it. She told me to calm him down, that she would talk to him about it. Then she said *she* was sorry, I said *I* was sorry and we both hung up. But Harding Lawrence was still in a beautiful lather. When I said, "It's really all a misunderstanding," he lashed out at me, more enraged than before: "You don't know what I'm talking about—and I don't want *you* to tell *me* what I did wrong a year ago, a month ago or a week ago." I was in the worst kind of hornet's nest: at my first meeting with the biggest account in my entire career I end up telling my client that his wife's work was wrong.

When Ron and I walked out we couldn't see straight. We had no idea where we stood with Braniff. On the flight back to New York I was convinced the ballgame was over.

Harding Lawrence obviously loved Mary more than me.

But while we were striking out in Dallas, Callaway was scoring big in Lima. He barged into the office on Monday morning and said, "Listen, listen—I did a *fantastic* job down there. In five days

I fired twenty-eight of the twenty-nine stiffs. I kept just one art director and hired an account man out of Buenos Aires. Then I rebuilt the agency from the ground up into a tight, beautiful seven-man operation. I hope you guys are *proud* of me!"

"That's *terrific*," I said. "Harding will just *love* what you did. First of all we had this meeting and I'm sorry to announce that I *think* we lost Braniff. And second, even if we didn't, we did *now*, because you just fired everyone that Mary hired." Callaway spent the next forty-eight hours on the phone trying to hire back the twenty-eight South Americans he fired. He ran up a phone bill that staggered our accountants, but he couldn't hire back a soul. By then Mary must have calmed down Harding in Dallas. We weren't fired after all, and a date was set to show Braniff our new campaign.

Mary's work for Braniff, with the sole exception of the hot potato that scalded me, was a tough act to follow. She took an airline with a name that was mistaken for a Canadian town and made it famous. To evolve a sizzling campaign for Braniff after she ended the "plain plane" with Pucci and pastels was a tremendous test of our creative powers.

We came up with: *"When you got it, flaunt it."*

Once we had the theme we fleshed it out with the most unexpected twosomes who "had it" in the history of advertising. Whitey Ford gabbed with Salvador Dali; Rex Reed talked about food and girls with "relentless" Mickey Rooney, a many-married guy; Hermione Gingold played gin with George Raft. We also paired Ethel Merman with Bennett Cerf; Mickey Spillane with Marianne Moore; and Dean Martin Jr. told Satchel Paige, "You got to live fast and hard because by the time you reach twenty-one, it's all over." In another commercial we showed Tab Hunter, Miss Universe, Leonard Lyons, Sugar Ray Robinson, Gina Lollobrigida and Joe Namath enter a Braniff plane, all in sixty seconds.

I was also determined that when we went to Dallas we would prove to Harding and his honchos that we three mavericks were the sharpest *businessmen* on Madison Avenue. I put our team at LHC through a cram course to memorize every flight and route of our new account. I drew a detailed system map over a map of the continent. For three weeks we went through quizzes and drill sessions on what flights came-and-went from any town that Braniff serviced.

Then we took our theme and showed how it could introduce every innovation that Braniff could fluant—jazzy terminal in Dallas, new computer system, new routes to Hawaii. We extended it to every piece of action on Harding Lawrence's airline.

When we left for Dallas I knew we had the answer to any question that could *possibly* come up.

There were about fifteen people in Braniff's boardroom. A few jokers too far from Harding for him to hear smiled at me and said, "How's it going, George? What do you think of Mary's stuff?" A tense session was at hand—after Mary's terrific work the odds were stacked against any campaign that would wow Braniff. They listened in total silence as I went through our work. I talked for two hours, with all stops out. I took that wild theme and explained how it was just right for an airline that had *made it*, how it was just right for a confident company to brag with those six easy words. If Braniff had it, I asked, why not *flaunt* it?

Not a word, not a cough for two hours. Harding's bushy-browed eyes watched every move and every gesture. Intently, he studied every ad and TV spot. His staff kept glancing at him for a clue, but he wasn't saying a thing. Finally I was done. The room was still. Harding Lawrence leaned toward Ron—and I could tell he was going to ask a question, not give an opinion. Good! We were ready for any question about Braniff—city, time, equipment—*anything* Harding asked.

"Tell me—what's the definition of *flaunt?*"

"Well . . . uh . . . umm . . . it's kind of . . ." stammered the fastest gun on Madison Avenue. We were prepared for everything except *that*. But Harding had that uncanny way of asking the obvious and drawing a blank. Finally Ron collected himself after Harding's karate and began to define it. The boss of Braniff still seemed uncertain, so I jumped in, then Jim. Harding Lawrence still seemed uncertain about the meaning of the theme. His staff all began to talk at once, but nobody seemed to love it—or hate it. We seemed to be drifting. Then Harding spoke up. This was *it*.

"I'll tell you what I think," he finally said. "I believe this has been the best goddam advertising presentation I *ever* saw. I think you fellows have done a fantastic job. And I think the theme is absolutely terrific."

Coming up with a winning campaign for Braniff was a very important juncture in my career, while the ad world was still slightly staggered by the news that our small new agency was awarded this formidable piece of business. In December 1968, *Fortune* wrote a long article on the shuffling of airline accounts. Its introduction floored me:

> Imagine a corner table at Manhattan's elegant Four Seasons restaurant, $9.75 steaks on the plate, a fine red wine alongside, and George Lois, as always, talking. George Lois is a man who is making a career out of starting advertising agencies. Listening to him talk is a little like getting a taste of pure garlic—pretty great, if you happen to like garlic. Lois eats at this table every day he is in town, only the conversation and the menu varying. Today the subject is Braniff Airways, a big, juicy account that has just landed at Lois' agency. How, he is asked, did you happen to get Braniff? "Well," he says, spreading his hands, "Harding Lawrence fell in love with me."

I was having dinner with Rosie a few weeks after the article appeared. She asked me how I happened to get by with that crack about Lawrence? "Well," I said, spreading my hands, "Harding Lawrence must *still* be in love with me."

He approved commercials that would have frightened off many men in his position—and particularly in his state of Texas.

One of our spots opened on a tight closeup of Andy Warhol giving this spiel: "Of course, remember there is an inherent beauty in soup cans that Michelangelo could not have imagined existed." Camera pulls back, showing him seated next to a big, brooding black man as the voice-over says: "Talkative Andy Warhol and gabby Sonny Liston always fly Braniff. They like our girls. They like our food. They like our style. And they like to be on time. Thanks for flying Braniff, fellows." Warhol winds up with our theme: "When you got it, flaunt it." Liston never opens his mouth, while giving Warhol a "What the hell are *you?*" look.

During the filming of that commercial, five years after Black Santa, I asked Liston, "Hey champ, do you remember me?" He glared at me with that unseeing look used by so many blacks only on whites. "No," he said, "don't know you, man." I stuck my face right in front of Liston and said, "You remember—Las Vegas,

Santa Claus, *Joe!—You* remember. Huh? Huh?" Liston smiled. "Yeahhh . . . man," he finally said, "that was hot shit."

But a few folks in Dallas hardly felt it was so nifty to show an underground oddball and a surly, uppity *nigger* in a Braniff TV commercial. Harding caught flak, but he told us, "I don't give a damn, I *love* the campaign." Mary put Braniff on the map, but now they were becoming *hot* and famous by running chancy ads that stuck in people's minds. "When you got it, flaunt it" entered the language, was used in movies, in comic routines, in daily talk everywhere.

Pressures, however, were building against it. The rich Dallas boys of LTV were *literally* flaunting it in their personal lives. Their mansions and fountains were being highly publicized, to their embarrassment. In an odd psychological way our theme may have struck home. Another curious aspect about the flying business: an airline is hated most in its home city, where most of its flights originate. At one time or another someone has a nasty experience—lost baggage, awful meal, late takeoff—the usual stuff. In New York you hear griping against Eastern, in Kansas City against TWA, in Atlanta against Delta, in Rome against Alitalia. Ron has a line that can apply to any airline: "Breakfast in New York, lunch in Los Angeles, baggage in Buenos Aires." When it happens, you never forget. And it usually happens in the airline's home base. The anti-Braniff feeling in Dallas spilled over onto Braniff's advertising, and "flaunt it" became a hotly controversial theme among many on Harding's staff—also in his social set. But when I flew on Braniff and complimented a stewardess about *anything*, the answer was always, "When you got it, flaunt it." A year later, as we were about to put "flaunt it" to work for the next phase of our program— Hawaii flights, new terminal, new computer, new routes—Harding said to me, "I must ask you to remove it from our advertising, much as I love that theme." He was visibly pained, but Harding Lawrence was the last tycoon in Dallas to give in.

He was one of those clients who genuinely understood advertising (some don't). He responded instinctively to good work— often with a "nifty," while rubbing his chest. He bombarded us with new facts that were hard to understand as his nose jutted forward while he grunted, "Huh? Huh?" always expecting a *yeah*,

yeah. He was rough on his staff, but they could always beat it out of Dallas on any flight they picked at any hour, which they did; when Harding Lawrence chewed you out he chewed you *up*.

Surprisingly he never mentioned a word about "Harding Lawrence fell in love with me" until more than a year after *Fortune* quoted me. When he raised the subject he did it obliquely. "Goddam you, Lois," he growled one day when telling me how hard he worked, "you and your goddam Four Seasons lunches. I don't go out for lunch. I work through the day. I never stop." I goddammed him back, telling him how hard I worked: "I come in at seven-thirty, I talk work at the Seasons, then I make ads until late at night. You work at lunch but you go home at *four*." A small clash, but a symptom of an ending honeymoon. We seemed to be headed toward an Indian wrestle of egos.

And as time went by, Harding Lawrence got to love me less.

But his relentless drive was a juicy challenge. My plans for Braniff went worlds beyond advertising campaigns and themes. When the first 747's were being readied, I told Harding to cut their seats from 364 to 299 and turn those flying warehouses into a flying *experience*. I designed a "privacy chair" for passengers who wanted to hide from the bustle. I worked out a multi-screen plan to give passengers a *choice* of movies. I suggested a lounge and a piano, with great entertainers like Bobby Short and Mabel Mercer belting out live entertainment. But again, I was more than thirteen weeks ahead of my time. "You're trying to destroy the economics of that airplane," said Harding, although he recognized its marketing sense. Unfortunately, 1970 was a lean year for airlines to invest in passenger comforts. Two years later the 747's are doing many of the "premature" programs that were created for Braniff. But 1970 was generally a brutal time for the airline industry. The economy was lousy, air travel was off, profits were down, budgets were cut, and the emphasis on advertising that marked the "flaunt it" period waned. Braniff is known today because Mary made them famous when fame was needed; George made them more so when the airline industry became more competitive.

When the recession hit hard, a lesser priority was given to ideas and bold campaigns. Changes were made in Braniff's executive suite as Harding Lawrence moved up to chairman. We grew more distant, the excitement ended—and two years after we got the account it was transferred to a conventional agency.

But "flaunt it" stuck in Madison Avenue's mind, and it became a subject of I-told-you-so post-mortems.

When we lost Braniff the ad community said *aha*, that silly campaign killed the crazy Greek and his two Irishmen. We were close to $30 million and dropped almost a third of our business. But the public is still using our theme in everyday talk—and Harding Lawrence was sold solid on "flaunt it"—plus our campaigns that followed. But when pressures that a client can't control kill a theme, your work begins to blend with the others, and the excitement ends. "When you got it, flaunt it" was the gutsiest advertising of my career, and my biggest gamble. I won when it ran because Harding backed it. I lost when it was killed, and only because it proved too powerful—because it *worked*. It was a blow to LHC, but when you have an airlines jinx it comes in threes. Now I've paid all my dues—American, National, Braniff.

"How," I was asked by Callaway at our luncheon wake at the Four Seasons, "do we explain the loss of an $8 million client? We were roasted in the trades for 'flaunt it' and now that we're out we'll be damned for one of the greatest campaigns in air travel."

"Perk up, James," said Ron. "Any attempt to explain this devastating blow will be regarded as protesting too much. This morning I was asked by a reporter to explain it and I disposed of it swiftly. I told him we lost the account because of *illness*." We stared at Holland as he waved to the waiter for another bottle of Chassagne Montrachet wine. "I told him they got *sick* of us," he explained.

I was still glum. It wasn't the size of the loss but the force of our work—ahead of its time, unorthodox, exciting, bold—and we end up looking like losers.

"George, why are you so quiet?" asked Ron.

"Well," I said, spreading my hands, "Harding Lawrence broke my heart."

"But not your balls, I hope," said the fastest gun in the Four Seasons.

"There's this Orthodox priest my father calls in to purge bad luck. I think I'll ask him to bring his holy water to the agency."

"Is your holy water more effective than ours?" asked Ron.

"One squirt lasts two years. But keep your flies zipped."

Professional athletes are a joy to work with in advertising. And the bigger the star the better he cries. We proved it with Maypo, a breakfast cereal for kids.

Unfortunately, Maypo was a *hot* cereal. There was no *instant* Maypo. Big problem. Hot breakfast cereals have been going downhill for years. To make Maypo an *in* cereal with the kids I assembled a team of famous athletes for a flight of TV spots on kids' programs. They were all superstars from the major sports. And they were all from different parts of the country to make Maypo famous nationally—but not with the usual testimonials, God no. When I put an athlete in front of a camera he'll never come on like a stiff in a locker room holding a package and mouthing a phony pitch.

Instead I had America's heroes *crying*. Through their tears, they all bawled, *"I want my Maypo."*

I started with America's classic hero, Mickey Mantle. He was tough to sign up unless you had a bundle to shell out. But his old Yankee roommate, Whitey Ford, had done a TV commercial for me at PKL on Puss 'n Boots cat food. Ford, whose nickname while he was on the mound pitching for the Yankees was "Chairman of the Board," spoke to Mantle and the tears flowed.

It was a gigantic put-on that kids would understand. (Kids are smarter than people.) As soon as the great Mickey Mantle was willing to cry for Maypo on TV we lined up Wilt Chamberlain, Oscar Robertson, Carl Yastrzemski, Johnny Unitas, Ray Nitschke, Don Meredith and Tom Seaver. They all bawled in front of the cameras in their uniforms, helped by a few glycerine tears from our makeup lady.

"*I want my Maypo*," bawled America's superstars. But most adults never saw the campaign because it was pitched at their small fry. Don Meredith showed up for a game with the Dallas Cowboys and was ambushed by a bunch of kids, all bawling, "I want my Maypo." His teammates were very confused. It was a put-on of the Maypo put-on that became a strangely successful campaign for a tough product. Sales went up about 10 percent because the kids understood. Their mothers didn't know Nitschke from Unitas, but they bought Maypo. All the athletes were happy to cry for Maypo—except one.

"Willie's fans don't want to see Willie cry," said the great Willie Mays. He was one of the last stars we signed up.

"You're kidding," I said. "I spoke to your man and told him the whole deal." I showed Mays the footage of all the others crying—Mickey, Wilt the Stilt, the Big O, Yaz, Johnny U.—but Willie Mays said, "Willie don't cry," always referring to himself as Willie. "I can *smile* and say, 'I want my Maypo,' but Willie don't cry."

I kept swinging and finally squirted the glycerine tears on Willie's smile. We finally got the footage, but I'd never nominate Willie Mays for town crier. Three years later Willie subbed as emcee for Dick Cavett one night. His guest was Leo Durocher, Mays' first manager when the rookie from Alabama joined the New York Giants. Durocher interrupted Mays at one point to tell a personal story about the Alabama rookie's disastrous first days with the Giants. Willie went hitless during his first twenty-four times at bat. His twenty-third and twenty-fourth zeros took place in a game with the Boston Braves. Here's how Durocher recalled what followed after that game (from the "Dick Cavett Show," December 3, 1971):

DUROCHER: We were beaten one to nothin'. And, as most managers do, you get a little upset and I came in the clubhouse and I kicked one shoe off and I was about to take the other shoe off and I was mad at everybody, and especially at Willie not gettin' the ball out of the infield or drivin' in a run for me, and Freddie [Fitzsimmons, the Giants' coach] said, "You better go down and talk to your boy." And I said, "What's wrong with him?" And he said, "He's sitting in front of his locker and he's crying." I know you remember this.

MAYS: I remember very well. You're telling the story, you go ahead on.

DUROCHER: And I walked down and I sat next to him. I put my arm around him, I said, "What's the matter, son?" And in those days Willie talked in a high tenor voice like a young girl would. I could never imitate it. But he never called me Leo or Mr. Durocher. He always called me "Missuh." "Missuh Leo . . ." [Laughter] "Missuh Leo," he said, "it's too fast for me. I can't play here." And the tears were streaming down his face. "I can't play here. It's too fast for me. They're gonna send me back to Minneapolis." And I put my arm around him and I said, "Willie, just go home now and get a good night's sleep," I said, "because as long as I'm here, you're my center fielder and you'll be there tomorrow and as long as you can walk you will go to center field." And the next day he came out against Warren Spahn and he hit that ball right on over the roof of the old Polo Grounds, it never touched anything, and from then on, believe me, ladies and gentlemen, he carried the then New York Giants right here right on his back right to the pennant in '51. [Applause]

When I saw that show *I* felt like crying.

Two years back, *Sports Illustrated* asked me to comment on the proper use of athletes in commercials. What I said then still holds: "There are only certain circumstances when an athlete is applicable. The ad must transcend the fact that you are using an athlete. You just don't say, hey, let's get a ballplayer for this. There must be a legitimate reason. You use an athlete only when it is apt to do so or, on the other side of the coin, in never-never land, when it is so ridiculous to use an athlete that it's a good bit for everybody.

That's what we did for Braniff when we used Sonny Liston listening to Andy Warhol talk about painting and Salvador Dali discussing 'baizboll' with Whitey Ford. The horrible thing is to catch the athlete between these extremes, when he is neither being himself nor putting the world on. No commercial in recent years, for instance, was more pathetic and artificial than a Brylcreem spot with Joe DiMaggio. There was Joe, all alone in that corny locker room talking with deadly seriousness about this hair thing, and you cringed with embarrassment. All you thought of was: How can poor Joe be that bad off? He must really need the money to do that."

While at PKL we had a client that made yogurt. They referred to their product as the yogurt that had more "cultures" in it. We turned it into "the more *cultured* yogurt." We chose the last guy in the world to sell a "cultured" product on television. Rocky Graziano wore a tux, but he spoke like Rocky Graziano should: "Goils, dis is Rocky Graziano tellin' ya how to keep in shape. Ya wanna develop a good left jab? Ya wanna have a good firm gut? Den ya gotta eat what I eat—Breakstone's Yogurt. Da more *cultured* yogurt." A perfect example of never-never land—like the crying heroes of Maypo.

Mickey Mantle cried for the kids, but he was pure Mantle for adults in a TV spot for Edwards & Hanly. Mickey just looked straight at the camera and said, "When I first came up to the big leagues, I was a grinnin', shufflin', head-duckin' country boy. Well, I'm still a country boy, but I know a man down at Edwards & Hanly. I'm learnin'. I'm learnin'.'"

I met Mantle on Maypo and Namath on Braniff.

I first met Joe Willie Namath after a shouting match with his red-headed Bronx Irish lawyer, Jim Walsh. I wanted Namath for Braniff's "flaunt it" commercial. I told Harding Lawrence I would try to get Joe Namath, the superstar of them all in 1969. Harding said, "You probably won't be able to get him, but if you can't I'll try." Harding Lawrence didn't understand that I had a certain way with Bronx Irishmen. On the day of the Braniff shoot, Walsh arrived with his Pennsylvania Hungarian. Sugar Ray was there, also Miss Universe, Tab Hunter, Leonard Lyons, Gina Lollobrigida, Mickey Rooney, Emilio Pucci, and Paul Ford (my upstairs neighbor).

At most shoots, the ho-hum film crews look at celebrities like any stiffs in the street. But the grips and gaffers swarmed over Joe Willie, begging for his autograph. "For my kid," they all said. He signed them all. I've worked with charisma types as electrifying as Bobbie Kennedy, but Joe Willie had it over all of them. "Joe Namath, Joe *Namath*," cooed Lollobrigida, "oooh, he's so *hondsummm.*"

He was also always his own man, and I loved him for that. He let his hair grow long and infuriated the front-office wheels of pro football. He wore white shoes on the field and grew a Fu Manchu mustache. He was cocky because he knew he had it and he wasn't afraid to flaunt it, but he was never a put-down artist. Neither was he a muscle-headed jock. When Joe Namath visited my apartment he was fascinated by my tribal sculpture and Oceanic art. As I explained each piece he soaked up every word.

He loved my Uli.

He was a gentle anti-hero, but tough. When we horsed around at shoots and I threatened to belt him in the mouth, he grabbed a bottle by its neck and held it like a guy who knew how to use it.

Joe Willie asked me to go with him to a taping for one of his first Johnny Carson shows. The kid from the steel mill country of Pennsylvania raised questions about the Vietnam war—not the sort of thing ballplayers were supposed to think about, especially then. And he never apologized for the life he led. "Athletes don't have to bullshit kids and say they drink only milk," he once mentioned to me. "I love kids but I live my life."

Ron was working with Joe Willie on a TV spot one afternoon. While waiting for the camera crew to get set up, Namath tossed an empty beer can across the long studio and it landed plunk in the middle of a garbage can. "Joe that's *very* good," said Ron. Joe Willie looked at Ron with his dreamy, cunning eyes and said, "That *is* my job, you know."

We added a kid's drink as a new client in 1971 when Dave Mc-Clain, a marketing hotshot at Alka-Seltzer, went to Ovaltine. I chose Joe Willie to describe the product on TV as "My o-o-o-old pal Ovaltine"—worlds apart from "straight" testimonials in a locker room. During the filming of this series Namath was asked by NBC's Dick Schaap, "Do you think it's going to hurt your image?" Joe Willie answered that one better than any ghost could have scripted for him: "Well as long as I drink it in the right places I don't think it will hurt my image too much. Looks kind of stupid going to Bachelors III and asking for it, so I don't think I'll go in there and ask for it." Everyone *knows* that Namath likes his booze; to show him talking about Ovaltine's nutritional value for kids makes the whole campaign *exciting*. By comparison, if Mickey Mantle were to speak about *his* old pal Ovaltine, the campaign would lose its edge. While he's an ace in front of a camera, his image is too wholesome to make Ovaltine stand out from TV's heavy load of advertising—and in 1971 no less than 42,000 commercials were produced for American television. The Ovaltine spots with Joe were an immediate success.

With some of the profits from sizzling LHC in 1968 we teamed up with Mickey and Joe Willie in an employment agency subsidiary, Mantle Men & Namath Girls. We opened three offices in Manhattan and quickly became one of the largest employment agencies in the New York area. In an industry that used only classified ads, we went on television. The stars of our commercials were Mickey and Joe—who else? At a shoot for Mantle-Namath, the Jet superstar mentioned casually, "I can type thirty words a minute." I put Joe Namath at the typewriter with Mickey leaning over his shoulder. They were great on camera, but off camera they were a peril; when I walked in Manhattan's streets with America's hero and anti-hero, my life was in danger.

After a shoot one day we stopped at the corner of Fifty-seventh and Fifth. A limo was due there to pick up Joe Willie. A passing secretary asked for his autograph. As he started to write his name a crowd suddenly swarmed over Namath and Mantle. It grew so big and unruly so fast that the window of the Manufacturers Hanover Bank on the corner began to buckle. A bank guard opened the door and we hustled Joe and Mickey out through the basement.

When we opened our third Mantle-Namath employment office in the Wall Street area, Callaway estimated that about six thousand people mobbed the area to see Mickey and Joe. Jim and Ron cut a path through the crowd after the ribbon-cutting and shoved our athletes into a cab. "As soon as they took off," said Jim, "Ron and I walked down the street and everyone was gone. Like *that*, we lost all our fame."

I love to be with ballplayers and I love to work with them.

They're the most honest professionals in the world. No trickery can help a ballplayer. It's what he does that counts. Period. Everything is down in black and white. He hits or he doesn't, he fields it or he boots it, he gets them out or he gets drilled, he scores or he misses. Their honesty as people is strengthened by the pressure of having to produce. They can't hide a thing.

I'm in awe of any man who can keep producing under the eyes of the world for ten or fifteen years. When he becomes a legend, like Mantle, there's a truth to the legend and usually a decency in the man. Mickey was a conservative southwesterner with a fine clarity about himself—and about others in his profession. "Why did you retire?" asked Ron. "Shit, it was like those kids on the mound were ten feet from me," said Mickey, "and when they pitched, their arms went right down my throat. I couldn't *see* the ball, I couldn't *hit* the ball, and I'm not gonna stand up there and be embarrassed." He once told me, "George, when I was sixteen I was the best ballplayer who ever lived, and it scared me." Then he stopped for a moment and drawled softly, "But you take a guy like Hank Aaron—he's twice as good as I *ever* was."

He understood the pressures that went with the role of America's hero. During a meeting at my office one evening he looked at his watch and ran for the elevator. He was booked on a flight to Dallas, where he lived, and time was running short. He was anxious to get home after having been away for a couple of weeks. His suitcase was in the checkroom at the nearby Hotel Pierre. We still had a few things to resolve. I ran after him, gabbing as we walked to the Pierre. At the checkroom, he peeled off a $100 bill for the hat-check lady, a woman in her fifties. She gave him back the hundred and handed him a blank sheet of paper and a pen. "Please, Mr. Mantle," she said, "I don't want the money, but if I could have your autograph for my son that would be wonderful." Mickey would much sooner part with a hundred than sign an autograph, but when she said her boy was a ballplayer, he asked her for the kid's name and wrote a long lovely note. She looked at Mickey's message and kissed America's superstar.

Now *I* was watching the clock. I grabbed his suitcase and hustled him into the revolving door. I shoved it hard and squeezed in behind him with the suitcase. When I got outside he was gone. I looked around to see if he was spun back into the lobby. But he was nowhere. Then I saw him. He was lying in the Fifth Avenue gutter, his cheek on the sidewalk, scraped and bleeding. I had pushed the revolving door too hard—he tripped on the way out and went into a dive, landing on his puss. "Holy shit, Mickey," I said leaning over him, "are you hurt?" He glared up at me and said, "Fahn place to be for America's *heero*."

Suddenly he bounded up from the gutter, wiped his face and grinned at me like a head-duckin' country boy who one-upped a city slicker. He had a very slight bruise. I hadn't hurt America's hero. *Heero*.

I'm learnin'. I'm learnin'.

21 Keep the big boys honest

Maggie. 1968.

He was Lois Holland Callaway's first political client. He was a sure loser.

Republicans in the state of Washington were licking their chops that summer. After twenty-four years Senator Warren G. Magnuson was a cooked goose. The polls gave him only 51 percent of the vote before the Republicans even chose their candidate—a terrible showing for an incumbent. Magnuson's fate was sealed and certified. The cards were stacked against him, particularly by the press back home. They said he was old and fat. They more than implied that he was stupid. They laughed at his baggy clothes. And they called him Maggie.

He came from a state with shifting blocs of transient voters. Companies like Boeing attracted new workers, many of them young. They were unfamiliar with his voting record and his accomplishments in the Senate, but these new voters were quick to learn that Senator Magnuson was an old, fat, stupid bumbler in a baggy suit. And wherever they turned, his name came up as *Maggie*—very undignified for a senator. He saw the handwriting on the wall. It was more like political graffiti. The odds seemed too much and the senator had just about tossed in the sponge. He was on the phone with Lyndon Johnson to line up a new job after young, trim Jack Metcalf—the sure favorite for the Republican nomination—would take away his Senate seat in November.

The senator's assistant, Gerry Grinstein, asked us to take on the advertising for Magnuson's "reelection" campaign. Nothing tests your creativity more than a sure loser for a client. But you must have belief in the candidate. Magnuson's voting record was one of the most liberal in the Senate. He hardly deserved to lose. He voted for Medicare and for the Test Ban Treaty. And he was an early fighter for consumer protection laws. All the issues were clearly in his favor. The Republicans had *no* issues. Instead they tried to portray him as the fool. As we sized up the senator's "predicament" we knew that our client was no cooked goose. Quite the reverse: the Republicans were sitting ducks.

When we presented our campaign to Senator Magnuson in a hotel room in Washington, D.C., he looked a trifle crotchety—in a sweet way. And he showed signs of wear. He sighed like a man who was resigned to defeat. He was totally silent as we outlined our strategy:

We took the name Maggie and used it boldly, as the endearing name that it was. We seized every rap they threw at him and tossed it back—with class. Baggy suits? Fat? Old? Trim, thin Ron Holland phrased it this way:

In his rumpled suit, carrying 20 extra pounds, and showing *some* signs of wear, Warren Magnuson remains a *giant* in the United States Senate.

We showed Magnuson facing the camera with a forlorn expression as a voice says, "Senator Magnuson, there comes a time when every young senator shows that he's putting on years . . ." Silent Maggie's hands jut out as if to say, "What can I do about it?" The announcer's voice continues: "Senator Magnuson, there comes a time—sure as fate—when slim senators assume a more 'impressive stature' . . ." The polite reference to his overweight destroys Maggie—(but so far in his Washington hotel room, the senator hasn't betrayed any emotion)—and he ruefully glances at his belly, very frustrated. The voice resumes: "So once youth is gone, once dash is gone, *what* can you offer the voters of Washington?" Maggie kind of reels back a bit at the question, then he regains his poise, looks straight at the camera and taps his head—once, twice, three times. The voice then ends the spot by saying:

"Let's keep Maggie in the Senate."

Ad campaigns don't win elections by being clever. We were turning the personal attacks against Magnuson into assets. These were the Republicans' only "issues." And they deserved to be deflated with our strongest weapons—truth and wit. *Then* we drove home the full story of Maggie's laws to protect consumers. This inspired the theme of our campaign:

Keep the big boys honest.

Let's keep Maggie in the Senate.

Not a word was heard from Maggie as we went through all the ads—not even when I showed him one that said "Senator Magnuson is a crackpot. He thinks kids' clothes should be fireproof. So he wrote a law that got rid of flammable materials and made manufacturers test each garment." He just listened. Slowly, a glint of hope sparkled in his eyes. We pulled out an ad with a testimonial from Teddy Kennedy. Maggie's face perked up sharply as he heard these words in Ron Holland's New England twang:

When I came to the United States Senate some six years ago,
I looked to one man for real leadership in that body . . . a
man of great power in that body . . . a man who uses this
power compassionately, humanely, and for the interest of
the people, not only of this state, but of the nation. I hope
you send him back to the United States Senate where he
belongs. That man is your own senator, right here from
your great state of Washington—the great . . . Warren
. . . G. . . . Magnuson!

The quiet senator suddenly leaned forward and said, "I like *that* one."

Our entire approach came as a shock to Maggie. But his young aides were fully fired up. They saw at once that our campaign could change people's minds about baggy Maggie by talking directly about his "faults." Maggie gradually warmed to the campaign, but he was still reeling from being assured that people *will* love you, Senator, because your record is remarkable—also because you're fat and old and because your name is Maggie.

After the commercials were shot, Maggie's wife dropped by the agency. I happened to be away from the office on a business trip that day. She scooped up all the rushes from our TV producer, who thought it was okay to let her have them—it's not an everyday event when a senator's wife barges into an ad agency. She hauled them over to CBS for Dr. Frank Stanton's opinion before we went ahead with the campaign. After seeing the rushes, Sttanton told Maggie that if *he* were running for the Senate he wouldn't approve that kind of advertising. But Maggie said to Stanton, "Well, Frank, I'll tell you. These young fellows really seem to know what they're doing. I think it's a new day and a new age. And I think I'm going to let them do what they want to do." I knew then that Maggie realized in his heart he could actually win.

We were also unorthodox in our timing. While we were readying our campaign the Republicans in the state of Washington were dominating the news with their upcoming primary. Since Maggie was a sure loser, it was like a pre-victory wingding for the Republicans and they whooped it up big. Jack Metcalf was expected to win the nomination by a huge plurality in a high-turnout primary. His big win would wow the fat cats, then he would hit tottering Maggie with the devastating clout of a bulging war chest. Our client's lousy showing in the early polls sunk further as the media blared about the upcoming primary and crowed about Metcalf while deriding "Maggie."

Most political advertising starts well after the primaries—not until late September or October. But we opened up with a blitz in August, three weeks *before* the Republican primary. We ran our ads and TV spots about *Maggie* and his rumpled suits. We hit the Republicans' "issues" head on, suddenly diverting attention from their primary race. They ended up with a very small turnout. As expected, Metcalf won, but as he never expected, he ended up with a half-empty war chest. His big contributors held back, not quite sure any more that they were backing a winner.

When the election campaign got underway it was a new ball game, a contest between endearing Maggie with a proud record versus no-issue Metcalf with no money. And Metcalf was no longer so eager to call Maggie old and fat, compared to his young, trim look. Then we came on strong with "Keep the big boys honest." After that, Metcalf never had a chance. Maggie won with a staggering 65 percent of the vote, the fourth highest plurality of thirty-two Senate races that year. But back in August of 1968 if anyone had said that Warren Magnuson would be reelected in November by two thirds of the votes, he would have been considered insane. All we did was tell the truth—the whole truth.

Two years later three Democrats named Lois, Holland and Callaway were invited to work for the Republican Senator Hugh Scott of Pennsylvania. We always went out of our way to let people know we were Democrats, and we never found out why in the world his staff contacted us. But our miracle for Maggie was no secret in the Senate Office Building. Scott was also no great favorite with the White House, having voted against the Haynsworth Supreme Court nomination while minority leader of Nixon's party. When we first met with Senator Scott in Washington, one of Nixon's staff was there. It was perfectly clear that *he* sure didn't like the idea of three Democrats helping the independent Republican senator.

"All right, boys," Scott asked at once, "what's the most important thing you're going to do for me?"

Callaway shot back, "The first thing we're going to do is make you *famous*." The room went into an uproar.

"You don't seem to understand, Mr. Callaway," said the man from Nixon's staff. "Senator Scott's name is a household word."

But Jim told it like it was: "Well I read a poll that says Senator Scott has only 55 percent recognition among Pennsylvania households after *thirty-two years* in the House and Senate, so I don't think that's the case at all."

Ron turned to Scott and asked, "Senator, do *you* think you're famous?

Scott smiled like a lovable Gene Hersholt, chugged on his pipe, and said, "Well I believe my name is a household word among the more *intelligent* households."

He was probably right. Hugh Scott was the most intelligent politician I ever worked for. He was an intellectual who collected Chinese art and had authored a first-rate book on that very complex subject. He was also a Gene Hersholt who worked with six Presidents, a great mix of fatherly warmth and national stature. We caught those qualities through a series of TV spots showing him talking to a twelve-year-old boy—like Gene Hersholt with the younger generation. I took a film crew into his Senate office, where he had a knockout grouping of photos with Franklin Roosevelt, Harry Truman, Dwight Eisenhower, John Kennedy, Lyndon Johnson and Richard Nixon. He pointed to those historic faces at the end of one commercial and told the boy, "I've worked with six different Presidents . . . all great men . . . and I got things done with all of them. C'mon Billie, I'll buy you a Coke."

"C'mon, Senator, I'll buy you a Coke," became a greeting to Scott on Capitol Hill after that campaign. We also called him "The Most Powerful Senator Pennsylvania Ever Had." That line plus the "C'mon Billie" approach showed Hugh Scott for what he was: a powerful senator with the heart of Gene Hersholt.

He was superb at shoots, always his open, honest self. And it came through on the screen. But before the commercials ran, another staff man from the White House came by to check them out. Having had my fill of Nixon's grim honchos, I was prepared for a rough going-over. When he opened his mouth I jumped in with both feet. The senator puffed on his Hersholt pipe and made it perfectly clear that *he* liked the campaign because it showed him as he was. Scott came across as "The Most Powerful Senator Pennsylvania Ever Had" who cared about the America he was shaping for the new generation. And he was always a joy to be with.

"Tell me some inside stuff, Senator," Ron asked him at lunch.

"Oh no, I couldn't do that," he said.

"Oh c'mon," said Ron. "Tell me your frank opinion about *something*—and I'll buy you a Coke."

"Well I will say this: my idea about nothing happening to nothing would be Martha Mitchell calling up George Murphy."

But I knew that after the voting he would be no different from all the other politicians I've worked with. Instantly, we would be three forgotten men. Politicians listen to you down to the wire, but once elected they forget you fast. When it's all over they can't let themselves believe that admen helped elect them. On election night, Jim, Ron and I voted straight Democratic tickets in New York, then we caught a plane for Philadelphia to watch the returns with our Republican client. Bob Maxwell, an ex-Peace Corps kid at our agency who worked as coordinator on the campaign, came with us. I made a point of preparing him for the cold towel. "Don't be shocked or disappointed," I told Maxwell in the cab to Scott's hotel, "if you get ignored tonight. That's the way it is with politicians. So just watch what's happening and don't expect a pat on the back if Scott wins." We expected our man to win, but in the race for governor the Democrat Milton Shapp was expected to pile up an enormous margin. We were afraid this might drain away enough votes to hurt Scott and possibly defeat him. To maintain his strength in the Senate he needed a clear win—by at least 100,000 votes. A smaller plurality would make the minority leader vulnerable to his conservative opponents. (There was talk of his being replaced by Senator Roman Hruska of Nebraska, who defended Nixon's Supreme Court nomination of Harold Carswell because he approved of Carswell's *mediocrity!*)

The hotel ballroom was packed with Scott's staff and campaign workers. They cheered wildly when returns from around the country showed a Republican winning—while Lois, Holland and Callaway winced. When a Democrat was ahead, Lois, Holland and Callaway cheered. The crowd wondered what was going on with these three Trojan horses.

At about eleven o'clock it was obvious that Scott had won, so I rounded up our group to return home. We were walking down the hall as the senator came out of his room, surrounded by reporters. He saw us through the crowd and shouted, "Hold it, hold it," waving his hand. He came toward us, put his arms around us and said to the crowd, "I want you to meet the boys who did it for me. These are my advertising men." He introduced us as I glanced at Maxwell. That had never happened to me before, and he dragged us back to the ballroom for the whole victory shebang. A few minutes later Senator Scott was staring into TV cameras from every major network. Midway through his victory speech he said, "And I couldn't have won without the help of the advertising that was prepared by that good firm of Lois, Dopsey, and Callaway."

Holland was stunned. "C'mon Dopsey, I'll buy you a Coke," said Callaway.

Milton Shapp was elected governor by 900,000 votes, the biggest margin since 1946. Hugh Scott won by 220,000 votes against Democrat William Sesler, a turnaround of more than a million votes.

After the election I received a framed photo from "The Most Powerful Senator Pennsylvania Ever Had." It was inscribed:

Genius! Thanks for 6 years of cake and
ale—and work. The M.P.S.Pa.E.H.

A year before we helped Scott win, we helped Howell lose, but Howell was so happy with our work that he hired us again. The second time we helped him win.

In 1969 Henry Howell, a maverick state senator in Virginia, was attacking the utilities and insurance companies in a series of populist speeches. He promised to "keep the big boys honest." He had heard the line from our campaign for Maggie and liked the ring of it. He borrowed it, used it—and came to New York to find Maggie's ad agency. He wanted to run in Virginia's Democratic primary for governor.

When Henry Howell and his staff came to LHC it was love at first sight. (Any politician who can borrow one of our best themes is obviously a man of fine judgment.) Howell was out to make the big boys honest. He didn't care how much heat he put on the powerful, as he demonstrated during our strategy dinner at the Four Seasons. We sat on the balcony in the club room. During our discussion Henry got so carried away he accidentally knocked a squat candleholder off the table. It landed on someone having dinner directly below our balcony table. We heard a deep, familiar cowboy voice bellow up, "Anyone up there want to say you're sorry?" We peeked down and saw Lorne Greene of "Bonanza" staring up. He looked ferocious. But Henry Howell had a fearless staff. The littlest guy on his team leaned over and said, "*I'm* sorry."

Henry Howell was the little guy of Virginia. He was determined to make the big boys honest by running for governor. But he was hampered by an awareness factor of only 6 percent when he entered the primary against two well-known politicians, William Battle and Lieutenant Governor Fred Pollard. Pollard was backed by the Byrd machine, but after we went to work for Henry Howell the three-way primary knocked out Pollard, a poor third. In a runoff with Battle our man lost, but he got 48 percent of the vote—incredible in view of his original 6 percent awareness. He was also bucking the entire Democratic organization. After that he was a power in Virginia politics. His populist coalition was so sold on Howell that in the general election many of them voted against the man who narrowly beat him in the runoff. As a result, William Battle lost to Linwood Holton, who became the first Republican governor in nearly a century. The switchaway by labor, blacks, rednecks, intellectuals and Wallaceites, who wanted the maverick Howell, elected Holton.

In 1971 the lieutenant governor died in office. Henry Howell made a run for that job. By this time he had an awareness factor of 88 percent in the state and the big boys were scared, so instead of a regular primary the Democrats nominated their candidate in a convention—which Howell, the populist maverick, couldn't possibly win. He ran as an independent, belting home the Maggie theme. As an example of how straight talk by an old Good Humor man can change the politics of Virginia, imagine that you're watching this TV spot in Newport News: "Eleven million bucks in school money disappeared every year until Henry Howell started sniffing around," says the announcer. Then Henry Howell comes on: "Where millions of dollars in tax money . . . education money . . . your children's money . . . is involved, I'll promise I'll watch it, and make sure it goes where it's supposed to go. Every last penny. *There's a lot of things that go around in the dark besides Santa Claus.*"

Henry Howell won the election in a three-man race with 40 percent of the vote and became Virginia's lieutenant governor. Now he's got the big boys more scared than ever. If he runs for governor in 1973 he's going to be a tough man to beat. He's already got Santa Claus working for him.

And nobody frightens Howell—not even Clyde. Henry had sponsored and pushed through a bill to legalize the serving of mixed drinks in Virginia. On the very night the bill went into effect, we went with Henry to a bar in Williamsburg. At precisely six o'clock the first drink could be served, but my Irish partners jumped the gun by sixty seconds. At 5:59 the micks from Missouri and Rhode Island bought the first mixed drinks in the history of Virginia. There was a festive air in the bar, and a few of the local customers got slightly looped. One neighborhood character was a three-hundred-pound tough, a Man Mountain Dean known as Clyde. He obviously hated Henry Howell and his politics. He needled Callaway about his longish hair, reaching over and tugging at it with his meaty hams. There were reporters present and Jim kept his cool, but Clyde kept tugging at his hair while loudly damning Howell and his "long-haired, Noo Yawk, Jew fag hippie yippies." While Clyde carried on, Jim shied away, desperately trying to avoid a brawl with a drunk in a bar attended by Henry Howell right after he put through the mixed-drink bill—especially with all those reporters around. Henry told Clyde to cut it out. Jim moved to the far end of the bar, but big Clyde got nastier than ever. Henry Howell—five feet nine, 160 pounds—warned Clyde again not to mess with his friends, and Clyde hauled back to take a swing at Henry. I jumped between them and got slightly dented by Clyde's enormous elbow, but I managed to wrap my arms around this huge, swinging drunk while calling over his shoulder, "Jim, *Jim!*"—I needed someone to grab him from the rear. Jim rushed over and put a Big Eight bear hug around Clyde. We finally had him sandwiched, and we hustled him out of the room in the most inconspicuous way, a tricky maneuver in view of his astounding size. But I was glad I jumped in—mostly to rescue Clyde from *Henry*. I then spent twenty minutes convincing the reporters that nothing happened. But boy, was I proud of our client!

At his 1971 victory celebration, Henry Howell introduced us as the advertising men who helped him win. Jim gave a short speech:

"This is only the beginning. In 1973 Henry Howell is going to be governor." The place burst into loud cheers. "And in 1976," Jim continued, "Henry Howell is going to be President." The cheers buckled the walls. Ron grabbed the mike and quieted the crowd. "Then," he added, "we're going to make him *Pope*."

Political advertising in the years ahead will have tighter rules—limiting the amount of money candidates can spend. Fine. But some people will always believe that political advertising is somehow un-American. I *do* know it's absolutely dishonest to compromise your beliefs for the sake of a new "account." I believed in Javits in '62, Bobby Kennedy in '64, Warren Magnuson in '68, Hugh Scott in '70. And I believe that Henry Howell understands the changes that must be made in America. They all won.

There will always be an advertising man ready to "package" a human being and fake out the public. But political advertising can be an art in its best sense when it conveys a truthful *"feeling"* about a candidate. And it can be done in ten seconds.

Telling the truth doesn't take long. It takes time to lie. "Selling" a candidate kills time—and conscience.

Javits, Kennedy, Magnuson, Scott, Howell: five honorable campaigns, five more reasons to be proud of my profession.

I was leaving the Four Seasons after a lunch with Ron Holland when I spotted Bernbach. The greatest advertising man of them all was having an animated conversation at a corner table with a renowned guest. This was one time I couldn't resist table-hopping. "Bill's on the board of the guy's research center," I said to Ron. "Let's go say hello. We'll always be able to say that we shook the hand of the great Jonas Salk." Ron didn't really know Bernbach and begged off. I ambled toward their table alone, with a ho-hum stroll, catching Bernbach's eye as he was gabbing furiously with Salk. His face broke into that warm, fatherly smile that was always so appealing about the man, ever since those first days at his agency way back in 1959 when I was the rookie art director who came to him with my ads for the Ear and the Matzoh.

He motioned for me to come quickly to his table, which I had every intention of doing, hoping he would introduce me fast so I could squeeze the hand of Jonas Salk and leave Bill to his distinguished guest. But the introduction took longer than I expected. Bill Bernbach described my work, my *ads*, to Jonas Salk. The minutes went by like hours—not that I expected Bill to describe the work of Jonas Salk to me. Salk listened *very* graciously, nodding his head and looking *very* impressed by Bernbach's praises of my advertising. Finally I cut Bill short and grabbed the hand of Jonas Salk. Then I took off with Ron, who was watching in disbelief from across the room.

It was awkward but touching. Bill Bernbach's respect for the art directors and writers who joined his crusade to revolutionize our industry had deepened over the years. Half a lifetime seemed to have gone by since my one incredible year at Doyle Dane Bernbach when I was twenty-eight. But Bill's pride in his creative descendants seemed richer than ever. His respect for artistry in our profession was profound—and his personal impact on the new generation of advertising men and women is still formidable.

Papert, Koenig, Lois was the first creative ad agency after Doyle Dane Bernbach. We were the first *red-hot* creative ad agency in the business, an important distinction. When Julian Koenig and I left the great Maestro in 1960 to team up with Fred Papert, we triggered a permanent breakaway from the establishment. After Ally the Turk left PKL in 1962 to start Carl Ally, Inc., a cluster of creative agencies sprang up. Many were started by the talented mavericks who were drawn to PKL. We proved that new ad agencies could be built on Bernbach's original model, and we created a small new world within our industry of some twenty new ad agencies plus isolated cells within a few of the giant shops, totaling perhaps a hundred creative nonconformists with common roots and a separate language from the oily mainstream of American advertising.

Among the Creative Hundred, competition has always been fierce. And it's probably true that among mavericks *and* establishment, the most loved ad agency is not Lois Holland Callaway. We might even be the most *hated* joint in the ad world—if jealousy can be measured. Our work is usually hard to avoid, which can pain anyone who vows to shut his eyes and ears to our ads. When the spectacular face of Joe Louis shows up on the tube, and he says in ten seconds, "Edwards & Hanly, where were you when I *needed* you?"—it connects. Our work is seen, it's written about in the trades and many admakers get miffed again when we cut through the smog. And it's quite a smog:

Forty-two thousand TV commercials were ground out during 1971, while the average adult American is said to be the target of at least a thousand advertising impressions every day in some way, shape or form—although he's largely *un*impressed. Most advertising is hot, stale, recycled air. Smog. Advertising in America flows from about 6000 ad agencies staffed by 75,000 people. Over $20 billion is spent annually in advertising. In that crowded field the odds are stacked against *any* ad agency scoring. Critics of advertising see it as a sinister influence on our personal values and an artificial prop of our economy. But some very reputable research has shown that over 80 percent of all advertising falls on deaf ears, on unseeing eyes and on bored minds. So before anyone knocks advertising for faking out the public by selling them on stuff they don't need, it should be borne in mind that most advertising is ignored because it's mostly *lousy*.

Of the small amount of advertising that works, much of it is due to heavy spending behind lightweight work—by an overkill of impressions. Big dough, small talent. There's no question that some highly successful corporations have moved their wares by sinking a fortune into shoddy ads. But there's a world of difference between the clout of impressions and the power of artistry. Yeah, *artistry*.

David Ogilvy needed less than $60,000 to make Hathaway Shirts a household name in 1951, a petty cash budget. Bill Bernbach needed less than a million bucks to sell Volkswagen in 1959, a poverty budget for any car advertiser. And LHC needed only $183,000 in 1967 to make Edwards & Hanly the third best known investment house in the New York area. "I warn you against believing that advertising is a science," said a famous innovator. "Artistry is what counts. The business is filled with great technicians, and unfortunately they talk the best game. They know all the rules. They are the scientists of advertising, but there's one little problem. Advertising happens to be an art, not a science."

Bill Bernbach said that in 1971, when the Creative Hundred was no longer an underground conspiracy of artists and writers against an establishment of management technicians. The zingy work of the Creative Hundred is no longer a freak sideshow off Madison

Avenue. Carl Ally made Volvo famous, Helmut Krone made Avis famous, Bob Gage made Dreyfus famous, Bill Taubin made El Al famous, PKL made Xerox famous—also Wolfschmidt, National Airlines, the *Herald Tribune* and those crazy Dilly Beans.

At my new agency I built an ad campaign for REA Express with the Lone Ranger theme ("Hi-Yo, REA! Awaaay!") and helped a failing old company back to health. A year after that campaign ran I was told by REA's president, Tom Kole, that when customers now complain about faulty deliveries (as they do with all companies) they often write angry letters telling REA to quit spending money on their TV ads and use the dough to speed up their service—convinced they've just seen REA's TV campaign. (No commercial had run for a year.)

And it's tough for any intelligent woman to tune out this kind of dialogue on television, from a campaign we've been running for another LHC client:

Voice-over:	Who's the greatest man in the twentieth century?
1st Young Mama:	I think Albert Einstein.
2nd Young Mama:	I think Albert Schweitzer.
3rd Young Mama:	I think Albert Foley! (He married me.)

This is from our "Young Mama" series, a campaign that appeals to motherly wit, and has helped *Redbook* prosper during a rough period for most magazines. We've also personalized the highly impersonal world of typewriters and business machines in an industry that has been dominated by IBM—by introducing the "Olivetti Girl." This campaign may well perform in the 1970s for Olivetti what our campaign at PKL in the 1960s achieved for Xerox. Carlo Alhadeff, the tenacious new president of Olivetti, is determined to make his worldwide brand a household name in the United States. His intuitive sense of breakthrough advertising is characteristic of that rare breed of corporate risk-takers who have accelerated the growth of their mammoth corporations by fearless, sprightly appeals to mass audiences. With the "Olivetti Girl" campaign we've brought feminine appeal to the industry's traditionally sterile, impersonal advertising. Our strategy for Olivetti, like our "Young Mama" campaign for *Redbook*, focuses on the American woman as a person of brains and wit.

Some of those 42,000 television spots try to sell cars. About $150 million a year is spent in local dealer advertising, but with rare exceptions I can't tell one car commercial from another. "Even my brother-in-law says they stink," I told Phil Dougherty in a 1969 roundup story he wrote on the opinions of advertising guys like me, without a car account in their shops. (Captain Ernie is usually right.) I was able to prove my point a year later. We took over the advertising for eighty-seven Pontiac dealers in New York and New Jersey. I invited all eighty-seven dealers to a shoot and created The Pontiac Choir Boys, singing their sales pitch. For example, to the tune of "My Bonnie Lies Over the Ocean" Pontiac's dealer choir belted out:

> *Last night you walked into my showroom*
> *We tried very hard to agree*
> *If you really want that new Pontiac*
> *Then bring back your money to me.*

Probably to a greater degree than most advertising, our work is seen, heard and remembered—certainly with a vengeance by my competitive colleagues, not excluding the Creative Hundred. Since they're more talented than the establishment majority, they're more jealous. Very understandable. A current example:

One of the creative shops that grew out of PKL is an outfit called David, Oksner & Mitchneck, headed by Bob David, formerly a management supervisor at my old agency. Bob is a very bright, tough, honest advertising professional. At lunch recently with Ron Holland he mentioned that some of his creative boys were laughing their guts off at one of *our* newest ads. According to Bob they were saying, "Look at that crazy shit. Lois doesn't know what the hell he's doing. . . ." Bob told Ron he remarked to his guys, "Well that may be so, but I can assure you that George Lois and Ron Holland are not sitting at *their* agency looking at one of *your* ads and laughing."

If the time ever comes when Madison Avenue stops saying, "Lois doesn't know what the hell he's doing," I'll know I've finally had it. In 1952 I was almost court-martialed for painting a white GI on a signal corps pole. In 1962 I was called an arrogant upstart when PKL became the first modern ad agency to go public. In 1972 I was called a nut for selling Ovaltine on television with America's anti-hero, Joe Namath. I've always been faced with a simple choice: be careful and go along or be free and go for broke.

But being free is a risky way to live. While I've had my triumphs, I also know how awful it feels to land head first—and I've made mistakes that were beauts. But I've buried the thought of them beyond recall. To see my work fail or falter has always been too painful to live with.

If I went along with the account executive at Doyle Dane and junked my matzoh poster, something inside me would have died.

If I went along with the bureaucracy that mushroomed at PKL after its early spontaneous years, something inside me would have exploded.

If I went along with the expected ways of advertising, something inside me would have suffocated.

Creative people feel these pressures every day of their lives, particularly in giant ad agencies. Young & Rubicam, for example, is one of the few monster-size agencies that has long been respected for its high creative standards. During the past few years Y&R's president, Steve Frankfurt (a gifted fellow alumnus of Music and Art, then Pratt), had directed a writer-artist nucleus of four top talents—writers Tony Isidore and Bob Elgort; art directors Marv Lefkowitz and Bob Wall. (Wall, coincidentally, was my old neighbor at Lennen & Newell during our getting-started days.) A top echelon shakeup at Y&R in 1971 led to the departure of Steve Frankfurt, who happens to be an art director. With Steve out of the picture, we asked this creative foursome to join Lois Holland Callaway. After the move was worked out, a trade newsletter wrote of our expanded agency: *"Like DDB of Old. Lois Holland Callaway will be the glamour agency of the seventies. The parallel is there."*

Tony Isidore, who did the memorable "Give a damn" TV campaign for the New York Urban Coalition, became LHC's new president. The florist's kid became, you'll pardon the expression, chairman of the board. When Phil Dougherty got the story—it was significant news in our industry, reflecting the growing clout of creative agencies—he said to me, "You're the most unlikely chairman of the board in the history of American business." (The Irish, the Irish—they're still out to get me.) We also brought in copywriter Rudy Fiala, who had worked at Doyle Dane with the big three art directors of my rookie days—Gage, Taubin and Krone.

Creative insiders in our business have said that Isidore and Lois in the same joint is the modern equivalent of Bernbach and Ogilvy in their primes under one roof. A gorgeous compliment. But it's tough to pair us off so the comparison makes sense. There's no doubt that I've got the same classy polish as the aristocratic, cultured David Ogilvy, you bet your sweet ass, may Meredith Hough be my witness. And while many suspect that Tony Isidore and Bill Bernbach buy their suits at Barney's, that's not the whole story. The comparison may be valid. Tony and I are mavericks. We made our careers in advertising without connections or family money. Bernbach had lived in plain old Brooklyn and Ogilvy sold stoves in Scotland, two outlanders who showed that great ads are not made on a golf course.

In 1971 I turned forty and became an old fart art director and a young fart statesman. My old buddy Joe Daly had by then become president of Doyle Dane Bernbach, with Bill Bernbach as board chairman. With a $270 million gone-public agency to mother, Joe Daly has to be even more respectable than me, which is going some. When our paths cross at the Seasons we greet each other courteously, like retired gunslingers. There's a toughness to Joe Daly that commands respect. Whenever we meet I can't help thinking of our 1959 shenanigans when I was a cocky punk at DDB, bristling for a showdown with this durable sonofabitch. Twelve years later, as we nod to each other, I know in my forty-year-old guts that tough, smart pros like Joe Daly add zest to the advertising life.

The first beautiful tyrant of my career, Bill Golden of CBS, died of a heart attack in 1959. Lennen & Newell, where I made my first mark in the ad agency world, filed for bankruptcy and folded in 1972. Herb Lubalin of Sudler & Hennessey now runs his own design studio. Massa Sam of Seagram died peacefully in 1971. Joe Baum left Restaurant Associates shortly after I started LHC and is now re-inventing the restaurant industry for the new World Trade Center; we still work for Restaurant Associates, the company he helped build with his genius. Julian retired from PKL, but Freddie is still active. When I left PKL in September 1967, my lovely den of Dilly Beans, "unbefouled by mannerism," had grown to a $40 million business. In March of 1972 the agency reported advertising billings of $6 million. Lois Holland Callaway is now billing $23 million.

I still do *Esquire*'s covers. And I'm still interested in politics. I'm working now with Bill Bradley of Princeton and the New York Knicks in whatever political activity he decides to pursue. When he runs for President in 1992, I expect to handle his campaign.

My fortieth birthday party back at our agency was a rounded moment. I was given a birthday cake in the shape of two large balls. I had come a long way from "greaseball." I was now known as "horseballs," a Greek in-joke about manliness and strength that the Irish have come to understand. The women in our office, including a Jewish bookkeeper, cut my cake. When she sliced my balls it was like Portnoy's mother turning the tables on Oedipus.

Also during 1971 I was elected president of the New York Art Directors Club. I'm now working with our five hundred members to push the art director beyond the drawing table—into social issues and art education. When I announced our plans, Phil Dougherty quoted me, accurately: "As a group they [art directors] care more than copywriters—they're more socially aware." The copywriters called a meeting of their club to strike back; better than watching them yawn.

Art will always be a core passion of my life, at work and at home. The same holds true for my wife. Rosie recently did a spectacular canvas showing the underside of a car. She worked on her sketches while standing in the grease pits of a Sixth Avenue gas station as cars were getting lubes. The painting was bought by Jim Judelson, president of Gulf & Western. He redesigned a stainless-steel office around Rosie's canvas (entitled *1966 Ford Chassis and Body*), and then placed it on his ceiling—the only way to look at the underside of a car.

On December 21, 1971, Ron Holland was one day short of his fortieth year. He threw a tremendous bash at Charley O's. "You are invited to the Last Good Day," he said in his invitation. "An era ends." There was an enormous turnout for Ron, what with his invitation offering "cocktails, hors d'oeuvres and midnight supper (in the style of the Middle Ages)." We gave the ancient copywriter a bicycle so he won't slow down. A famous advertising man sent Ron a copy of his book, *Confessions of an Advertising Man*, inscribed:

> To Ron Holland, a volcano erupting,
> from David Ogilvy, a volcano extinct.

Hardly extinct. David Ogilvy is still one of the world's best. He was always a bold and witty innovator. He sold a lot of Rolls Royces by talking up their *clocks*. He made Schweppes famous by bringing on a limey aristocrat with a beard. When PKL went public, David Ogilvy saw its validity while the establishment harrumphed. He referred accounts to PKL when many moguls on Madison Avenue thought we were jokers and jocks. Advertising needs more extinct volcanos like David Ogilvy. Ron answered Sir David in style:

> I'll be able to keep your inscribed copy
> in its pristine condition because I've
> already committed my old copy to memory.

Someday Callaway will reach thirty-five, when we'll put him on a new diet. As of this writing he's up to 240, but investing another small fortune to slim down the same huge Irishman could destroy the economics of our agency.

Since the days of St. John's parish I've led an exciting life because there's no business like the ad business. Its goal is to sell products by reaching people in a convincing way. The tougher the product the tougher the people behind it, pitting me against the most varied and exciting personalities of our age. And while my craft is an art director's, my best work has always flowed from the right words as much as from strong "visuals." Certainly Bill Bernbach was one of the men who made it possible.

Toward the end of 1971 I was having lunch at the Seasons with a talented art director, Aristides Kambanis, known as just plain Steve. Suddenly Steve grabbed my sleeve and said, "Look George, *look*—there's Bill Bernbach!" Bill had just come from a farewell luncheon for his partner Maxwell Dane, who was retiring. I waved to the Maestro and he came to our table, brimming with excitement —and with a certain sadness about this new milestone for his great agency. But his open enthusiasm again took me by surprise. As the years passed, the great Bernbach, now sixty, seemed to savor more and more his memories of those early years when we changed an industry.

And this time it suddenly struck me: now was the moment for a homage long overdue. With Aristides Kambanis as my Greek witness, plus all the other diners at the Four Seasons, I slid to the carpet on one knee and grasped Bernbach's hand. He was baffled, as well he should have been—especially when I said, "No, no, Bill, the *other* hand." I took Bernbach's other hand and finally kissed his ring.

I was on one knee, but only for Bernbach. I was in mid-career with new worlds to discover in the wonderful world of advertising.

"*Work . . . family . . . father . . . son,*" Haralampos, my father, still chants at Easter. Like my father, work has always come first in my life. And like my father, being Greek runs through everything I do, every ad I make, every breath I take.

But in my style, in my way.

The turning point, the time of discovery, occurred on a vacation. In Greece, wearing sneakers.

As we rumbled up the single-lane dirt road, we seemed to be hugging the rusty wall of mountain sod while keeping our distance, what there was of it, from the bottomless drop off the open side. We were moving toward the sky, piloted by a trained peasant driver, over a road that must have been carved out of the mountainside by one scoop of a small bulldozer. When passengers choked up at the incredible altitudes, the drivers pasted Greek newspapers against the car's side windows so they couldn't look out.

We were about a hundred miles west of Athens, heading toward my father's village, up the winding rocky road, higher and higher through the awesome Greek light until the trail came to an end at a small clearing with a ramshackle inn and a few decrepit houses. I spotted four Greek letters on the inn and my eyes popped. "That's our *name*," I shouted to my father. "It says LOES." Haralampos nodded, half listening. His eyes were searching for something beyond the inn, on the peak of a hill in the upper distance. Finally he found it. He grabbed my arm and pointed to a small house silhouetted on the mountain crest. "I was born there," said Papa.

"But what about this place—LOES?"

"It started here. Cousins . . . all cousins. Goes back to the Turks." During the centuries when the Turks occupied Greece they seized all the fertile flatlands. To escape their savage occupation, many Greeks left their houses and fled into the safe remoteness of the country's tough mountains. In the 1600s a few families named Loe (singular) scrambled up the mountain above the town of Nafpaktos on the northern rim of the Isthmus of Corinth. They settled in a clearing and named it Loes. After three hundred years there was still no road beyond Loes, where the bulldozer quit and the peasant drivers unloaded their passengers. Over the centuries, as other Greeks made their way up the mountain to escape the bloody Turks, they moved above Loes to even higher ground. This new sanctuary became the village of Kastania, Greek for chestnut.

The inn at Loes was by now just a lookout point, a link with a phone between civilization below and Kastania in the distance. Kastania was a village of forty families. There was no plumbing, no electricity, one telephone, a few stores, a one-room schoolhouse, a taverna and a Greek Orthodox church.

They phoned ahead from the inn at Loes to announce that *he* had arrived—and from house to house in Kastania the villagers shouted the news. Kastania was a long steep trek from Loes without a flat square inch along the trail. The village encircled a small valley that was nestled in the high mountain. Most of its forty families were direct descendants of the handful that fled the Turks in the seventeenth century and sunk roots in Loes. As a result of much intermarriage, many Kastanians looked like children of the same parents. But the inbreeding must have strengthened these mountain peasants. The most common cause of death was too much life—old age was usually the reason when a Kastanian gave up the ghost. And *slipping*.

As we climbed the treacherous trail to the birthplace of my father, a woman in her nineties came down to greet him. She was almost blind but her footing was firm as she clutched at her black shawl of mourning for the aging Kastanians who were dying off. Many of the remaining villagers were in their eighties and nineties and a few were more than a century old. She touched my father's face with her coarse, wrinkled fingers and whispered, "Hara-lampos? *Haralampos?*" She had nursed Papa's dying father during his last years when he was completely blind; Haralampos thought that she herself had died years ago. They embraced on the rocky trail. As this nearly blind peasant woman in her nineties kissed him, and as they both wept under the piercing sunlight of Greece, I could see that my father, Haralampos, was all the way home.

The last time Papa had seen Kastania was in 1951, when he returned to Greece with Vasilike after thirty years in New York. During that trip, while I was eloping with my Polish-American Rosie in the Baltimore Lutheran's home, Mama had her first stroke.

The visit I'm now describing occurred in 1965, fourteen years after that fateful year for our family. Papa had sold the store two years before and Mama was a permanent invalid. They had moved from Kingsbridge and were living with Ricky and Ernie. The new Greek owner of my father's store on 231st Street and Broadway was selling gladiolas to a new ethnic mix—still largely Irish plus black and Puerto Rican. The fumes of burning incense from the icons in our skinny corridor were by then probably buried in chili smells and the bite of soul food.

The trip to Kastania in 1965 was my first vacation while at PKL since we started the agency in 1960. My unhappiness at the agency was becoming a strain on me and a plague on my partners. In June, when the mountain region is usually sunlit without a speck of cloud to hold back the brilliant Greek light, I took my father and my wife to Kastania. I was in Greece at last, my first visit. A pilgrimage.

A year prior to our trip, Rosie completed a course in Athenian schoolgirl Greek at Berlitz. When we stepped off the 707 in Athens she was sporting a rich vocabulary and a highbrow accent. But the distance from Berlitz Athenian to the peasant village of Kastania is centuries long. Up the trail from Loes a childhood friend of Hara-lampos came scampering down; he was in no mood for embraces, swearing in a passionate rage. His donkey had just slipped off a cliff, a common accident among Kastania's mules and people. Hara-lampos' mother had fallen to her death by slipping down the mountainside when he was a young boy. (When surgery is needed to save a life in the remoteness of Kastania, a helicopter plucks the sick peasant off the mountain and flies down to the flatland, to a hospital in the city of Patras across the Isthmus.)

"*Haralampos? Haralampos?*" was all we heard in Kastania's square, a small open plaza in the valley below the ring of houses on the surrounding hills. The villagers were embracing their prominent son who had returned after fourteen years. The retired florist from Kingsbridge was a rich man to them. He had achieved wealth and status in the new world. Now he was home again—and he had brought along his little boy, still wearing sneakers, and his boy's wife. Some of the villagers seemed oddly fascinated by the wife of Haralampos' son before she popped a single word of Greek in her classy accent. Their interest in Rosie seemed hypnotic.

My father's house on the horizon was the highest above the village plaza, a clue to the prominence of Haralampos' father in Kastania. He had been their most prosperous citizen, with the largest herd of goats and the most land, the man of status in that poverty-ridden mountain village. The Kastanians regarded him as their leader, prophet and wise man. He was also their "doctor" because of his folk skills at healing with herbs and setting broken bones with twine and shaved branches—the skills that Haralampos retained so well among the Kingsbridge Irish.

Haralampos had been raised as a shepherd, tending the family's flock of mountain goats while playing a flute (the Greek *floghera*) among the cypress trees, dreaming of new horizons. His family grew grapes, bottled *retsina* from their harvest and distilled *ouzo* from its residue. They also built walls, an ancient mountain habit —there were always Turks who might come by, then the Nazis came close. Over the centuries, life on the mountain began and ended according to an unchanging pattern of primitive survival against the toughness of nature, butchery by Turks, the Nazi savagery—and between wars, against the boredom of their isolation. For restless young men like my father at fifteen or for visionaries like Spiridon, the boredom bred dreams.

I first heard of Spiridon Loues while reading an article on the Olympic Games before we left for Greece. That historic event had been revived in 1896 after fifteen hundred years. The words in that historical fragment leaped off the page:

> Suddenly a courier galloped into the stadium and up to the royal box where King George I of Greece was seated with the royal family and guests. Seven kilometers away Spiridon Loues had taken the lead. The word went quickly

through the great crowd and a wild cheer went up. . . .
The leading runner had been sighted. It was Spiridon
Loues. The other Greek runners had been gaining as the
stadium was approached. The crowd was in a frenzy of enthusiasm. Prince Constantine and Prince George of Greece
hastily left the royal box and stationed themselves at the
head of the stretch as Loues trotted into the stadium. The
little Greek shepherd from the hills ran to the finish line
with Prince Constantine on one side and Prince George,
6 feet 5 inches tall, on the other side. Thus royally escorted,
Spiridon made a glorious finish for Greece while the stadium and the hills around resounded with the cheers. . . .
Honors were heaped on the humble hero from the hills.
. . . These were things that Spiridon Loues, the visionary,
had not dreamed when he set out from the hills to run for
the honor and glory of Greece. But in a philosophical spirit,
he quietly accepted the honors and offers that were thrust
upon him.

I called Haralampos that night. "Hey Papa, listen—you got
somebody in your family named Spiridon Loues? The runner who
won the Olympic marathon? The first man in the world to win it
after fifteen hundred years?"

"Oh yes," said Haralampos. "Yes, yes. From Kastania. Let's see
—second, maybe third cousin. Like me, a shepherd. Played the
floghera—like me. How's business, George?"

We stayed for three days in my father's white stucco house, now
the dowry of his niece. We slept on feathered mattresses. The villagers prepared feasts for us, always careful to store away every
remaining food scrap. One of the women hauled water in wooden
kegs from a well in the valley. She strapped the heavy kegs across
her breasts and carried them up the steep hill to our white house.
For breakfast we were served hot goat's milk with a steaming
curdle. As the relatives darted back to the kitchen for sausage and
home-baked bread I inched toward the window and poured the
precious milk, which I couldn't drink or refuse, against a cypress
bark.

The village was without plumbing or privies. During the lovely
summers, when it rarely rained, and during the bitter winters, the
family toilet was Kastania's woods. But our visit was short and my

constipation was severe, so no plumbing was no problem. And you rarely ran into a stranger in the woods; anyone you met in the cypress grove was probably a relative. In Kastania it was all in the family.

My father's name was engraved on the schoolhouse marker. In 1920 it was built with the money he saved during his early years in Coney Island selling hot dogs, then as an apprentice florist. Now the wealthy Haralampos was back, loaded with riches—in envelopes. He brought envelopes of cash from every Kastanian's relative in New York; he also had his own envelopes for his relatives and kinfolk, a ritual of giving when a visitor from the new world comes home to the mountain. Much of Kastania's economy, like so many Greek villages, depends on these envelopes from America. Haralampos went from house to house, delivering the relatives' envelopes first, saving his for last. As he visited with the envelopes, he was losing himself in memories and tears. The man from the new world was in another world, in *his* world. He would never leave it no matter how many oceans he crossed.

In the evening we went to the village taverna, off limits to women. An exception was made for Rosie, but the villagers stared at her in an intense, curious way. There was more to their interest than the sight of a woman crashing the men's saloon. The zesty jabber of folk Greek filled the taverna while we all drank *ouzo*. Before long a ninety-six-year old villager came in and stared suspiciously at Rosie. He propped his cane against the table and joined the party. Unaware that she understood Greek, he turned to me and said, "I heard that you married a black woman."

I nodded to the old man. He leaned toward Rosie and punched her hard on the shoulder—a mean right if you're almost a century old and spent all those years in the Kastania hills. "She's not *black*," he said to me in Greek, chuckling. When I had married out of our faith and nationality fourteen years before, the word went across the ocean and the Isthmus and up the mountain from house to house until Rosemary Lewandowski had become the most famous American Negro among the natives of Kastania.

"How old is she?" the old man asked me. Before I could say she was old enough to lie about her age, she finally uncorked her classy Athenian dialect. "*Theka octo*," she said loud and clear, Greek for eighteen. It was worth a year's tuition at Berlitz to see those gorgeously shocked peasant faces in Kastania's taverna when my black wife gave it back to the boys with their *ouzo* in Athenian spades. During the rest of our stay the men in the village greeted her with a rap on the back and a hearty, "*Theka octo!*"

Kastania's cemetery sat behind the houses, up another hill. The village priest led us up a small cliff with "stairs" made of horizontal lumber strips, lodged like a ladder into the tough vertical sod and rocks. As Rosie climbed the cliff to visit the graves of Haralampos' family, the priest mentioned that the "ladder" was called *golo-vlepo* by the townsfolk. In Berlitz Greek that phrase may not come up until post-graduate studies, and Rosie made a mental note of it. But *I* sure knew *golo-vlepo* from my Kingsbridge around-the-house vocabulary. Standing among the headstones of my grandparents, I told Rosie in English, rocking on my heels as though I were chanting a prayer for the dead, "It means *I see your ass*. You gotta be careful with these Fellini priests, especially if they're Greek Orthodox."

By the last day of our visit the villagers were jumping out of their skins, waiting for the patient and thorough Haralampos to hand out *his* envelopes. He had planned to give each relative $25, an absolute fortune for primitive Kastania. Most of the envelopes he had delivered from Greeks in America were thin by comparison, mostly a few bucks, five at most. But the poverty and primitive ways of Kastania were so overwhelming that I persuaded Haralampos to put away his envelopes and give the village $4,000—then let them decide how to use it for the betterment of the full community. I put up the money, but as far as Kastania was concerned it was a gift from Haralampos, not from his big kid in sneakers. In the eyes of Papa's townfolk, I was benefiting from a successful father (and of course they were right). Haralampos had been looking forward eagerly to the ritual of distributing his envelopes, but he agreed to my suggestion. He called a meeting of all the men in Kastania on the last night of our visit. It was held in the taverna.

The *ouzo* flowed as he announced the donation instead of the usual envelopes. He asked that all present decide how the $4,000 should be spent. The two "officials" of the village were the priest and a bright young teacher. Prior to the meeting I had caucused with the teacher to line up support for a new road before the priest moved in with a pitch for church improvements. And sure enough —as soon as Haralampos mentioned the unholy sum of $4,000— the priest's Rasputin eyes popped. He snuggled up to my father and began to plump for a *new* church. I was about to pull my father aside and speak my piece, but I was distracted by an unfamiliar phrase that kept shooting out through the jabbering and shouting. The taverna was booming with the throaty sounds of peasant mountain Greek, laced with *ouzo*. "What's that?" I asked Rosie. "What's that goddam *apo hotirion* they're all getting so excited about?"

"Washroom," said Lewandowski Berlitz.

"You gotta be wrong, Rosie. They say *meros* for that—*the place*."

She reminded me that all over the johns in Athens there were signs marked *apo hotirion*. I had come a long way to learn the proper way to say *toilet*, but the priest was short-cutting the meeting by collaring Haralampos to say *church*. I leaned over to my father and told him in English, "If this guy thinks he's gonna get the dough for a new church when nobody here has a pot to piss in, I'm taking back the four grand and you can go back to the envelopes." My threat was unnecessary. Haralampos was devoutly religious, but he was also a very practical Greek. He pointed out to the priest—with respect for the cloth as he spoke, but with a tough sense of what four grand could do for Kastania—that in his opinion forty families without a toilet or a paved road hardly needed a second church. When Papa finished his speech, the priest went for the toilet. In fact, he went further: he proposed an enlarged schoolhouse that would include an *apo hotirion* plus a kitchen. The kids could eat at the school in winter instead of climbing the cold hills for lunch—and the village would have its first john. While he was pitching for the bigger schoolhouse, a gnarled-looking Greek in the taverna sidled up to the priest and goosed him with a dozen extra reasons for the *apo hotirion* and kitchen.

"Who's that man whispering to the priest?" I asked the teacher.

"The carpenter of Kastania."

"Listen—if they vote for the washroom-kitchen, who gets to build it?"

"The carpenter of Kastania."

At that point I told the teacher to start selling the road before someone suggested a bowling alley. The teacher took the floor and ticked off the benefits of a paved road: faster travel to the next town where medical care was available . . . profitable farming through easier transportation . . . the poverty of Kastania would be eased and the younger generation wouldn't run off to Rhodes and Athens . . . the Greek government would match the $4,000. It was one helluva *presentation*—and the road was now winning the crowd. But not completely.

Those $25 envelopes of Haralampos were still a lot more appealing to a bloc of villagers with unmarried daughters. They wanted the $25 for dowries or they might end up burdened for life with spinsters to support. They appealed to Papa and he almost seemed ready to forget my "modern idea." He was about ready to pull out his envelopes, but the teacher kept plugging away, and a vote was finally taken. The road won.

The next day we had planned to visit my mother's village of Perista by mule. I woke up early and announced to my wife, "Rosie, you won't believe this, but I think I'm going to live. I'm ready to go to the bathroom." Suddenly I heard a great clap of thunder and a ferocious downpour hit the mountain. I grabbed an umbrella and took off for the cypress grove.

But time was running out. With the rain coming down, the dirt roads would be washed out fast and we might be stranded in Kastania for months. Our driver was getting ready to take off fast. We had no choice but to leave with him. Our mule trip to Perista was now impossible, but before we left, a visitor from my mother's village came to see us in Kastania.

Cousin Katerin was the celebrated spinster of Perista. She refused to marry all the men who were brought to her. No man could ever measure up to her perfectionist standards. She was a proud, arrogant woman, known all over the mountain as the Spinster—and she didn't care who said it. Rosie gasped when she saw the thirty-four-year-old Katerin, exactly my age. She turned away to squelch a laugh. I couldn't see what was so goddam funny—Cousin Katerin was a remarkably handsome woman with a fine patrician nose and a very aristocratic manner.

"Quit laughing and say something sensational in your expensive

Berlitz Greek," I commanded my wife in English, "and don't embarrass me in front of my mother's *one* relative we'll meet in Greece or I'll call a meeting in the taverna and tell Polish jokes."

"I'm at a loss for words," she said, still in English, but smiling sweetly now at the magnificent Katerin. "Just look at her *incredible* face."

"I'm looking. It's spectacular. *She's* spectacular. Now start talking Greek, and I mean Park Avenue, Athenian Berlitz, Four Seasons, Nikos Kazantzakis *Greek!*"

I was working myself into a lather, but always smiling warmly at the noble Katerin. There was something I couldn't put my finger on that appealed to me deeply about this proud, fearless lady. Well finally, *finally*—in the most ballbusting Athenian ever heard on the mountain, Lewandowski Lois said, "It's such a great pleasure to meet you, dear Cousin Katerin, particularly since we shall not be able to visit Perista and will therefore miss the great joy of being with all our relatives of the Thanasoulis clan. But I shall never ever forget your face, dear Cousin Katerin, because from now on whenever I look at my beloved husband George, I will always think of you. The resemblance between you is truly astonishing."

They embraced nobly on the mountainside. Through our fourteen years together I never had one regret. Now I was positive beyond a doubt that my marriage to Lewandowski was as solid as the Greek rocks under our feet.

When we left Kastania in the rain, Haralampos Lois was the saddest man in Greece. He hated to leave and he was deeply disappointed by the rain—terrible luck. He seemed to be searching for a reason as we squeezed into the little car near the inn at Loes, where the road home began. As the villagers wept and waved, we started down the mountain. Rain pelted the car and melted the sod off the shaved mountain passes. My father blew his nose, wiped his eyes and sank back against the seat between Rosie and me into his private world. As we rounded a curve and a fresh gust of rain sprayed the windshield, he said softly in Greek, "There's an old saying, 'When the son comes home to the mountain, the mountain cries.' "

Soon we were in Athens. On the morning before we left for our plane I visited the Acropolis. There in the brilliant light after the mountain's tears, I kneeled on the steps of the Parthenon and gazed in awe at its fluted Doric columns. Had I been born in Kastania I would have left it—for the glories of Athens.

From the parish of St. John and the village of Haralampos, the visitor to the Acropolis blew a kiss and left for the 707.

Then I flew back to the life that was mine—New Yorker, ad-man, Greek.

Can't mention everyone, but I tried.
Some will say thank God he left me out.
You're welcome.
But special mention is due those who've enriched
the Lois Holland Callaway scene
but were not included in this book:
Bob McCann, our traffic boss;
Ed Murphy, who produces our television commercials;
John Murray, our ad production chief.
Good men.
Cathy Cresci is a mainstay of our administrative staff;
Davine Izen is our pluperfect copy editor and researcher.
Good women.
Al Evans is a splendid account supervisor.
Jim Curnutt, the only Mormon I ever worked with,
is a fine advertising man, and a friend.
Special thanks to those mentioned too fleetingly in these pages
who are still with me:
Tom Courtos, Dave Hotz, Denny Mazzella, Ed Rohan,
and the great Kurt Weihs.
(I love them and I hope they love me.)
Marlene McGinnis: you I adore.
And there are others:
Felix Kent, our attorney,
whose counsel to me was always
"George, be yourself."
John Veronis, a clairvoyant Greek, who saw the value
of this effort when others didn't.
To my basketball cronies
(notably Phil Suarez, Steve Berkenfeld and George Kokines)
who put up with my shenanigans,
this word of warning:
nothing will change.
Shirley Baker Boterf, a Kansas WASP on MacDougal Street,
was a swell typist on the manuscript.
Corinne Boni of Woodmere also rates a thank you ma'm
for her superb typing.
Soulful apologies to His Holiness the Pope
for having swiped the divine hand by
Michelangelo.
(I love Italian artists with great hands.)
And thank heaven for my new good friend, Bill Pitts.
Meeting him is one of the great things
that has happened to me.
Peter Pitts, Bill's kid, rates a pat on the back
for checking stuff in his World Book of Knowledge.
Much gratitude to Jimmy Ayvaliotis of our staff.
A good Greek.
Bless the world's Hellenes.
Also the Irish and the Jews.
And God bless the advertising life.
A fine adventure.
Tea roses and retsina for Madison Avenue.
(And tip the kid who delivers the flowers.)

G. L.
July 1972